Dr. Saif Mahmood is a New Delhi-bas
literature critic, commentator, translator,
Advocate of the Supreme Court of India. Founder of the South
Asian Alliance for Literature, Art & Culture (SAALARC), Saif has
won particular acclaim for his passionate recitations of Urdu
poetry, especially of such progressive and contemporary poets as
Faiz, Majaz, Sahir and Jaun Elia. His writings on literature and law
and his English translations of Urdu prose and verse have appeared
in several prestigious Indian and international publications.

'Hum sub ke mehboob shaayar Firaaq sahab marhoom ne apne ek mazmoon mein badi patey ki baat likhi thi, ke agar muarrikh Hindustan ki taareekh ke liye qalam uthaaye, toh usey hamaare classiki adab ka sahaara lena hoga, khusoosan Urdu ghazal ka. Yoon toh Dilli par beshumaar kitaabein likhi gayi hain aur likhi ja rahi hain, magar Saif ki kitaab is lihaaz se judagaana haisiyat rakhti hai ke ye kitaab is ahad ki shayari aur taareekh ka ek khubsoorat imtizaaj hai.'

('Our beloved poet, the dear departed Firaq sahib, had once written something very important in one of his essays, that if a writer is to pick his pen to write the history of Hindustan, he will have to take recourse to our classical literature, especially the Urdu ghazal. Many books have been written on Delhi and are being written but Saif's book occupies a distinct position insofar as his book is a beautiful admixture of the poetry of this age and its history.')

—Zehra Nigah

'Saif Mahmood hamaare ma'ashre ki rooh ko bhi samajhte hain aur Urdu zabaan-o-adab ki qadron ka bhi gehra shaghaf rakhte hain. Is kitaab ki shakl mein unhon ne apne parhne waalon ke liye ek khoobsoorat aur waqe'e tohfa pesh kiya hai.'

('Saif Mahmood understands the temperament of our society and also has a deep passion for the values of Urdu language and literature. In the form of this book, he has offered his readers a beautiful and precious gift.')

—Shamim Hanfi

A Mughal City
and Her Greatest Poets

SAIF MAHMOOD

SPEAKING
TIGER

SPEAKING TIGER PUBLISHING PVT. LTD
4381/4, Ansari Road, Daryaganj
New Delhi 110002

First published in India by Speaking Tiger 2018

Copyright © Saif Mahmood 2018
All photographs (except Jama Masjid) copyright © Anant Raina
Photograph of Jama Masjid copyright © Subinoy Das
Image on p.29: Diwan-e-Khas by Ghulam Ali Khan,
between circa 1852 and circa 1854. Source: Wiki Commons

ISBN: 978-93-88326-04-9
eISBN: 978-93-88070-55-3

10 9 8 7 6 5 4 3 2 1

The moral rights of the author have been asserted.

Typeset in Sabon Roman by SURYA, New Delhi
Printed at Sanat Printers, Kundli

All rights reserved.
No part of this publication may be reproduced, transmitted,
or stored in a retrieval system, in any form
or by any means, electronic, mechanical,
photocopying, recording or otherwise,
without the prior permission
of the publisher.

This book is sold subject to the condition that it shall not, by way of
trade or otherwise, be lent, resold, hired out,
or otherwise circulated, without the publisher's
prior consent, in any form of binding
or cover other than that in
which it is published.

To Naani Ammi, Begum Nayyara Hasan,
the most liberal woman in my life ever,
every conversation with whom had a
flourish of Urdu poetry.

Maqdoor ho toh khaak se poochhoon ke ae laeem
Tu ne vo ganj-haaye gira-maaya kya kiye

If I were given the power, I would ask the Earth, 'O miser!
What have you done to those precious treasures [that
   were buried in you]?'
                                                    —Mirza Ghalib

CONTENTS

Foreword

POLITICS AND POETRY ARE SAID TO BE INTERWOVEN, EVEN IF they aren't equivalent. In the Delhi of the nineteenth century, everybody—from the king down to the impoverished vagrant singing in the koocha and bazaar—was smitten with poetry. Before 1857, before the long twilight of the Mughals had turned to dark night, poets had dominated the city's cultural and intellectual landscape; they were held in greater esteem than the later emperors, whose 'rule' extended no further than the shabby grandeur of the Qila-e-Moalla, or the Exalted Fort, as the Red Fort was then called. After 1857, the political climate became far too volatile for poets to write of Delhi with the old flair and confidence. They could, at best, defend or decry—depending upon their lot after the cataclysmic events of the Great Revolt—the causes and effects of the annus horribilis that was to change their city and their lives irrevocably. And this they did in prodigious amounts of poetry written in Urdu during and after 1857.

Even prior to 1857, there existed a body of poetry known as shehr-ashob, literally meaning 'misfortunes of the city', to express political and social decline and turmoil. The first proper shehr-ashob is said to have been written by Mir Jafar Zatalli, one of Urdu's most incendiary poets, who is believed to have lived between 1658 and 1713. The shehr-ashob of Zatalli's period had elements of satire and humour and flashes of political insight; Zatalli himself was unsparing in his criticism of all authority, including the emperor, for which he was sentenced to death by Farukkhsiyar. But with time the lighter, sharper elements were leached out of shehr-ashob and what was left was highly romanticized, poignant, pathos-laden protest poetry, usually about the city the poet dwelt in. And yet, while this genre of poetry became largely melodramatic, self-pitying and exaggerated—with a great deal of rhetoric and play upon words in the best traditions of elegiac poetry such as nauha, marsiya and soz—it also provided ample opportunities for the poet to paint graphic word pictures of what he saw and experienced at first hand. Twinned with the conventional imagery of the Persian-Arabic tradition, shehr-ashob allowed the poet to bemoan a crumbling social order while speaking, ostensibly, of his personal sorrows and losses. This was what the greatest exponents of shehr-ashob finally managed to achieve: Hatim, Sauda and Mir, each in his own way, pulled Urdu poetry out of the thrall of romanticism and—while retaining the classical idiom and syntax of the ghazal, masnavi and qasidah forms—made Urdu poetry speak of newer concerns.

Pioneers and innovators like Hatim, Sauda and Mir may have been the best chroniclers of Delhi in verse, but it must be noted that even the most traditional among the poets of Delhi have always had a finger on the pulse of the city. There is something about the fiza and maahaul—the very air and general climate—of the city that its poets have never been ghaafil—oblivious—to the political fault-lines that have marred the tenor of its social and cultural life through the centuries. The great Urdu poets of Delhi always took note of the disarray, mismanagement and decline around them and it is this, coupled with their mastery over the intricacies of the ghazal, that makes their poetry so distinctive. Rooted in the topical and the contemporary it might be, it continues to speak to us across time and circumstance.

Poetry, it has been said, flourishes when all else withers.

When there is political chaos, when the social fabric tears, when corruption and poverty become rampant, when—in the words of that other great poet, Yeats—'the centre does not hold', it is usually the poet's finest hour. And so it was in the last years of Mughal rule in India. From the middle of the eighteenth century, events conspired to give plenty of fodder to the Urdu elegist's mill. There was the decline and dismantling of the Mughal empire with each successive incompetent ruler. There was the sack of Delhi by Nadir Shah; the series of invasions of the city by Ahmad Shah Abdali and plundering raids by the Marathas and the Rohillas; the establishment of British control over Delhi in 1803; and the most cruel blow of all—the annexation of Awadh in 1856—which turned even loyal Muslim supporters of the British in Delhi and elsewhere into discontented, suspicious malcontents, if not ardent jehadis. With each fresh catastrophe, the Urdu poet evolved a vocabulary to express his angst, clothing his sorrow in a time-honoured repertoire of images and metaphors. Some favourite synonyms for the Beloved—sitamgar, bu't, kaafir, yaar—now began to be used mockingly for the British. And so it went on—two worlds colliding, or waiting to merge and fuse—one dying and the other waiting to be born!

The book you hold in your hands encapsulates this twilit, churning world: it not only documents the life and often turbulent times of some of the finest poets the city of Delhi has produced, but also gives you a sample of their most representative work in English translation. The photographs accompanying the text do an admirable job of connecting the modern reader almost immediately with a past that lingers in the by-lanes of Purani Dilli and catches us unawares every now and then.

A book such as this was waiting to be written. I am very glad that Saif Mahmood has filled this much-needed lacuna in our city's literary history, and done so with his characteristic enthusiasm and attention to detail.

Rakhshanda Jalil

Urdu Hai Jis Ka Naam

A Preface and a Short History of Delhi's Urdu

THE IMPULSES THAT LED EVENTUALLY TO THE EVOLUTION of the language that is known today as Urdu go back to the ancient past. And that is where we must begin our story.

Mahavira and the Buddha (commonly believed to have lived in the sixth or fifth century BCE) were the first major figures to challenge the hegemony of Sanskrit in matters spiritual. They can—and should—thus be recognized as the two main catalysts for the processes, spanning several centuries, that led to the evolution of a large number of languages of the people of South Asia. Urdu was one of these languages, though, comparatively speaking, it followed a more tangential trajectory.

The processes referred to above unfolded across the dusty plains of North India in an epochal sweep and carried with them an amalgam of beliefs, traditions, rituals, cultures, mythologies, music, food, literary expressions and much else besides. The mainstream, with its many tributaries and distributaries, was a celebration of diversities; a river flowing across centuries, meandering, stumbling and bursting through obstructions. The cultural and social upheaval that truly powered this river was unleashed by the revolutionary decision taken by both Mahavira and the Buddha to communicate with their growing number of followers in the natural languages of the people, the so called prakrits, and not in Sanskrit, the enriched language of the ruling elite.

This one act dislodged Sanskrit from its pre-eminent

position as the sole arbiter of spiritual matters and made it possible for languages and dialects of the common folk to become mediums for serious intellectual enquiry. For the first time, questions about who we are and what is the purpose of our existence began to be debated and pondered over by the plebeians, by those who were hitherto considered incapable of understanding the subtle nuances of spirituality. The hegemony of the tiny Sanskrit-knowing coterie was challenged in a fundamental way as the peasant, the potter, the metal worker, the carpenter, the weaver, the stone mason, the carver, the tanner, the butcher, the cobbler, the basket weaver, the entertainer and many others began to discover new shades of meaning in their daily vocabulary, even in the names of the humble instruments of their craft. Gradually, over the next many centuries, the spoken dialects of the common people enriched their experience and expression and many new languages began to evolve.

The purists continued to maintain that only Sanskrit, 'the language of the gods', was meant for discussions on spiritual matters and derisively referred to these emerging languages as apabhramsas, or fallen languages, unfit for any meaningful dialogue.

One apabhramsa, which linguists call Shurseni, had spread across North India by the tenth century CE, and over time its different strains were to grow into a host of languages spoken in present-day Gujarat, Rajasthan, Himachal, Punjab, Haryana, UP, Bengal, Assam, Bihar, Central India and other adjacent areas. A mixture of Haryanvi, Punjabi and Braj—all born of Shurseni—emerged in and around the area we now know as Delhi.

By the late twelfth century CE, North India also began to receive a set of languages that belonged to the Indo-Iranian group, principally, Turkish, Persian and Pashto. Languages of the Indo-Aryan group, which had held sway in the South Asian Subcontinent until now, began to draw upon this new reservoir of terms and vocabularies and were gradually transformed in the process. Of these, the language spoken around Delhi was influenced the most, and this happened because Delhi had by now become the most important political centre in North India and an important centre of trade, a magnet for both traders and soldiers of fortune.

The idea that such incursions from across the Khyber beginning in the tenth century were introducing alien and inimical elements into the subcontinent is rather short-sighted and of recent vintage. The purists and zealots who champion this idea either lack or deliberately ignore a basic understanding of how civilizations and cultures evolve. Migrations and intermixing are woven into the very fabric of humanity—indeed, of all life. The Aryans, too, came from beyond the Khyber, as did the Greeks, the Huns and the Mongols. People from the east of the Khyber also travelled across—how else do we explain Ashokan edicts in Qandahar and the now destroyed Bamiyan Buddhas?

When civilizations meet, they do not always meet to clash and to try to destroy each other. Destruction happens, but it is not the only thing that happens. Civilizations have resilience and they learn to adapt, accommodate, absorb and appropriate. The destructive streak burns itself out rather quickly, while the creative impulse sustains through the initial upheavals and eventually overcomes the forces of destabilization, and then begins the slow, laborious, lumbering, stumbling effort to imagine and create and recreate.

The speakers of the Indo-Iranian languages who were moving into North India and into Delhi were a diverse mix. There were those who came in search of the famed wealth of Hindustan and were in a hurry to fill their pockets with what they could find, through means fair or foul, and depart. But they were not the only ones. In fact, they were a small minority of the new arrivals. Among the majority were traders who came in search of a market for their goods and to buy stuff that they could take back and sell at a profit, and there were craftspeople and men of letters in search of employment in the growing markets and urban centres. There were men of faith and seekers of knowledge, there were those who came to find a shelter and build a home, and there were those who came in the hope of building empires.

The new arrivals brought with them new lifestyles and knowledge systems, all of which began to be gradually absorbed, adapted and appropriated by the older inhabitants of the subcontinent. This interaction between two civilizational streams, the Central Asian and the South Asian, led to hybridization of all markers of cultural identity and eventually to the emergence of new music, architecture, cuisines, attires, etiquettes of social discourse and—most important, in the context of this essay—new languages.

The seeds of expression scattered in the fertile polyglot soil of the Indo-Gangetic plains, harvested and replanted again and again across centuries in varying soils and climes, were to grow into newer and richer strains. One such journey began from Delhi in the period between the late twelfth and early fourteenth centuries—the evolving, hybrid language spoken here, often referred to as Hindavi or Hindi, moved to Gujarat, Deogiri, Deccan, Gulbarga, Golconda, Bijapur, Aurangabad and returned, richer and more vibrant, to Delhi again. And it was here that the verse of Rekhta (a mixture of Persian and Hindavi) and the Prose of Hindi fused together to emerge as Urdu—just one of the innumerable products of the creative energies unleashed by the coming together of different civilizations in our ancient land over millennia.

—

The journey of Hindavi out of Delhi began almost simultaneously at many locales, almost all of which can be clubbed together in four broad categories: battlefields or camps; shrines; market- and work-places; and night-shelters or caravanserais. Some of these places or sites regularly doubled up to serve two purposes—the shrine or hospice of a Sufi would turn into a night-shelter for the weary traveller, while the caravanserai, aside from providing board and lodging to merchants, could also turn into a market for their merchandise. Locals and new arrivals met and interacted constantly in all these places, and a syncretic tradition and a culture of synthesis began to develop.

Those wishing to build empires recruited their armies from among the peasantry, and the army camps resonated with the sounds, among others, of Awadhi, Bhojpuri, Maithili, Maghai, Hadoti, Mewari, Marwari, Gujarati, Kathiawadi, Sindhi, Multani, Punjabi, Haryanvi, Ruhelkhandi, Bundelkhandi, Malwi and Braj—the languages of the recruits—while the 'kamaandaars' who led them spoke Turki, Farsi, Dari and Pashto. The need for commands to be issued, understood and quickly followed amidst the din and clamour of metal striking against metal, the galloping of horses, the grunts and shouts of combatants and the shrieks of the wounded, led rapidly to the development of a form of communication common to this disparate group of men—Lashkari, the language of the Lashkar, the army camp.

Lashkari had several variants. Its grammar and syntax

relied on local usage but its vocabulary drew many words and phrases from Turki, Farsi, Dari and Pashto. Sandooq, bandooq, tafang, zarrah baktar, band-o-bast, kamaan, kamaandaar, sipahi, pyada, gasht (trunk, gun, muzzle-loaded rifle, armour, arrangement, bow, commander, sepoy, foot soldier, beat) and hundreds of other words travelled and became a part of the vocabulary of common people as soldiers dispersed after battles and returned to their villages. The Pashtoon soldiers gathered every evening to recount the events of the day in extempore poetry in chahaar bait, a form consisting of four stanzas of four lines each, sung in chorus to the beat of the duff, the tambourine. Chahaar bait arrived with the Afghans and continues to be sung almost 700 years later in annual competitions among the Pathans of Bhopal, Tonk, Amroha, Rampur, Moradabad, etc., to this day.

Meanwhile, the merchants and artisans thronged the marketplace selling their wares or their skills and a language of exchange gradually evolved in a continuity that linked the streets and lanes of Mehrauli, Siri, Tughlaqabad, Jahanpanah, Ferozabad, Dinpanah and eventually Shahjahanabad—the seven cities of Delhi—through five centuries. Terms for measurement, weighing and counting and names for professions and products began to gain currency. Qaaleen, girah, wazan, taraazu, gaz, safar, manzil, bahishti, saazindah, mashaalchi, baawarchi, kaarkhana, kaarigar, ustad (carpet, knot, weight, scale, yard, mile, journey, destination, stone mason, water-carrier, [musician's] accompanist, torch-bearer, cook, workshop, craftsman, teacher [or foreman]) and such other terms began to find space in the conversation of the common population of Delhi and also reached other areas, near and far, touched by these linguistic impulses.

The practice of gifting robes and head gear to soldiers, officers, nobles, courtiers and ambassadors, initiated by Alauddin Khilji (1296-1316), one of the most powerful rulers of the Delhi Sultanate, led to the setting up of kaarkhanas where hundreds of weavers, cutters, tailors, embroiderers worked continuously to keep the toshakhana—a gift house or a store for garments—constantly supplied with the wide range of robes that were needed in the thousands every year. Terms like bazzaz, darzi, kasheedakar, zardoz, zargar, khil'at, jubba, dastaar (cloth merchant, tailor, embroiderer, gold embroidery, gold worker, robe, shirt, headgear), found their way into the local vocabulary.

Just as the tourist guide at Khajuraho, the Taj, Sikri, Mamallapuram, Konark and Ajanta can communicate in half a dozen or more languages, the keeper of the caravanserai too began to pick up words from the languages of the travellers he or she catered to, and gradually they became part of a pidgin or creole spoken along the caravan routes that eventually came to be identified as Sarai ki Zabaan—the language of the sarai—or Saraiki.

Those with imperial ambitions were accompanied by their armies, officers, hangers on and camp followers, but there were others who at times accompanied the soldiers of fortune and at other times moved independently, and their agendas did not necessarily coincide with the ambitions of those that wished to conquer lands. There were curious travellers egged on by wanderlust, and scholars keen to learn about these ancient lands. And there were Sufis seeking spiritual solace and wishing to share their ideas of the uncertainty of existence with others like them.

The Sufis believed in the unity of the human race, the unity of all they observed and the unity of being itself; they hoped for universal harmony and sought to conquer the hearts of people. They found resonances across the Subcontinent in the indigenous ideas of maya and advait—and thus began a dialogue between the Nirgun poets, like Kabir and Nanak, who celebrated a formless egalitarian God, and the Sufis, who believed in a formless, merciful, benevolent God.

Four silsilas (orders or traditions) of Sufis found a foothold in different parts of India—the Qadris, the Suhrawardis, the Naqshbandis and the Chishtiya. The influence of the Sufis on our spiritual and cultural life continues to resonate well over 800 years after the first of them set foot in Hindustan. The Chishti Silsila introduced to India by Khwaja Moinuddin Chishti in the twelfth century grew to be the most influential among the Sufi silsilas in India, especially during and after the time of Nizamuddin Auliya, the fourth head of the Silsila and one of the most prominent Sufis of South Asia, who made Delhi his home.

The doors of the Sufi khanqah (hospice or monastery) were open to all creeds, classes and castes. The khanqahs became centres of dialogue, debate and exchange of ideas and of music and poetry. This culture of inclusion and openness produced some of the finest literature and music of the medieval period. The Sufis, who mostly spoke Turki, Persian, Dari or Pashto, wished to communicate with the growing number of new adherents in their own languages. As they travelled far and wide and settled across the length and breadth of the subcontinent, they acquired new languages. Those who settled in Punjab and Multan and neighbouring areas chose Saraiki, Sindhi, Multani and Punjabi as the languages of their discourse, just as those who travelled to the east chose Awadhi. In Delhi, Nizamuddin Auliya asked his favourite disciple, his mureed, Yamin ud Din Khusrau—whom we know as Amir Khusrau—to write in the language of the people, so that 'we are able to better communicate our message'. As it turned out, the mureed did much more than that.

———

Amir Khusrau is one of the most influential and transformative figures in the cultural history of northern India—a history that is also tied in significant ways to that of other parts of the subcontinent, like the Deccan. Born in the mid-thirteenth century to a Turk father and an Indian mother, Khusrau was a polyglot, poet, musicologist, composer, vocalist, chronicler and soldier who described himself as Turk-e-Hindustani. He epitomizes the coming together of the genius of the South Asian and Central Asian creative processes; it was in his persona that the diverse streams of the two worlds came together like never before.

Khusrau is the first—and best—known poet of Hindavi, the language that was to later evolve and, unfortunately, get divided into Hindi and Urdu. These two languages, the music and poetry of India—especially of North India—and much of what went into making us an inclusive society, owes a lot to Khusrau.

The language that Khusrau used was the spoken language of Delhi and it drew from diverse linguistic sources. Khusrau travelled extensively—to Bengal, Multan and other places as the official chronicler with one king or another; to Ajodhan (now Pakpattan) in Punjab, with his pir, or spiritual guide and master, Nizamuddin, to visit the latter's pir, Baba Fareed; and to several places as a curious traveller, including a sojourn at Ayodhya where he wrote a beautiful Persian ghazal in praise of the city, comparing it to Paradise. It was in these journeys that he picked up words from different languages and used them with great felicity and imagination in his compositions—poems and songs, of course, but also riddles, which have become part of everyday speech in large swathes of South Asia.

This one riddle, popularly ascribed to Khusrau, that straddles the territory between physical and spiritual love—the playground of both the Sufi and the poet (and Khusrau was both)—is also a fine example of the kind of vocabulary and usage that was in vogue in Delhi in the late thirteenth century:

Bakhat Bakhat moe wa ki aas
Raat Dina oo rahat moe paas
Mere man ko sab karat hai kaam
Ai sakhi saajan, na sakhi Raam

(I am restless without him all the time,
he is by my side day and night,
he fulfils all my wishes.
'Is he your beloved?' No, my friend, He is God.)

The Persian 'waqt' (time) is used here in its colloquial form of 'bakhat' (in use even today); 'moe' for me or I, is typically Braj; 'dina' is Haryanvi and Braj for day; and 'karat'—to do—is common to both Braj and Awadhi. 'Raam' is not specifically a reference to Lord Ram, but is used as a synonym for God, a usage common to Kabir, Nanak and Mahatma Gandhi, aside from many Sufi and Bhakti poets across centuries.

Words and ideas that deal with the spiritual, with notions of right and wrong and heaven and hell, were constantly crossing the fluid boundaries between languages even three hundred years after Khusrau, as can be seen in this doha (two liner) by Daadoo Dayal, the sixteenth-century Nirgun Bhakti poet of Gujarat:

Jor na kare, haraam na khaaye
So momin bahisht mein jaaye

(He who doesn't oppress nor consume what is prohibited
Is a Momin [Believer] and will go to heaven.)

'Zor (jor) haraam', 'momin' and 'bahisht' are Persian and Arabic words, but they had long become part of the vocabulary of artisans and peasants by Dadoo's time. Daadoo was himself an artisan.

So a common language, drawing upon diverse linguistic and cultural sources (both secular and religious), had begun to take shape in the khanqahs of the Sufis and the akhadas of the Nirgun poets as early as the twelfth and thirteenth centuries. And it is this language in which Khusrau composed his poetry, most of which he just gave away to whoever had asked him to write. He wrote riddles of many types, he wrote devotional poetry in praise of his pir, and he wrote bandishes (compositions) for Indian ragas. He is also believed to have introduced ragas like aiman, zilaf and shahhana to Hindustani music, and of course the qawwali— the gift for which he is most loved in the Subcontinent.

The qawwali had its beginnings as the Qaul (which translates as 'the word', or 'saying') recited in the khanqah of the Chishtiya Sufi Khwaja Qutubuddin Bakhtiyar Kaaki in Delhi in the early thirteenth century. The Qaul travelled with Bakhtiyar Kaaki's successor, Baba Fareed, to Punjab and changed in shape and content under the influence of the vibrant music of Punjab. Khusrau is credited with bringing the form back to Delhi and turning it into a vehicle for communicating his love for his pir, Nizamuddin Auliya. This form was to evolve into the qawwali as we know it today. Qawwali democratized faith and spirituality, diluting the power of purists, priests and clerics, and breaking down some of the barriers between communities, religions and cultures. This development was to contribute in a fundamental way to the emergence of a syncretic 'people's language' like Urdu.

One notices a very interesting development in both the Sufi and Bhakti movements during this entire period. The love for God and the love for the beloved seem to become one, God becomes the beloved and the devotee the lover, and in the process the attributes of love, kindness, benevolence, clemency, mercy associated with God begin to be highlighted, as opposed to the idea of God as punishing, vengeful and unforgiving. The device of turning God or the pir/guru into the beloved and the devotee into an unabashed lover made God more approachable, more sensuous and therefore more real. God was no longer a dreadful, punishing, censorious presence but a being that one could approach, beseech, cajole and even argue with. This idea and approach is central to qawwalis and Urdu poetry, and to Bhakti and Sufi poetry.

Around the time when Amir Khusrau began writing in Hindavi, Alauddin Khilji had spread the Delhi Sultanate to Gujarat and he despatched some of his Turk commanders to administer the newly conquered territories. The Turk commanders shifted with their household staff and retainers, and Hindavi—Zuban-e-Dehli, or the language of Delhi— found a toehold in Gujarat, and over time, intermixed with Gujarati to emerge as Gujari or Gojri.

In 1327, two years after he became ruler of the Sultanate, Mohammad Bin Tughlaq shifted his capital to the Deccan—to Deogiri in present-day Maharashtra. A large population of Hindavi speakers settled in and around Deogiri, which was renamed Daulatabad, and Zuban-e-

Dehli reached Maharashtra. Just twelve years later, the capital was shifted back to Delhi, but many original Delhi-walas decided to stay back. About half a century later, the then head of the Chishti Sislsila, Khwaja Bandanawaz Gesu Daraz, chose to leave Delhi in the wake of Taimur's invasion and sack of the city, and headed for Daulatabad with many of his disciples, and the population of those who spoke Zaban-e-Dehli in Daulatabad was replenished with this fresh infusion. Gesu Daraz was to later shift to Gulbarga (in present-day Karnataka) at the invitation of the Bahmani Sultan Tajuddin Feroze Shah. The Bahmani Kingdom had been set up by one of the Turk Sardars who had broken away from the Delhi Sultanate in 1347. The arrival of Gesu Daraz and his disciples in Gulbarga further strengthened the spread of Hindavi, and the cultures and sensibilities associated with it, in this region and adjoining areas of the Deccan, like Bidar and Telangana.

Thus, from the time of Alauddin Khilji's despatch of his Turkish Sardars and their retainers to Gujarat to the setting up of the Bahmani kingdom, Hindavi had spread from Delhi to present-day Gujarat to different parts of the Deccan, absorbing words, phrases and expressions from Gujarati, Marathi, Telugu and Kannada and enriching these languages, too, with words, expressions and phrases from Hindavi, Gojri, Persian, Dari and Turkish. This exchange and intermingling gradually led to the rise of a dialect called Dakhani—a flexible, adaptive language of daily life in large parts of the Deccan. The Sufis are believed to be the first group of people to write in this language; the earliest known text written in Dakhani is the Sufi masnavi *Kadam Rao Padam Rao* by Fakhruddin Nizami of Bidar.

While the languages of the court at Delhi and Agra (where the capital shifted under Sikandar Lodi) from the early days of the Sultanate were Turkish and Persian, the

Bahmani kingdom made Dakhani the official language. Later, the Bahmani kingdom broke up into different Deccani sultanates, but two of these, the Qutub Shahi and Adilshahi Sultanates, continued to use Dakhani as the court language. It was in the Qutub Shahi Sultanate of Golconda, particularly, that Dakhani evolved most impressively, not only as the official language, but also as a language of the people and as a language of literature.

Up in the north, the Mughals, who replaced the Delhi Sultanate, retained Persian as the language of the court. While they did extend patronage to indigenous languages like Braj, which was the language most widely spoken in and around their long-time capital Agra, the tongues of the street and mohalla were not heard at the high table. Persian was the language of the court, and also of literature—in Agra and then in Delhi, which became the seat of the Mughal Empire after Shahjahan shifted the capital there.

It was a voice from the Deccan that would change this situation, and change it radically.

—

Dakhani arrived in Delhi as an almost fully developed language with the poetry of Wali Dakhni, also known as Wali Aurangabadi and Wali Gujarati, there being no consensus on his place of birth—some sources mention Aurangabad and others mention Ahmedabad (where he was buried and where his mausoleum was destroyed during the killings of 2002 and a road built on the site overnight). Wali Dakhni came to Delhi in 1700, bringing with him his extraordinary verses, the likes of which few in Delhi had ever heard.

Delhi was at this time home to some of the finest poets of Persian, not only in India but in all the lands where the language was spoken. Scholars of Persian literature have

lately described this era as Sabk-e-Hindi or the Indian style
of Persian Poetry. Some of the leading lights of this style of
poetry were Hatim, Abroo, Arzoo and Bedil, all residents
of Mughal Delhi. Most maintained that the only language
for meaningful poetry was Persian and the poetic style of
the great Persian poets like Saadi, Haafiz, Jami, Khaqani
and Urfi set the tone and tenor of poetry in the city.

It was into this milieu that Wali brought his poetry.
Dakhani, the language in which Wali wrote, was derisively
called 'Rekhta' or mixed language. It was considered
a language of the marketplace and therefore lacking
refinement and unfit for civilized discourse. Despite the
stakes being loaded so heavily against him, the sheer force of
Wali's expression and his skilful use of the Indian idiom as
opposed to the world-view crafted in the Persian discourse,
made the great masters of Delhi not only sit up and take
notice, but also acknowledge that here was a language and
diction fit for poetry. The imagery of Wali's poetry, especially
his ghazals, was fresh and vital, drawn as much from the
earthy experience of the street and mohalla as from the
ideas of Sufi and Bhakti mystics. All the master poets of
Delhi were soon trying their hand at writing in a language
that had started life in their own city and virtually been a
gypsy for 350 years, before returning to the land of its birth.

The story of Urdu as we know it today begins here.

And from here, too, it is a long story. There is much
that remains to be told and all of it cannot be contained
within the covers of a single book. The parts that need
to be narrated include the evolution of Rekhta into Urdu
and its rise from a language spoken in the streets to a
language of beautiful poetic expression; its flowering into a
language that has articulated longing, separation and pain
like few others known to humanity; its transformation by
the repeated invasions and plunder of Delhi through the

eighteenth and nineteenth centuries, and the loss of a culture
of tolerance and inclusion; its growth into a language that
captured the passing of an entire way of life in 1857; and
its ability in later years to give voice to the anger of the
oppressed.

A significant part of the story that remains to be told
is to be found in this volume—a bird's-eye-view of the life
and work of some of the great masters of Urdu poetry, and
through them, of the great city of Delhi. The compilation is
the result of years of painstaking research and selection by
Saif Mahmood. A young legal luminary, itinerant traveller,
inspired raconteur and one of the most popular reciters of
Urdu poetry, he has put together a work of remarkable
depth and feeling and a wide sweep.

Hopefully his work will reach the growing number of
those who wish to know more about Urdu and wish to
cut through the communal divide that has prevented them
from accessing one of the finest products of 800 years of
interaction between South and Central Asia.

One hopes that this volume will be followed by a
companion volume where the story of Urdu from the
nineteenth century to the present will also be told by Saif
in the style and format of the present volume.

*Sohail Hashmi**

---

*I must thank my dear friends Dr Akhlaque Ahmad 'Ahan' and Dr
S.M. Anwar Alam 'Pasha' from the School of Languages Literature
and Culture Studies, JNU—the former from the Centre of Persian
Studies and the latter from the Centre of Indian Languages—and
Dr Ali Javed, Department of Urdu, Delhi University, for clearing the
cobwebs of doubt that regularly blurred my vision during the putting
together of this essay. For any missed out details, mistakes, sweeping
generalizations or overstatements found in the article, however, I alone
remain responsible.

Author's Note

THE EIGHT POETS PROFILED IN THIS BOOK WERE, OF COURSE, NOT the only poets of Mughal Delhi. But they are widely regarded, if I may use a contemporary term, as the 'first rung poets' of their times and their stories interest the general Urdu lover more than those of others.

Beginning from the early 1700s, when the story of Urdu properly began in Delhi, to 1905, when the era of the Classical Urdu poets ended, the book broadly covers two time-periods—the eighteenth century and the nineteenth century. Deciding the sequence of poets for the first time period was easy: I could keep it chronological. However, for the poets of the nineteenth century, this kind of sequencing was an impossible task because all of them (except Daagh) lived and gained prominence at exactly the same time. I finally decided that the best way to place them was in order of their prominence in their times. This was also the most engaging way in which the story of Mughal Delhi could be narrated, without the sequence of historical events becoming too confusing. The book ends, as it should, with Daagh, who was the last poet of Mughal Delhi, much younger than all the others and the one who died last.

Finally, a word about the Roman transliterations. I have tried, as much as possible, to spell Urdu words the way they would be pronounced in Urdu, but without using diacritical marks. At first, I had thought I would make an exception for the nasalized 'n'—or what is called 'noon ghunna' in Urdu. For example, depending on where and how it has been used, and also on the poetic metre, the word 'jahaan' (world) can be pronounced either the way it is written—simply 'jahaan' (with a full 'n' sound at the end)—or with a nasalized 'n'. I'd thought I would italicize the 'n' wherever it should be a nasal sound. But in the end, to keep things as simple as possible, I decided against doing this as well. I'll trust my readers, and leave it to them to figure out the correct pronunciation.

Introduction

Dilli Jo Ek Shehr Tha

Tazkira Dehli-e-marhoom ka ae dost na chhed
Na suna jaayega hum se ye fasaana hargiz

(Don't talk to me of Late Lamented Delhi, my friend
I don't have the heart to hear this story.)

—Altaf Husain Hali

'DELHI GIVES ME PERMISSION TO BE OBNOXIOUS'—THIS WAS
the reply I got from a Pakistani friend when I asked her
why she insisted on living in the city even though her Indian
husband did not want to. Delhi's charms are unpredictable.
The chaotic streets, the unruly traffic and polluted air, the
aggressive inhabitants and their hurried life, the tolerance
for the obnoxious—all of these constitute an integral part
of this phenomenal city. In beauty resides horror, and vice
versa.

Inextricably intertwined with Delhi's complicated
present is her violent history—a history of invasions and
assaults, even massacres. It has been 'late lamented' many
times through the centuries, yet it lives. Each time it was
razed to the ground, it came back to life with startling
vivacity. Nothing dies in Delhi, the ghosts of its past lives
roam the streets or bide their time in half-ruined buildings,
and they rise up to speak in a thousand stories that are still
told about the city.

Struggling to breathe under the angry modern façade of
the megalopolis is another one, timeworn and easily missed,

that teems with art, heritage and poetry. It is the Delhi of
Mir and Ghalib, the Delhi of the fabled Seven Cities, all of
which have risen and fallen and risen again, or been changed
beyond recognition over time. Delhi's indestructible spirit
has haunted writers and poets for generations; some of
them have written out of love, others in awe and yet others
out of bewilderment. In the eighteenth century, Mir said:

> Dil-o-Dilli donon agar hain kharaab
> P'a kuchh lutf is ujde ghar mein bhi hain
>
> (My heart and my Delhi may both be in ruins
> There are still some delights in this ravaged home.)

In the middle of the twentieth century, Percival Spear
compared Delhi with Rome:

> Delhi can point to a history as chequered and more
> ancient than the 'eternal' city of Rome; it was a famous
> capital before the days of Alexander, and it has survived
> all the vicissitudes of time and fortune to become one of
> the youngest and certainly the most magnificent of recent
> imperial cities. For it has undergone transformations as
> numerous as the incarnations of the God Vishnu; if it
> has frequently changed its site, its character and even its
> name, it has preserved through all a continuous thread of
> existence...Like most ancient cities it has succumbed to
> the magic of the number seven, but as the plain of Delhi
> is too flat for even the most exuberant imagination to
> discover seven hills on which the city can rest, historians
> have played with the idea of seven consecutive cities.
> The 'seven cities' of Delhi are in fact no more accurate
> description of Delhi history than the seven hills ascribed
> to many other places.[1]

And at the beginning of the new millennium, Rukmini Bhaya
Nair wrote (in her essay 'City of Walls, City of Gates'):

> There are many etymologies that have been offered for
> Delhi, but perhaps one of the most appealing is the
> philosopher Ramachandra Gandhi's suggestion that its
> name could derive from the words 'dehri' or 'dehli',
> both meaning 'threshold'—a permanent point of entry
> and departure but forever resistant to any stamp of
> permanence...
>
> The city Delhi most resembles...is Athens—with its
> monumental, crumbling history strewn all around, its
> ramshackle, seething present.[2]

In this 'seething present', Delhi is bigger, more sprawling than it has ever been. Officially called the National Capital Territory of Delhi, it is the third largest city of India in terms of size—covering an area of approximately 1500 square kilometres—and the second largest in terms of population—home to more than 25 million people. And in the heart of this mega city, in the north east of its central district, lies Purani Dilli, Old Delhi, where the tale of its glory and ruin and haphazard regeneration is best perceived. It is this 'walled city' of narrow, crowded and cacophonous alleys—where it is impossible to walk a few paces or even stand still without touching, literally, at least ten other human beings—that this book is about. Or rather, about a few great men of verse who internalized the spirit of this remarkable patch of the Earth so deeply that they were Dilli, and Dilli was them.

And together, Purani Dilli and its iconic poets tell a 300-year-old story; the story of one of the most evocative languages ever known to humankind: Urdu.

The city of Shahjahanabad, or what is now commonly known as Old Delhi or Purani Dilli, was built by the fifth

Mughal emperor, Shah Jahan—whose name has become synonymous with Mughal architecture. The Mughals ruled India for 331 years, and in this period, gave the country nineteen emperors of different dispositions and propensities—strong, weak, liberal, bigoted, pious, debauched, scholarly, illiterate. However, what ran like a golden thread throughout the Mughal fabric was the desire to build new cities and structures. Shahjahanabad was the last prominent city to be built by the Mughals.

Shah Jahan (1592-1666) wanted to be remembered as an Indian ruler who built a capital as grand and majestic as the one built by his Timurid ancestors in Samarqand, three centuries ago. The royal desire started being translated into action in 1639 when the emperor directed his architects and planners to look for a site to build the new Mughal capital, not too far away from the existing capital, Akbarabad, as Agra was then called. A spot on the bank of the Yamuna river was selected for its climatically, geographically, politically and, perhaps, also astrologically strategic location. It lay next to the centre of the larger area of Delhi, which had been the capital of various dynasties in previous centuries. Shah Jahan's great grandfather, the second Mughal Emperor, Humayun, had himself ruled from Delhi until his death in 1556. The area was also considered auspicious by both Hindus and Muslims since a large number of Sufi saints, including Qutubuddin Bakhtiyar Kaaki (d. 1236), Nizamuddin Auliya (d. 1325) and Naseeruddin Mahmud Chiragh-e-Dehli ('Light of Delhi') (d. 1356), lay buried here. Then there was Nigambodh Ghat on the banks of the Yamuna, one of the holiest cremation ghats for Hindus that is believed to have found mention in the Mahabharata and been blessed by Lord Brahma, the Creator. What better site to build a new capital on?

An ambitious plan was laid out for the new city. A royal fort—qila—would be built to house the Mughal royalty and a sprawling city would come up just outside its precincts. Work began on 29 April 1639 and was completed in nine years. On 19 April 1648, Shah Jahan, who had personally supervised the construction in many parts, entered the new qila and formally declared Shahjahanabad as the capital of Mughal India.

Shahjahanabad was shielded by a stone wall twenty-seven feet high, twelve feet thick and almost four miles long. The walled city could be accessed through seven large gates—Kashmiri Gate, Mori Gate, Kabuli Gate, Lahori Gate, Ajmeri Gate, Turkmani Gate and Akbarabadi Gate. Just outside the qila came up a grand and vibrant city with wide streets, large squares, specially carved-out bazaar areas and residential localities, a garden and a water channel fed by the Yamuna. Shah Jahan's eldest daughter, Jahanara Begum, had inherited considerable wealth from her mother, Mumtaz Mahal, who had died in 1631 (and for whom Shah Jahan built the Taj Mahal). Out of that bequest, Jahanara commissioned an octagonal square with a large pool of water in its centre. At night, moonlight would reflect in the water and the place came to be called Chandni Chowk (Moonlight Square).

As a gift to his third wife, Izz-un-Nisa, commonly known as Akbarabadi Begum, Shah Jahan got another beautiful garden laid out to the west of the city. It was named Shalimar Bagh, perhaps after the magnificent garden of the same name that his father Jahangir had built for his last wife, Noor Jahan. Izz-un-Nissa later, out of her own funds, built a sarai, or inn, within the garden complex.

With its pivotal position in the city—geographical as well as societal—the qila from where the emperor ruled soon began to be called the Qila-e-Moalla, the Exalted Fort[3], familiar to us as the Red Fort. On one of the walls of the Qila's Chamber of Honour—Diwan-e-Khaas—was inscribed a Persian verse attributed to the legendary poet Amir Khusro:

> Gar firdaus bar ru e zameen ast
> Hameen ast o hameen ast o hameen ast!

> (If there is paradise on Earth
> It is here, it is here, it is here!)

By 1656 was built, just outside the Qila, the largest mosque of the Mughal Empire, Jama Masjid (Congregational Mosque). Around the mosque came up mohallas (residential neighbourhoods) and katras (commercial enclaves), many of which were named after the occupational identities of their inhabitants: for instance, the area where bangle-makers lived came to be called Churiwalan, and the one where butchers lived was called Qassabpura.[4] With time, some mohallas came to be inhabited almost exclusively either by the Hindus or by the Muslims—Koocha Pandit became the domain of Hindu Brahmins, Bazar Sita Ram of the Kashmiri Pandits and Ballimaran of Muslim nobles and Hakims (Unani physicians). The new capital soon became home to people from all walks of life, including traders, artisans, writers, poets and scholars and, within a few years, its population surged to around six million.[5] As the emperor periodically gifted largesse to his favourites and even named streets after them, a new class of aristocrats and nobles was also created, some of whom also began to settle outside the new city. (It is worth clarifying here that while Shahjahanabad was the name of this new capital founded by Shah Jahan, the larger city around it, which embraced not only the new capital but also all the smaller pre-existing settlements, was called 'Dehli' or, colloquially, 'Dilli', which later the English started writing as 'Delhi'. The distinction now remains academic.)

In 1657, Shah Jahan fell ill and entrusted most of his responsibilities to the eldest of his four sons, Dara Shikoh. The emperor's illness and consequential absence from the court created unrest and soon a war of succession among his sons became inevitable. In 1658, Shah Jahan's third son, Mohiuddin, not only defeated Dara Shikoh at the Battle of Samugarh but also imprisoned him and the ailing emperor in Agra. Having thus incarcerated his father and brother, Mohiuddin returned to Shahjahanabad and, on 31 July 1658, at a grand coronation ceremony held at Shalimar Bagh, declared himself the new emperor. Thus began the reign of the sixth Mughal Emperor, Abul Muzaffar Mohiuddin Muhammad Aurangzeb Alamgir, today known to the world as the harshest of the Mughal rulers.[6]

Within a year of his coronation, Aurangzeb ordered the execution of Dara Shikoh. Shah Jahan remained imprisoned in Agra for another eight years and died in captivity in 1666. Aurangzeb ruled India from the Mughal throne in Shahjahanabad for almost fifty years, till he died in 1707. An authoritarian ruler, he presided over an era of territorial expansions, and by the time he died, the Mughal Empire extended across almost the entire Subcontinent. Though puritanical, Aurangzeb was neither a religious bigot nor did he despise the fine arts. Highly educated and erudite, he was well-versed in history and Persian literature and was a religious scholar of great eminence.

By now, Shahjahanabad had become quite the centre of art and literature. It was home to some of the best poets of Persian who, though deeply influenced by the great

Persian poets Saadi, Haafiz, Jami and Khaqani, had firmly established their own syncretic style of poetry called Sabk-e-Hindi or the 'Indian Style'. Prominent among these poets were Sirajuddin Ali Khan 'Aarzu', also known as Khan-e-Aarzu, and Maulana Abul-Maáni Mirza Abdul Qadir 'Bedil'. While Khan-e-Aarzu was the first scholar to draw similarities between Sanskrit and Urdu, Bedil was a Sufi mystic and philosopher, whose works would later inspire not only great poets like Ghalib and Iqbal but also Central Asian scholars from Tajikistan and Uzbekistan, where even today he has a cult-like following. Bedil died in 1720. He is believed to be buried in what is today called Bagh-e-Bedil (Bedil Garden) at Mathura Road, across Purana Qila and next to the gates of New Delhi's Major Dhyan Chand National Stadium. Some historians have, however, disputed the claim that he was interred in the grave located in Bagh-e-Bedil. They maintain that it is Khwaja Nooruddin Malik Yar-e-Parraan, a Sufi saint, who lies buried there and Bedil's mortal remains were carried to Afghanistan by some of his disciples soon after his death.

In or around 1700, Wali Mohammad Wali Dakhni, who is widely believed to be the father of the Urdu ghazal, visited Delhi from his native Deccan. His poetry was romantic and his expression typical of his home-region:

> Tujh lab ki sifat laal-e-badakhshaan su kahoonga
> Jaadu hain tere nain ghazalaan su kahoonga
>
> (The beauty of your lips I'll extol before the Ruby of
>   Badakhshan
> I'll tell the gazelle how magical your eyes are.)

Disdainfully called Rekhta or 'assorted dialect', Wali's language was considered rustic and inappropriate for something as refined as poetry which, till then, was exclusively monopolized by Persian. But Wali's expression was so powerful and evocative that he ended up setting the tone for what would soon develop as the Urdu ghazal.

—

Following Aurangzeb's death, his eldest son, Azam Shah, became the emperor for less than three months. He was succeeded by Bahadur Shah I, who till then was the governor of Akbarabad, Kabul and Lahore. The new emperor dreamt of expanding his territories and busied himself in fighting battles outside Shahjahanabad. He was brought to the Capital in 1712 only to be buried next to the Shrine of Qutubuddin Bakhtiyar Kaaki in Mehrauli, then in the outskirts of Delhi. He was followed by Jahandar Shah, who had barely ruled the gigantic empire for six months when, after killing him in a bitter war of succession, his nephew Abul Muzaffar Moinuddin Muhammad Shah Farrukhsiyar succeeded to the Mughal throne. Upon his coronation in February 1713, Farrukhsiyar was presented with an India that was standing at the precipice of fragmentation. Of his two immediate predecessors, Bahadur Shah I had spent all his time outside the Capital and Jahandar Shah had only made a name for his debauchery and decadence. As a result of those six years of neglect, the territories which had been consolidated by Aurangzeb were now in danger of being wrested by provincial chiefs desirous of being rulers of their own independent kingdoms. Farrukhsiyar wasn't up to the difficult task of keeping the empire together and was entirely dependent on his political advisors, some of whom told him that the only way to restore the fading Mughal glory was to unleash fear and crush dissent of all kinds.

In Delhi, meanwhile, what is now called Urdu was

still in the early stages of developing into a language of poetry. It was still called Rekhta, or sometimes Hindi, and was used only by a few native poets. Among them was Mir Jafar 'Zatalli', a satirist who did not shy away from calling a spade a spade, and did that in rather derisive verse. The word 'Zatalli', it seems, had been specially coined by the poet himself to refer to a person who spews nonsense—'zatal'. The mayhem surrounding the decaying Mughal Empire and the incompetence of the emperor and his advisors and officials in dealing with the unfolding crisis kept Zatalli's incensed mind sufficiently nourished and he frequently expressed his anger and frustration in verse. Farrukhsiyar had just ordered the minting of a new coin to mark the beginning of his rule. On the coin was inscribed a Persian couplet:

Sikka-zad az fazl-e-haq bar seem-o-zar
Padshaah-e-bahr-o-bar Farrukhsiyar

(By the grace of God, [he has] minted coins of silver
    and gold
The Emperor of the earth and the oceans, Farrukhsiyar.)

In a parody of this couplet, also in Persian, Zatalli lashed out at the Emperor, referring to rampant corruption, even in the distribution of public supplies and food:

Sikka-zad bar gandum-o-moth-o-matar
Padshaah-e-tasmakash Farrukhsiyar

(He has minted coins even of wheat and lentils and peas
The Emperor whose face is inscribed on the coins—
    Farrukhsiyar.)

The enraged Emperor pronounced a death sentence on Zatalli, and in the very first year of Farrukhsiyar's rule, Zatalli was hanged to death.

In this politically intimidating milieu was born, in 1713, Mirza Mohammad Rafi 'Sauda', who would later be known as Mughal Delhi's first classical Urdu poet and the greatest satirist ever. A fearless poet who raised his voice against the growing decay of the Empire, he was famed for his razor-sharp tongue. Among his contemporaries was Shaikh Ghulam Hamdani 'Mushafi' (1750-1824), a prominent poet who spent his initial years in Delhi. It seems that the name 'Urdu' was first used for the language by Mushafi sometime in the 1780s:

Albatta Rekhta mein hai Mushafi ko daava
Yaani ke hai zabaandaan Urdu ki voh zabaan ka

(Mushafi does claim expertise in Rekhta,
Which means he's a whiz of the Urdu language.)

It is generally believed that Urdu was born in the army camps of Delhi as a language that borrowed words from different languages so that soldiers from different parts could easily communicate with each other. Those who subscribe to this belief think that since in Turkish the word 'Urdu' refers to an army camp, and the language was a product of interactions between soldiers in army camps, it was called Urdu. Noted critic and author, Shamsur Rahman Faruqi, however, dismisses this claim:

The belief that Urdu originated in Muslim army camps and cantonment bazaars helped generate and sustain two myths: Urdu was the language of the Muslims, and being originally the language of camp and cantonment, it stood in natural need of being refined and gentrified, and this process was initiated by the master poets of Delhi in the second half of the eighteenth century. Small wonder, then, that the name 'Urdu', which didn't come into use for the language before the

1780s, is invariably invoked by our historians to 'prove' that since 'Urdu' means 'army, army camp, or the market of a camp', the Urdu language was born as a result of 'foreign' Muslims and local 'Hindus' interacting with each other for petty trade and commerce. None stopped to consider that the only foreign armies in India during and from the 1780s were British (and some French). There were no Arabic or Persian or Turkish-speaking armies in India from the 1780s, and the language of Urdu had by then been in existence for several centuries. Thus the name 'Urdu' which first came into use apparently in the 1780s could not have been given to the language because of the putative army connection.[7]

The name 'Urdu', Faruqi maintains, refers to the language spoken by the inhabitants of the Qila-e-Moalla and its neighbourhood, the area which, because of its elevated position, was called Urdu-e-Moalla-e-Shahjahanabad (Exalted City of Shahjahanabad). 'Urdu'—or 'Oordu' (as it was also called), he says, is a shorter version of the expression Zabaan-e-Urdu-e-Moalla-e-Shahjahanabad (language of the exalted city of Shahjahanabad).

Whatever be the origins of the name, Urdu by now had become the lingua franca of Delhi. It was spoken by everyone, from poor men begging for alms to members of the royalty. Urdu was not just a language, it had become a way of life in Delhi. Urdu poetry was mostly a spoken-word occupation and one did not have to be literate to be a poet or a lover of Urdu poetry. The common man on the streets of Delhi was, thus, as much taken by Urdu poetry as were the royalty and the elite. According to Faruqi, poetry was not 'an activity of literature, but of life'.[8] The disconnect between life and literature, he complains, 'is so great today that people do not appreciate that poetry can be a part of life. Here it was, it was life itself.'[9]

—

Mughal rule continued for one hundred and fifty years after the death of the last of the great Mughals, Aurangzeb, and Delhi remained the seat of the Mughal Empire, with the Qila-e-Moalla as the symbol of its grandeur. But it was a long saga of decline, of chaos, corruption and tragedy.

As the Empire disintegrated, weakened by wars of succession and Mughal nobles asserting independence and declaring themselves rulers of the provinces they governed, large territories were captured by the Marathas, Rohillas and other rising local powers. Delhi was raided and plundered frequently. But none of this compared with the brutal invasions of the city by Nadir Shah in 1739 and by Ahmed Shah Abdali later. In 1739, three years after he became Shah of Persia, Nadir Shah crossed the Indus, drawn by the fabled wealth of Mughal India. He defeated the army of Muhammad Shah and entered Delhi. His soldiers took over the city, and when some residents fought back, Nadir Shah ordered a massacre. In a single day, 22 March 1739, over 20,000 men, women and children were slaughtered in the streets of Shahjahanabad. Ahmad Shah, one of Nadir Shah's generals at the time, was to plunder Delhi and its surrounding areas repeatedly some two decades later.

Delhi recovered from this loot and savagery, too.

Meanwhile, a new power was rising: the British East India Company. Having defeated Nawab Sirajuddaulah at the Battle of Plassey in 1757, the Company had been granted the right to collect revenue in Bengal and Bihar. By 1773, the Company had turned into an almost parallel government in much of India and had set up its 'capital' in

Calcutta. How, then, could the Mughal capital escape the Company's attention?

By 1803, the Company had firmly established its presence in Delhi, and began curtailing the powers of the Mughal Emperor. Farrukhsiyar's successors turned out to be more feeble and more incompetent than him. They also seemed indifferent to the changing power balance in the Capital. By the time Akbar Shah II took over the reins of the Mughal Empire in 1806, sovereign command had literally been usurped by the Company. It did not take the British very long to demonetize the Mughal currency, and by 1835 they had begun minting their own coins without any reference to the Mughal Emperor.

While in the political scheme of things the supremacy of the Qila-e-Moalla was fast shrinking, Delhi was playing capital to a parallel empire. It had become the most vibrant centre of Urdu literature in India. Though the language and its poetry were being patronized by the ruling Nawabs in Lucknow and Nizams in Hyderabad as well, because of it being the home of the Mughal rulers and nobles and because of its cosmopolitan society, Delhi was the Urdu poet's chosen destination. With the rising control of the Company, Delhi's elite had begun to cultivate the English officials and traders who had taken up residence in the city. Since Urdu transcended boundaries of religion and ethnicity, it acted as a secular bridge between the different communities of Delhi, and this led to the white man's interest in Urdu poetry and, occasionally, its patronage by the English sahib. Young officers would be invited to lavish poetry evenings by prominent Dilliwalas. Some of them even took to formally learning the language and trying their hand at poetry. Thus, while Mughal power and influence diminished, Urdu continued to grow and evolve.

Boasting of unique idioms and inimitable figures of

speech, Delhi's Urdu had an atypical flavour, different from the character of its Awadh or Deccan sisters. The city's women, especially courtesans, who were women of independent means, often widely read and remarkably self-possessed, had adopted Urdu enthusiastically. They enriched the language with their own vocabulary and mannerisms. They could either be very proper and decorous or sardonic and even coquettish. Mushafi had famously said:

Ae Mushafi tu in se mohabbat na kijiyo
Zaalim ghazab hi hoti hain yeh Dilli-waaliyaan[10]

(O Mushafi! Don't fall in love with them
These damsels of Delhi are damn cruel.)

The Qila-e-Moalla, too, occupied a dominant position in the literary life of the city. Its customs were different from those of the city outside. Its syntax was distinct, and it influenced Urdu just as much as the vocabulary and syntax of the street, salon and pleasure house.

It was customary for Urdu poets to adopt a *nom de plume* or takhallus. One of the first Urdu poets of Delhi was Shaikh Zuhuruddin (1699—1792) who adopted the takhallus 'Hatim' and is, thus, known as Shaikh Zuhuruddin Hatim. Fed up of the anarchy and chaos that followed the city's incessant invasions, it was he who had remarked:

Pagdi apni yahaan sambhaal chalo
Aur basti na ho ye Dilli hai

(Take care of your turban here
This is no other city but Delhi.)

Hatim was followed, in the eighteenth century, by Mirza Rafi 'Sauda', Khwaja Mir 'Dard' and Mir Taqi 'Mir', and in the following century by Shaikh Mohammad Ibrahim 'Zauq', Momin Khan 'Momin', Mirza Asadullah Khan

'Ghalib' and Nawab Mirza Khan 'Daagh' Dehlvi. Of course, there were a number of others too. Many of the later Mughal Emperors themselves were poets. Shah Alam II wrote under the takhallus 'Aftab' and the last Mughal Emperor, Bahadur Shah, called himself 'Zafar'. Delhi also saw a surge of visiting poets through much of the eighteenth century and up to the mid-nineteenth from nearby areas. Among them were Qayam 'Chandpuri', Insha Allah Khan 'Insha', and many others, most of them aspiring poets hoping to make a name for themselves. It was common practice for senior poets to accept young poets as pupils or shaagird. The senior poet, acting as ustaad, or tutor, would supervise and mend verses composed by his pupils. In common parlance, this would be called 'ghazal banaana' or 'mending a ghazal', though the more sophisticated ones would call it 'islaah karaana' or 'getting it improved'.

The elite would organize mushairas, social gatherings where poets would be invited to recite their verse. The mushaira soon became an important institution of Urdu literature, offering poets a secular space to not only showcase their poetic talent but also vent their anger and frustration with political, social and economic affairs. To this day, the mushaira continues to occupy a central position in Urdu poetry across the world. Certain customs became attached to the mushaira. It would be presided over by a senior poet or a member of the royalty who was also a poet. The junior-most poet would be asked to recite first and the one presiding—sadr-e-mushaira—would recite last. A big candle or a lamp called shama-e-mehfil would be placed in front of the poet who was reciting, indicating that he was 'on'. There were some basic genres or forms of poetry, the romantic ghazal being the most popular one.

A ghazal is a collection of many couplets—sher—of the same length and following the same metre. These couplets are thematically autonomous of each other. Sometimes, though, a few of them can be read together, indicating a single theme, and when this is done, the cluster of couplets is called qita or qata. Each line of a sher is called a misra and the first sher of a ghazal is called the matla. In the matla the two lines rhyme with each other, whereas throughout the rest of the ghazal only the second lines of the sher rhyme with each other. The last couplet of the ghazal, in which the poet's takhallus appears as a signature, is called the maqta.

Poetry is figurative and allegorical and Urdu poetry is no exception. With the growth of the ghazal form, founded almost entirely on the theme of love, a new lexicon evolved with its distinct metaphors, similes and allusions. For instance, the beloved would be referred to as 'kaafir', which literally means 'infidel' but can also mean heartless or merciless. When the beloved's beauty was being extolled, she, sometimes he, would be called 'sanam', which literally means 'idol'. Agnieszka Kuczkiewicz-Fras, a Polish scholar of Urdu linguistics and literature, has compiled a formidable list of terms metaphorically used in the ghazal. They include maikhaana (tavern), baada or mai (wine), jaam, pyaala or paimaana (goblet or peg), saaqi (wine-bearer), badmasti or khumaar (intoxication), shama and parvaana (candle and the moth), gul and bulbul (flower/rose and the nightingale), bijli or barq and aashiyaana (lightning and the nest), and historical or legendary figures like Yusuf (Joseph, famous for his beauty), Isa/Eesa or Ibn-e-Maryam (Jesus Christ or Mary's son), famous Arabian lovers Laila and Majnu or Qais, or their Persian counterparts Shireen and Farhad. All these, she says:

> ...used as catalytic agents, are arranged and employed according to a poet's imagination and sensibility with only one aim: to describe his love and the whole range

of associate feelings like sadness, loneliness, yearning, longing, desire or devotion. Love is the central theme of the ghazal and its conception is highly idealistic and sensuous. However, love depicted in the ghazal is first and foremost one-sided and unrequited, platonic (or even spiritual) but at the same time irresistible, sublime and idealizing both the object of love and the lover's emotion. The probable crucial reason which has motivated the evolution of such a concept of love was the fact that love pictured in ghazals was illicit in its character, as for the member of the purdah society there existed only three possibilities to experience love, and all three of them were socially not allowed: love for a woman betrothed or married to another man, love for a courtesan, and homosexual love for a young and beautiful boy.[11]

As Delhi was ravaged by frequent invasions, many of its best poets migrated to other parts of the country. Despite their resilience, some of them could just not bear the sight of their beloved city being plundered and devastated. Naturally, they expressed their sorrow in poetry. Thus, they tried their hands at a genre called shehr-ashob— also referred to as sheher-e-ashob (literally, 'misfortunes of the city')—a poem lamenting the loss of a city's soul. There was also elegiac poetry in the form of nauha and marsiya.

Since royalty and aristocracy played an important role in patronizing poets, there arose a tradition of odes called qaseedah, as well. All in all, Delhi of the eighteenth and nineteenth centuries was overflowing with Urdu poetry.

Ironically, this was happening as Mughal Delhi, the great theatre of Urdu poetry, was losing its eminence. By the time the frail sixty-two-year-old Bahadur Shah Zafar ascended the throne in September 1837, the grandeur of the Mughal Empire had completely faded away. The people of Delhi still looked up to Zafar as the Zill-e-Subhaani (Shadow of God), and poets still sought his appreciation and patronage, but he was Emperor only in name, reduced to a mere employee of the East India Company, surviving on an annual stipend that barely covered the costs of running the Qila-e-Moalla which, by now, shorn of its erstwhile splendour, had begun to be referred to as Lal Qila or Red Fort.

The year 1857 changed Delhi forever. In May that year, Indian sepoys of the British East India Company rose against the Company in what they thought was a gigantic rebellion. They marched to Delhi and proclaimed Bahadur Shah Zafar as their Emperor without poor Zafar playing any significant role in the proclamation. Called the Great Indian Mutiny or Ghadar, the revolt was soon crushed by the British forces. It was a bloodbath. Thousands were killed in Delhi alone. As the city was reclaimed by the British within four months, its katras were razed to the ground and its mohallas were wiped out. The Emperor's sons were captured and killed and the Emperor himself was sentenced to life imprisonment in Burma. A large number of residents fled the city to safer environs. Amongst them were writers, poets, artists and scholars. The two major poets who survived the Delhi holocaust were Ghalib, who was over sixty by then, and Daagh, who was in his mid-twenties. While Daagh later migrated to Rampur and then relocated to Hyderabad, Ghalib continued to live in the city, till he died in 1869. Both were distraught and heartbroken. An era had come to an end, and a rather bloody end. The poet Mohsin Naqvi wrote:

Mohsin hamaare saath bada haadsa hua
Hum reh gaye hamaara zamaana chala gaya

(Mohsin, a great tragedy struck us
Our time went by, we were left behind.)

What was this bygone era all about? What was happening in that era in Mughal Delhi? It is said that a narrative is never more enchanting than when it is in verse. The times we live in, the dreams we see and the heartbreaks we suffer resonate in the songs we sing and the poetry we hum. Should we, then, not make an effort to peep into that era through the lens of its songs and poetry?

In Urdu, we can find a number of biographical accounts of the poets of Mughal Delhi and their times, including commentaries written by authors who witnessed those times first hand, the foremost amongst them being *Aab-e-Hayat*[12], authored by Maulana Muhammad Husain Azad in 1880. The Maulana was a shaagird of Zauq, for which reason he depicts the life and work of his ustaad with a certain exaggeration, but this bias apart, his record is of great historical value. In a sense, the Maulana was following in the footsteps of his equally illustrious father, Maulvi Muhammad Baqar, who had purchased a lithographic printing press (which cost a fortune at the time) and launched Delhi's first Urdu newspaper, *Dehli Urdu Akhbaar*, in 1836 at a monthly subscription of two rupees. During the 1857 revolt, the *Akhbaar* published fierce criticism of British brutality. Maulvi Baqar was arrested and sentenced to death without a trial.[13]

Many years before *Aab-e-Hayaat*, the British East India Company had commissioned Mirza Sangeen Beg to draw a list of the important structures then existing in Shahjahanabad and in the ruins of the earlier cities. Beg did far more. In his Persian book *Sair-ul-Manazil*[14], not only did he describe these structures but also copied the Persian and Arabic inscriptions carved on their stone tablets containing the names of their builders, architects, calligraphers and others. In 1847, the great educational reformer Sir Syed Ahmad Khan had published a book on the monuments and history of Delhi titled *Asar-ul-Sanadid* (Remnants of Ancient Heroes). In 1853 he published another book with the same title albeit with different content. Then there was Mirza Farhatullah Baig Dehlvi, who wrote a dramatic presentation of Mughal Delhi's fictionalized last mushaira and called it *Dehli ki Aakhri Shama* (The Last Lamp of Delhi). Though fiction, the book gives vivid descriptions of the poets of nineteenth-century Delhi, their homes, their sartorial sense and their mannerisms. Many more biographical accounts of the Urdu poets of Delhi were published in later years, but most of them are available only to readers who can read the Urdu script and have access to the few Urdu libraries that exist in university departments or small-time Urdu institutions. And even these readers have to contend with a serious drawback—while some poets have dozens of books written about them, others are subject matters of a slim volume or two. In some cases, even these slim volumes turn out to be mere collections of their poetry rather than narratives of their lives and times.

Delhi has witnessed immense, radical change in the last three hundred years. It is completely transformed from what it used to be at the turn of the nineteenth century. However, what has not changed is the popularity of its Mughal poets and their poetry. Delhi's classical Urdu poets, from Mir to Daagh, remain the most quoted poets of the language ever. Often, people quote them without realizing that what is being quoted was actually penned some two hundred years ago. That this poetry remains relevant today bears testimony to the great skill of these poets, the universality of their themes and the enduring quality of their compositions. They were great thinkers, far ahead of their times. It is a pity that their lives and the life of the city they lived in—and which shaped them and their poetry—have not been documented in a single volume for the general

English reader. Even though short biographies of some of these poets may be found in larger works on Delhi written in English, there is hardly a book in the language which captures their fascinating world in detail. The book in your hands is the result of an effort to do exactly that. It seeks to give you an overview of the lives, times and works of the poets you quote or hear quoted so often.

What this book also intends to do is to tell you what we have done with the heritage that these poets have left behind for us—their homes, their haunts, their graves. Have we even a vestige of pride, love or even compassion in our hearts for this treasure-trove?

The photographs in the book of the places, as they exist today, where these poets lived, composed, recited and died provide the answer.

Perhaps Sahir Ludhianvi (1921-1980) spoke not only of himself but of the greats who preceded him, who, too, must have known what their fate would be:

Kal aur aaeinge naghmon ki khilti kaliyaan chunne waale
Mujh se behtar kehne waale tum se behtar sunne waale

Saagar se ubhri leher hoon mai'n saagar mein phir kho
     jaaonga
Mitti ki rooh ka sapna hoon mitti mein phir so jaaonga

Kal koi mujh ko yaad kare kyon koi mujh ko yaad kare
Masroof zamaana mere liye kyon waqt apna barbaad kare

(There will be others tomorrow to pick the blossomed
     buds of poetry
Better composers than me, better listeners than you,

I'm the rising wave of an ocean, I'll be lost in the same
     ocean
I'm a dream of the earth's soul, I'll be buried in the same
     earth,

Someone might remember me tomorrow—but then again,
  why?
Why would this busy world waste its time on me?)

I am neither a historian nor an Urdu scholar. But I have
grown up around dining-table conversations not only about
but also *in* Urdu poetry. This book is the culmination of
my love of those conversations. Poetry is love and there
are two ways to study love. You can either read scholarly
texts on its metaphysical aspects, or you can read notes
written by lovers themselves, in which they bare their souls,
the passion and longing that beat in their hearts and flow
in their veins. I urge you to place my book in the second
category. Please read it only as you would a book written by
a lover. Read it also as a taster's menu for those who love
Urdu, its poetry and cadence, but have little or no access
to it. The scholarly job of narrating the history of Urdu I
have left to Sohail Hashmi saheb, who has performed it
with his trademark erudition in the Preface.

Talking of love, in the subtitle of this book, Delhi has
been ascribed the feminine gender—'A Mughal City and
Her Greatest Poets'. In English and many other languages,
countries and cities have traditionally been seen as feminine.
This is truer of Mughal Delhi because the city was a female
'beloved' for the great Mughal poets—as far as one can infer
from their verse and the conventions of their time. Today,
this might be contentious. So I bow to the old convention
on the cover, and then use the safer 'it' for the city through
the rest of the book.

The job of selecting verses to be included in this book,
especially those of Mir, Ghalib and Daagh, was quite
onerous. Even more difficult was deciding which verses to
keep out. The selection exposes my personal biases and I
can do no better than to fall back upon Ghalib:

Khulta kisi pe kyon mere dil ka muaamla
Sheron ke intekhaab ne rusva kiya mujhe

(Why would my heart's affair be revealed to anyone?
My selection of verses has made me notorious.)

A word about the translations—they are all mine. However, I am skeptical about calling them 'translations'. I firmly believe that poetry defies translation. Therefore, I have made the English rendition of the verses mainly explanatory and illustrative of the poets' intent in the original. I am no poet, so that is the best I can do. I would only ask you to not judge my book by its 'translations'.

There are innumerable books on Delhi and its history, but no work on the city can ever be called 'complete', for Delhi does not cease to charm or surprise. Even after years and centuries, it continues to bewitch its lovers. In 'India Remembered', Percival and Margaret Spear have beautifully unveiled Delhi's truth in just two sentences:

> Full understanding is granted to no one. For those who seek, there are rewarding glimpses of 'The gorgeous palaces, the cloud capp'd towers' but always *'Dilli dur ast'*, the Delhi of full knowledge is far away.[15]

The magical spell of Delhi endures. As I continue to remain beguiled by the city, the Dilliwala in me offers you its story through the words of her eloquent poets:

Hamin hain maujib-e-baab-e-fasaahat hazrat-e-Shaayar
Zamaana seekhta hai hum se hum vo Dilliwaale hain[16]

(We are the cause of that chapter on eloquence, O Poet
We are Dilliwalas, the world takes lessons from us.)

Saif Mahmood

August 2018
New Delhi

MIRZA MOHAMMAD RAFI SAUDA

The Great Satirist
(1713–1781)

Sauda ko agar poochho, ahwaal hai ye uska
Do-chaar ghadi rona, do-chaar ghadi baatein

(If you ask Sauda, he'll describe his condition thus:
He cries for a while, he talks for a while.)

—

Dair-o-haram ko dekha, Allah re fuzooli
Ye kya zulm dhaaya dil sa makaan banaaya

(I see their temples and mosques—O God,
what extravagance!
You've been so cruel to them, making Your home in
our hearts.)

I

ONE OF THE MOST PRIZED POSSESSIONS OF THE INDIA Office Records in London's British Library is an eighteenth-century handwritten manuscript containing some Urdu verses. The manuscript is believed to have been personally presented by its illustrious author to Richard Johnson, the British Assistant Resident in Lucknow, in recognition of the Englishman's love for the Urdu language.[17] The author of the manuscript, whose signature appears on the cover, was none other than Mughal India's greatest Urdu satirist, Mirza Mohammad Rafi Sauda who, along with Mir Taqi Mir and Khwaja Mir Dard, is considered one of the 'three pillars' of Delhi's classical Urdu poetry. He was a courageous poet, with an acerbic tongue and razor-sharp wit, and it is a pity that his name has not travelled beyond the corridors of Urdu academia and literary history. In the twenty-first century, when writers are being brazenly persecuted for their audacity to even speak up, Sauda astounds us with a voice that could not be silenced by brutal kings or drowned in the pandemonium of an empire in spectacular decline.

Sauda was born as Mirza Mohammad Rafi in Delhi in 1713 to Mirza Muhammad Shafi, an Afghan aristocrat who had migrated to India for trade. Shafi's wife was the daughter of Niamat Khan Ali, a celebrated writer known for his works describing the decay of Golconda after its siege by Aurangzeb in 1687. This illustrious parentage gave Sauda 'the advantage not merely of an affluent background, but also of close association with the literary and intellectual atmosphere of the age'.[18] It is widely believed that his takhallus, 'Sauda', denoted his father's profession—that of a merchant, or saudaagar. However, Maulana Mohammad Hussain Azad, in his magnum opus on the classical Urdu poets, *Aab-e-Hayaat*, has rubbished this claim and maintains that the word 'Sauda', in this case, means 'madness':

> The truth is that the poets of Asia, in every country, live and breathe through love; and 'sauda' [=madness] and 'deewangi' [=madness] are born together with love. Thus, madness too is a cause of pride to lovers. So with regard to this he chose 'Sauda' as his pen-name, and thanks to 'saudagiri' [=merchandizing] the verbal device of punning came as a 'special free offer' into his poetry.[19]

Sauda was born and lived in Delhi's Kabuli Darwaaza (Kabul Gate) area—close to what is today known as Naya Bazar, near Khari Baoli—which was an upmarket neighbourhood back then, inhabited by the city's elite and connoisseurs of art and culture. Those were the times when the 'domni', or courtesan, had a distinct place in society. Courtesans were not only trained in music and dance but also well-versed in poetry and would often receive influential guests for exclusive evening performances. The easiest route to reach the Qila-e-Moalla (now the Red Fort), the seat of the Mughal Empire, from Kabuli Darwaaza was through Chawri Bazar, then an avenue on which stood the elegant mansions of some of Delhi's best-known courtesans. Such was the splendour of this avenue that it inspired the poet Rasikh Azimabadi (b. 1748) to compare it to the famed Mount Caucasus of West Asia:

> Chawri qaaf hai ya khuld-e-bareen hai Rasikh
> Jhamghatey hooron ke, pariyon ke pirey rehte hain
>
> (Is Chawri Mount Caucasus or is it Paradise, Rasikh?
> Swarms of houries and fairies are woven into this
>   tapestry.)

Many years later the neighbourhood also became home to the last poet laureate of the Mughal Court, Shaikh

Mohammad Ibrahim Zauq. It is said that when Zauq would enter the Kabuli Darwaaza area on his way back from the Qila-e-Moalla, he would invariably speak of the greatness of Sauda and his poetry to his companions and pray for the peace of his soul.

Kabuli Darwaaza got its name from the caravans going to and returning from Kabul that regularly passed through it. The gate known as Khooni Darwaaza, located in the centre of today's Bahadur Shah Zafar Marg in Delhi, opposite the Maulana Azad Medical College and just ahead of the Times of India building, is often mistaken for the Kabuli Darwaaza—one of the many misconceptions about the remnants of Mughal Delhi. But such errors and disregard are par for the course in our part of the world.

There are hardly any reliable historical accounts of Sauda's life, but it is generally believed that he began trying his hand at poetry in his very early twenties. Emperor Farrukhsiyar had died in 1719 when Sauda was just six years old and, after short stints of three months each by two of Farrukhsiyar's ineffective successors, his cousin Naseeruddin Muhammad Shah (born Roshan Akhtar) had taken over the reins of the Mughal Empire.

Though an incompetent ruler whose reign saw rampant corruption, Muhammad Shah was a great patron of art and literature. During his rule, Nawab Nizamul Mulk Asaf Jah I, the autonomous Governor of Hyderabad and the Emperor's most trusted lieutenant, came to Delhi on an extended visit, from June 1738 to July 1741. Travelling with the Nizam was his official chronicler, Dargah Quli Khan, who wrote a detailed record of his travels with the Nizam and called it 'Risala-e-Salar Jung', which was re-published in 1926 as a travelogue titled *Muraqqa-e-Dehli* (Images of Delhi)[20]. The *Muraqqa* suggests that the Emperor literally lived on and for music, poetry and dance. In fact, he was formally trained in music himself, by the great master of his time, Nemat Khan. He also liked to wear women's dresses and footwear, take off into the jungles on hunting expeditions, watch elephant and partridge fights, and organize performances by Delhi's best courtesans, jugglers and mimics in his private chambers. Shah's colourful personality earned him the epithet 'Rangeela', or 'the colourful one', and he is popularly known to this day as Muhammad Shah Rangeela.

In 1748, Nawab Asif Jah I died and, it is believed, Rangeela succumbed to the tragic news. He was buried next to the mausoleum of Delhi's presiding Sufi saint, Hazrat Nizamuddin Auliya, where his tomb still exists. Sauda was thirty-five at the time. Almost his entire youth, then, had been witness to the charmingly bizarre indulgences of an emperor oblivious to the ruination of the mighty empire he had inherited. It was the strangest and most contradictory of times: as one of history's grandest empires was being obliterated, there was a great flowering of poetry, painting and the performing arts. Perhaps Muhammad Shah Rangeela came to the throne at the wrong time. He might have been remembered for presiding over a remarkable cultural renaissance—he was a patron not only of miniature painters, calligraphers, poets, musicians and dancers, but also supported scholarship and science, abolished the jiziya tax imposed by Aurangzeb, reintroduced qawwali singing in the Mughal court and replaced Persian with Urdu as the official language of the Empire. But as it happens, he is remembered only for the invasions and plunder that devastated Delhi and other parts of North India in his time.

Between 1737 and 1757 Delhi was plundered and looted repeatedly by one invader after another. At the young age of twenty-four, Sauda was witness to the siege of Delhi by Maratha forces led by Bajirao I. This was followed by the gory invasion of Delhi by the Persian King Nadir Shah.

In 1721, Roshan-ud-Daula Zafar Khan, a Mughal noble, had built a beautiful mosque in Chandni Chowk near the Kotwali Chabutra next to the present-day Gurudwara Sisganj Saheb. The mosque soon became a popular centre for religious gatherings and later began to be called the Sunehri Masjid because of the golden coating on its domes and turrets. On 22 March 1739, Nadir Shah rode into this mosque and from here gave orders to his troops to begin a brutal onslaught on the unarmed people of Delhi. Michael Axworthy, in his book *The Sword of Persia: Nader Shah, from Tribal Warrior to Conquering Tyrant*, writes:

> On the morning of 22 March, Nader mounted his horse and rode from the palace to the Roshan-od-Dowala mosque [the former name of Sunehri Masjid]. As he arrived there with his men about him, some people threw stones from balconies and windows around the mosque, and a shot was fired, killing an officer beside him. He had already made up his mind, but this final insult may have added fury to Nader's frustration. He went to the roof of the mosque and stood by the golden domes, looking out over the houses, shops and roofs of the Chandni Chowk district. He ordered that no one should be left alive in any part where any of his soldiers had been killed, and then drew his sword as a signal that the massacre should begin.[21]

The carnage went on for a number of days, till such time as Emperor Rangeela accepted defeat and handed over the royal treasury, the royal throne—later to be called the Takht-e-Taaoos (Peacock Throne)—and various Mughal jewels, including the Koh-i-Noor (Mountain of Light) diamond, to Nadir Shah.

After some years, Ahmad Shah Abdali, who had accompanied Nadir Shah to India in 1739 as one of his generals, attacked Delhi and ordered another mass massacre.

Yet again, Delhi was pillaged and blood ran through its streets.

This, then, was the climate in which Sauda matured as a poet.

Sauda originally wrote in Persian for many years. It was at the insistence of a great Persian poet and Urdu scholar of the time, Sirajuddin Ali Khan 'Aarzu', known to history as 'Khan-e-Aarzu', that he started writing in Urdu. Aarzu was the author of two highly regarded Urdu dictionaries and ustaad, or teacher, to many an aspiring poet, including Mirza Mazhar Jan-e-Janaan and the young Mir Taqi Mir. Of Khan-e-Aarzu it has been said that 'his relationship with Urdu literature is equivalent to Aristotle's place in the tradition of philosophy (that is, he laid down the rules for later generations)'[22]. Unfortunately, none of his verses have been preserved. Khan-e-Aarzu would sit in the Zeenat-ul-Masjid, a mosque built by Emperor Aurangzeb's daughter, Zeenat-un-Nisa, and young poets would congregate there to meet him. Now popularly known as Ghata Masjid, the mosque still stands on a street just off Ansari Road in Daryaganj. In fact, the street is named after the mosque.

Though deeply inspired by Khan-e-Aarzu, Sauda never formally became his shaagird, or pupil. Sauda's first formal ustaad in poetry was Sulaiman Quli Khan 'Vidad', a Persian poet in the court of Rangeela. After some years as Vidad's shaagird, Sauda sought the mentorship of Shaikh Zuhuruddin 'Hatim', who had written numerous poems in praise of Rangeela's regime but later lamented the swift turn of providence:

> Kaho kis tarah koi ho khush yahaan ek dum aise daur
>   mein
> Na vo bazm hai na vo saaqi hai na vo shauq hai na
>   firaagh-e-dil.

(How does one remain happy for even a moment in these
    times, pray tell me
When nothing survives; no gathering, no wine-bearer, no
    passion, no large-heartedness.)

Hatim outlived Sauda and, in one of his compilations which
gives a list of his pupils, has recorded Sauda's name with
immense pride.[23]

While Sauda's poetry had started becoming popular
around 1745, when he was in his early thirties, his fame
seems to have reached the Mughal court only after two
decades or so. In these two decades, much had changed in
Mughal Delhi. Rangeela, the great patron of the arts, had
died after ruling for twenty-eight years, and after three of his
successors came and went in quick succession within eleven
years, Shah Alam II had ascended to the Mughal throne. In
those days, rulers and aristocrats who were fond of poetry
and wanted to improve their poetic skills would request
established poets or scholars to 'mend' their poems ('ghazal
banaana'). Though this meant changing an occasional word
to either enhance the musicality or quality of a verse or to
correct its metre, it is widely believed that under the cloak
of 'mending', many rich young princes and nobles would
actually get their poetry ghost-written for a fee. It was a
fantastic arrangement—while the broke poet, who could
(or would) do nothing other than composing verse, would
not mind infusion of additional income, his rich benefactor
would earn 'poethood'. In or around 1765, impressed by
Sauda's literary prowess, Shah Alam II invited him to the
Qila-e-Moalla and sought his help with his poetic skills.
However, this relationship did not last long. Sauda was a
no-nonsense man. Soon the Emperor's royal demands began
to irritate him. It is believed that one morning, the Emperor
was insisting that Sauda recite a particular ghazal for him
and Sauda was avoiding the recitation. The Emperor finally

asked him: 'Mirza, how many ghazals do you manage to compose every day?'

Sauda replied, 'My Lord, I manage to compose only three or four verses.'

To this, the Emperor condescendingly said, 'My friend, I compose three or four whole ghazals while I am in my bathroom every morning.'

'No wonder they smell so bad,' said Sauda, and came away.[24]

The Emperor sent for him a number of times after that and offered to appoint him as the Malik-ul-Shoara, or Poet Laureate, of his court. But Sauda turned down the offer, saying his poetry would make him the Poet Laureate and not some royal decree. Sauda firmly believed that his poetry spoke for itself. Of his own rising popularity, he says:

Sukhan mera hai muqaabil mere sukhan ke hi
Ke mai'n sukhan se hoon mash'hoor aur sukhan mujh se

(My poetry is rivalled only by my own poetry
For I am famed for poetry, and poetry is famed for me.)

Having inherited considerable wealth from his father, Sauda was financially sound and there was no dearth of nobles and the elite in Delhi who appreciated his poetry and held him in high esteem. Sauda, therefore, lived a comfortable life without having to bother about his source of livelihood or curry favour with anyone.

By the mid-eighteenth century, the law and order situation in Shahjahanabad had become appalling. Thefts, robberies and armed assaults had become routine. In *Three Mughal Poets*, Khurshidul Islam and Ralph Russell describe this period as one where the city was 'swarming with thieves and robbers, who go unpunished because the police are in league with them; the danger of assault is always present so that men go out in the evening to a mushaira fully armed,

as though they were going to a battle'.[25] Disgusted with
this law of the jungle, Sauda, past fifty by now, laments:

> Is zamaane ka jo dekha toh hai ulta insaaf
> Gurg azaad rahein aur ho shubaan pehre mein
>
> (Justice in this age is turned upside down
> Wolves are free and shepherds under guard.)

Almost two centuries later, the great Faiz Ahmed Faiz would
give vent to his disgust with the situation in Pakistan under
military rule using a similar metaphor:

> Hai ahl-e-dil ke liye ab ye nazm-e-bast-o-kushaad
> Ki sang-o-khisht muqayyid hain, aur sag aazaad
>
> (For the compassionate, there is now a new order:
> Stones and bricks are locked up, and rabid dogs set free.)

With Delhi having been repeatedly vandalized, Sauda felt
distressed and decided to leave his beloved city. The numbers
of his patrons and fans in Delhi had also diminished.
During those days, there were only two places of refuge
for Urdu poets and scholars—Awadh and Hyderabad-
Deccan. Hyderabad was far away. Awadh was being ruled
by Nawab Shuja-ud-Daula, with Faizabad as his capital.
Sauda's mentor, Khan-e-Aarzu, had already left Delhi in
1750 and settled in Faizabad under the patronage of the
Nawab. Sauda was close to Imad-ul-Mulk, a nobleman
to whom Ahmad Shah Abdali had assigned the task of
collecting revenue from Awadh. On Imad-ul-Mulk's advice,
Sauda accompanied him to Awadh and, in or around 1770,
they reached Farrukhabad. Sauda stayed in Farrukhabad for
some months with its ruling patron, Nawab Ahmed Khan
Bangash, and his prime minister, Meherban Khan, who was
a great admirer of Sauda's. It is believed that Sauda was
so content with his life in Farrukhabad that when Nawab
Shuja-ud-Daula sent him a personal invitation along with

travel expenses to join his court in Faizabad, he declined
the request and sent his regrets in the form of a qita, telling
the Nawab that life was too short to keep relocating for
material pleasures:

> Sauda pae duniya tu bahar-su kab tak
> Aawaara az een koocha baan ku kab tak
> Haasil yahi is se hai ke duniya hove
> Bil-farz hua yoon bhi toh phir kab tak

> (Sauda, for worldly desires, how far will you run?
> How long will you wander from one place to another?
> All you can gain from this is the wealth of the world
> Assuming you get it, how long will it last?)

In 1771, Nawab Bangash died and with him died Sauda's
royal patronage. Sauda now decided to take up Shuja-ud-
Daula's offer. He relocated to Faizabad. When he arrived
in Faizabad, the Nawab welcomed him to his court with
great honour. However, the Nawab committed what later
turned out to be the grave mistake of reciting the qita that
Sauda had sent him long ago, adding: 'Mirza, aap ka ye
qita mere dil mein ab tak naqsh hai' ('Mirza, this quatrain
of yours is still engraved in my heart'). Sauda thought the
Nawab was taunting him about his financial constraints
which had finally made him change his mind. He bowed
and went away, never to return to the court in Shuja-ud-
Daula's lifetime.[26] When Nawab Asaf-ud-Daula succeeded
Shuja-ud-Daula, he invited Sauda to his court and Sauda
finally accepted the invitation.

When the capital of Awadh shifted to Lucknow in 1775,
Sauda moved to the new capital too and was awarded an
estate yielding an annual grant of six thousand rupees,
a rather handsome sum at the time. Sauda remained
in Lucknow till his last. He died on 26 June 1781 and

was buried at Imambara Agha Baqar in what is now the Yahyaganj area of Lucknow.

It was in the Awadh court that Sauda first met Richard Johnson, the British Assistant Resident who was a great connoisseur of Urdu literature and to whom he presented the manuscript of his collected verse just before he died. Johnson was later instrumental in getting Sauda's works published.

II

SAUDA'S BITING SATIRE REMAINS UNPARALLELED. THE MID-nineteenth-century Shahjahanabad, it is said, reverberated with instances of his razor-sharp wit and people would be careful not to get on his wrong side. Sauda would often use ingenious invective. Once a young poet, anxious to meet him, was brought to his house in Kabuli Darwaaza by a friend. The youngster recited some of his couplets and expressed his desire to enrol as a pupil of Sauda's. After listening to him for a while, Sauda asked him what takhallus he had chosen for himself. The young man replied, 'Ummeedvaar'. The word 'ummeed' in Urdu means 'hope' and, consequently, the word 'ummeedvaar' means 'one with hope'. However, in another connotation, the word ummeed is also used to denote pregnancy and an expectant lady could be referred to as being 'ummeed se', or 'one with hope'. On hearing the eager young man's takhallus, Sauda grinned and mumbled:

> Hai faiz se kisi ke shajar unka baar-daar
> Iss vaaste kya hai takhallus 'ummeedvaar'?

> (His tree will bear fruit with the triumph of another,
> Is this why his takhallus is 'ummeedvaar'?)

Embarrassed, the young man immediately decided to look not only for another takhallus but also for another ustaad.

Sauda was also famed for his quick-temper. Wherever he would go, a man-servant would follow him carrying pen, ink and paper. If he was unhappy with someone, he would immediately compose a satirical verse making that person the object of his anger. One of his favourite targets was a gentleman called Mir Zaahik, father of Sauda's contemporary and well-known poet Mir Hasan, who, like Sauda, had also migrated to Awadh. Once Sauda and another poet, Sikandar, were visiting Prince Mirza Sulaiman Shikoh, son of Emperor Shah Alam at the Qila-e-Moalla in Delhi when Mir Zaahik arrived. The Prince, well-aware of Sauda's dislike for Zaahik, turned to Sauda and asked if he would like to recite something for the guest. Sauda replied that he had not composed anything but Sikandar had, and then recited the following verse:

Ya rab tu meri sun le, ye kehta hai Sikandar
Zaahik ke uda deve kisi ban mein qalandar
Ghar us ke tawallud ho agar bachcha-e-bandar
Galiyon mein nachaata phirey vo Bangley ke andar
Roti toh kama khaaye kisi taur mucchandar

(O Almighty, listen to my pleas, says Sikandar
Let a magician make Zaahik lose his senses in a forest
And should then a baby monkey be born to him
He can make it dance in the streets of Bangla [Faizabad]—
At least the moustached fellow will earn his bread.)

It was a nasty, crude comment, and on hearing it, Zaahik pounced upon Sikandar. While others tried to separate the two, Sauda stood in a corner grinning.[27] According to Islam and Russell, 'Sauda enjoyed all and more of the licence that is still granted to the modern political cartoonist, who may ridicule the personal appearance and habits of his target, though these have nothing to do with the point of his cartoon.'[28]

Despite his aversion to Zaahik, Sauda had a genial relationship with his son, Mir Hasan, who would publicly acknowledge Sauda's hospitality and affection. This strengthens the belief among many biographers that Sauda's targets were not his literary rivals but those who sought to acquire an elevated place in society by masquerading as scholars or poets.

Another victim of Sauda's satire was a self-proclaimed Kashmiri intellectual, Nudrat. There is no individual who has fallen prey to such repeated attacks by Sauda for his literary pretensions as Nudrat:

> Faazilon ki toh bazm mein hotey ho ja ke sheyr-khvaan
> Shaairon paas aap ko kehte ho nehv-o-safrdaan
> Dono ho jama jis jagah phir tumhein vaan jagah kahaan
> Bolo jo vaan kuchh aan kar sab kahein tum ko meherbaan
> Ghodey ko do na do lagaam, muhn ko tunak lagaam do.

> (In the assembly of scholars, you recite poetry
> In the company of poets, you are a grammarian
> How would you find a place in a gathering where both
>   are present?
> If you speak something there, the generous gathering
>   might say,
> 'Whether or not you harness your horse, you must leash
>   your tongue.')

Sauda carried his sarcasm and satire with him to Awadh. Once, while he was a court poet with Nawab Asaf-ud-Daula, he heard that the Nawab had killed a lion in one of his hunting expeditions and had been continuously boasting about it. Sauda immediately composed a couplet and sent it to the Nawab:

> Yaaron ye Ibn-e-Muljim paida hua dobaara
> Sher-e-Khuda ko jis ne bhelon ke ban mein maara

(Friends, here is Ibn-e-Muljim reborn
He has killed the Lion of God in the forest.)

There is serious pun and double entendre intended in this couplet. Sher-e-Khuda (Lion of God) was the title of the fourth Caliph of Islam, Hazrat Ali, who was the Prophet's cousin and son-in-law and is held in exceptional reverence by the Shia sect of Muslims, to which the Nawab also belonged. Ibn-e-Muljim was Ali's assassin who is abhorred by the Shias. Sickened by the Nawab's bragging, Sauda had compared him to the much-detested assassin of Hazrat Ali. When the Nawab heard the verse, he questioned Sauda. The poet calmly replied: 'Ji, baja hai. Sher khuda hi ka toh tha. Na aap ka tha, na mera' ('Well, it's a fair comparison. After all, the lion did belong to God; it was neither yours nor mine').

Fearless, mischievous, even irascible, and impatient with the arrogant and the self-righteous, Sauda was the voice of the voiceless. Islam and Russell point out that Sauda's attitude in his poems helps in explaining why he was popular in his times:

> People saw and condemned the degeneracy all round them, and wanted to see their feelings expressed, but were too conscious of their human failings to sympathize with the conventional moralists.[29]

Once, an acquaintance advised Sauda not to make friends easily as few live up to one's expectations. Sauda showed him the proverbial mirror:

Ye sun ke us se kaha muskura ke Sauda ne
Shikaayat itni kisu ki koi bayaan na karey
Bhaley-burey ke tujhe imtehaan se kya kaam
Ye shukr kar jo koi tujh-ko imtehaan na karey

(Having heard this, Sauda smiled and said to him:
It isn't good to complain so much about anyone.
Why should you bother about the test of good and bad?
Just thank your stars if no one puts *you* to the test.)

—

Being contemporaries, Sauda and the other great, Mir Taqi
Mir, have often been compared with each other for the
apparent similarities—or dissimilarities—in their work. Both
were born poets, both loved Delhi and exiled themselves
from their beloved city, and both towered above other poets
around them wherever they went. But very little beyond
this is common to them. Each had his own distinctive style
of writing, very different from the other. Mir, though an
extraordinary poet, was a declared pessimist who, but for
minor exceptions, remained buried in penury and cynicism
all his life and died in gloom. Sauda, on the other hand,
was an optimist with a vivacious sense of humour and is
celebrated as the master of wit, satire and humour. It is
said that when a Lucknow nobleman, known for his love
for Urdu poetry, was asked to spell out the differences
between the works of Mir and Sauda, he gave a short but
memorable reply:

> Mir ki shairi aah hai
> Sauda ka kalaam waah hai

> (Mir's poetry is 'aah' [a cry of pain or longing]
> Sauda's verses are 'waah' [an expression of delight].)

And yet, although known best for his delightful satire,
Sauda is also, like Mir, a traditional romantic, affected by
every move of his beloved—pleased by her coquetry and
perturbed by her indifference:

Jab yaar ne utha kar zulfon ke baal baandhe
Tab maine apne dil mein laakhon khayaal baandhe

Bosey ki toh hai khwaahish par kahiye kyon ki us se
Jis ka mizaaj lab par harf-e-sawaal baandhe

Sauda jo un ne baandha zulfon mein dil saza hai
Sheron mein us ke tu ne kyon khatt-o-khaal baandhe

(When she gathered her curls and tied them up
I wove together a million thoughts in my heart.

Yes, I yearn for a kiss, but why should I tell her
Whose temper only brings blame and questions to her
     lips?

Sauda, it's a curse to have my heart tied up in her curls
Why did you have to paint her figure and form in verse?)

He's game for love, though he knows the rules:

Dildaar usko khwaah dil-aazaar, kuchh kaho
Sunta nahin kisi ki mera yaar, kuchh kaho

Ghamza ada nigaah tabassum hai dil ka mol
Tum bhi agar ho iske khareeddaar, kuchh kaho

Shireen ne Kohkan se mangaayi thi joo-e-sheer
Gar imtehaan hai is se bhi dushwaar, kuchh kaho

(Call her a sweetheart, call her a tease, call her what
     you like
My beloved listens to no one, say whatever you will.

Gesture, style, sight, smile—this is the worth of a heart
If you too are a buyer of things like these, you may say
     something.

Shireen had asked Kohkan* to dig a stream of milk
If you want me to take a tougher test, just say so to me.)

---

*Another name for Farhaad. Shireen and Farhaad are the protagonists
of a famous Persian tragic romance.

The sweetheart's killer-arrow spares no one:

> Naavak ne tere saed na chhora zamaane mein
> Tadpe hai murgh-e-qibla-numa aashiyaane mein
>
> Sauda khuda ke vaaste kar qissa mukhtasar
> Apni toh neend udd gayi tere fasaane mein
>
> (Your arrow has spared no one in the world
> Even the compass needle [pointing to Mecca] trembles
>   in its nest.
>
> Sauda, for God's sake! Now cut your story short
> I've already lost much sleep listening to your account.)

And love, of course, is always lost, and grief is inevitable:

> Marta hoon mai'n is dukh se yaad aati hain vo baatein
> Kya din vo mubarak thay kya khoob thiin vo raatein
>
> Sauda ko agar poochho ahwaal hai ye uska
> Do-chaar ghadi rona do-chaar ghadi baatein
>
> (Grief kills me when I remember those times
> How lucky were those days, how lovely those nights.
>
> If you ask Sauda, he'll describe his condition thus:
> He cries for a while, he talks for a while.)

Speaking of the complications of romance, he advises the devout to tread carefully in the city of love:

> Aashiq ki bhi kat'ti hain kya khoob tarah raatein
> Do chaar ghadi rona do chaar ghadi baatein
>
> Is ishq ke kooche mein, zaahid tu sambhal chalna
> Kuchh pesh na jaaweingi yaan teri manaajaatein
>
> (In what astonishing ways a lover's nights are spent!
> For a moment or two he cries, for a moment or two he
>   speaks.
>
> O pious ones, this is the lane of love, tread carefully
> Know that your supplications will yield no result here.)

Sauda's ghazals give us an insight into the spoken Urdu of Delhi in the mid and late eighteenth century. Characteristic of his verse, as of Mir's, are words like 'kabhu' (an early form of the word 'kabhi'), 'ku' (a variant of the word 'ko'), 'tuk' (predecessor of the word 'zara'), 'un-ne' (used instead of the word 'unhone'), 'tujh' (used instead of the word 'tere') and 'teein' (another word for 'tera'). Here are three couplets from a ghazal (the complete ghazal—'Gul pheinke hain auron ki taraf'—is included in the final section of this chapter):

> Ae abr qasam hai tujhe rone ki hamaara
> Tujh chashm se tapka hai kabhu lakht-e-jigar bhi
>
> Ae naala sad-afsos jawaan marne pe tere
> Paaya na tanik dekhne teein roo-e-asar bhi
>
> Sauda teri fariyaad se aankhon mein kati raat
> Aayi hai seher hone ko tuk tu kahiin mar bhi
>
> (O Cloud, I ask you in the name of my sorrow
> Tell me, have you ever cried tears of blood?
>
> O lament, my sympathies on your untimely death
> We barely saw your face, and you were gone.
>
> Sauda, your constant pleas kept me awake all night
> It's almost morning now—go, get lost!)

In a classic example of using colloquial Urdu bordering on slang that typifies the language of his and Mir's Delhi, Sauda describes the beauty of the object of his affection and how he yearns for her. Expressions like 'bastiyaan hain', 'tarastiyaan hain', 'dhanstiyaan hain', 'barastiyaan hain' would have been unique to the Rekhta spoken in the streets of Shahjahanabad:

> Ve sooratein ilaahi, kis mulk bastiyaan hain
> Ab dekhne ko jinke aankhein tarastiyaan hain

Kyon-kar na ho mushabbak sheesha sa dil hamaara
Us shokh ki nigaahein patthar mein dhanstiyaan hain

Barsaat ka toh mausam kab ka nikal gaya par
Mizhgaan ki ye ghataaein ab tak barastiyaan hain

(Those lovely faces, Lord, which country are they from?
For just a glance of whom, my eyes yearn like this.

Why would my heart of glass, not be a nest of splinters?
That saucy beauty's gaze can bore a hole through stone.

The season of rains passed by so long ago, and yet
The clouds of her eyelashes are still pouring down.)

—

Urdu poetry has been historically liberal in its criticism of both religion as well as the religious, but Sauda took this to another level. He could be sacrilegious like no one else. When it came to chiding the preacher, he was a genius. But Sauda was neither prosecuted for blasphemy nor persecuted for his open irreverence of the Almighty. Had he dared to compose such verses today, he would have been executed or imprisoned in some countries, or had numerous fatwas passed against him in others. Sample this:

Jalwa toh khudaayi ka dekha hai bu'ton hi mein
Samjhaute ko phir aagey kuchh baat bana li

(I have seen Divine Glory only in idols, but
For the sake of compromise, I agreed to another version.)

In one of his ghazals, Sauda renders some rather audacious advice to the mullah, asking him to keep his arrogance and pride aside when he sits down to pray:

Amaame ko utaar ke parhiyo namaaz, Shaikh
Sajde se varna sar ko uthaaya na jaayega

(Take off your turban before you go to pray, O Shaikh!
Lest you aren't able to raise your bowed head again.)

It is the same idea that resonates in a couplet by Agha
Sarosh, a twenty-first-century poet:

Ye ibaadaton ka ghuroor teri jabeen-e-shauq ko dass na le
Ye hai saanp isko bila-jhijhak tu namaaz tod ke maar de

(This pride of worship, I fear, will sting your eager
    forehead
It's snake; break your prayers and kill it without
    hesitation.)

Going back to Sauda, in that ghazal, he then goes on to say
that the sanctimonious devout man will not stop sneering
at the joys of those who drink till such time as he is himself
forced to taste alcohol:

Zaahid gile se maston ke baaz aane ka nahin
Taa maikade mein la ke chakhaaya na jaayega

(The pious won't stop condemning the joys of drinking
    wine
Until he is taken to the tavern—and made to taste it.)

Again, in a short couplet, he unequivocally tells the mullah
that religion is a menace, and piety nothing but a mental
disorder:

Dikhaoonga tujhe zaahid us aafat-e-deen ko
Khalal dimaagh mein tere hai parsaayi ka

(I'll prove to you, O devout, religion is a menace
Your poor mind suffers from the disorder of piety.)

In a scornful comment on the orthodox Wahabis who claim
to be the only pure Muslims, Sauda compares his heart to
the holiest place in Islam, the Kaaba, and the disquiet within
it to the siege of the Kaaba by the Wahabis:

Dil-e-sitamzada betaabiyon ne loot liya
Hamaare kaabe ko wahaabiyon ne loot liya

(My oppressed heart has been ravaged by anxiety
[As if] my Kaaba has been looted by the Wahabis.)

In all of this, Sauda is only following a tradition—perhaps with greater daring than other Urdu poets—of taking serious liberties with the concept of an omnipotent, omniscient unseen God—an unassailable power that decides the fate of all humans. However, there has also always been a tradition of never taking similar—or even lesser—liberties with the Prophet Muhammad. There is a well-known Persian saying:

Ba khuda deewaana baash o ba Muhammad hoshiyaar

(Say crazy things about God, but beware what you say about Muhammad.)

Sauda, however, defies this ultimate tradition as well. In one of the boldest and most intrepid couplets in the history of Urdu literature, while referring to the fact that the Prophet's first wife, Khadija—a rich and successful merchant—was also his employer, Sauda declares that love is not intimidated by the stature of the lover, even if the lover is God's own Prophet:

Bazar-e-mohabbat mein nuboowat ka baha kya
Ek zan ne liya mol nabi chandd dirham se

(In the market of love, what value does prophethood have?
A woman bought the Prophet with a few Dirhams.)

To the hidebound, this couplet may seem to be disrespectful of the Prophet. But, contrary to orthodox interpretation, it is not a remark on the Prophet or his marriage at all. It is a bold comment on the majesty of love, which does not distinguish between a common man and a prophet.[30]

Ritual and orthodoxy did not find favour with Sauda, compassion and genuine humanity did. Like many Urdu poets, he seems to have drawn inspiration from Sufi and Bhakti ideals. God resides in our hearts, he says, and does not need temples or mosques:

> Dair-o-haram ko dekha Allah re fuzooli
> Ye kya zulm dhaaya dil sa makaan banaaya

> (I see their temples and mosques—O God, what
>   extravagance!
> You've been so cruel to them, making Your home in our
>   hearts.)

Urdu has a rich history of composing panegyric poems or odes—called qaseedah—in praise of kings or nobles. Sauda lived for less than seventy years, and in this time he witnessed the rule of ten Mughal emperors. Like his contemporaries, he also eulogized the emperors and his aristocratic patrons in verse. Sauda's qaseedahs in praise of Alamgir II are some of the finest examples of the tradition of eulogy in Urdu poetry. However, Sauda was also eyewitness to the decline of the Mughal Empire, which he blamed on bad leadership. Though he did eulogize the Emperor, and despite being aware of the fate of poets like Zatalli, Sauda's conscience would not allow him to refrain from giving the Emperor a few lessons in governance. Sauda, of course, did not use profanities like Zatalli while addressing the ruler.

In this simple and straightforward qita, Sauda renders some valuable advice on fundamental principles of governance and human rights. His advice seems even more relevant and appropriate today:

Kisi gada ne suna hai ye ek sheh se kaha
Karoon mai'n arz gar is ko na sarsari jaanein

Umoor-e-mulk mein awwal hai sheh ko ye laazim
Ki har ek khurd-o-kalaan mein barabari jaanein

(We hear a beggar once said this to a king:
May I say something, if you don't consider it frivolous—

Foremost, in state affairs, it is incumbent upon the king
To treat everyone as equal, no matter how high or low.)

Even in Sauda's days, as now, positions of importance were occupied by the incompetent and the corrupt on account of their proximity to the powers that be. Sauda is happy for not having acquired a position of importance in a society where usually the undeserving are in positions of authority:

Pahunche vo log rutbe ko ki mujhe
Shikwa-e-bakht-e-naarasa na raha

(Such people have occupied lofty positions that I
No longer regret not having reached those heights.)

Sauda believes that only the knowledgeable should be allowed to judge or give their opinion on matters of significance; the inept and ignorant should be kept away. In this age of twitterrati and Facebook-scholars, his two-hundred-year-old counsel seems prophetic:

Jauhar na howe jis mein, jauhar-shanaas kyon ho
Jo sahib-e-hunar ho vo hi hunar ko parkhe

(Why should a man without the ornament of knowledge
    evaluate jewels?
Only a master should judge a skill.)

Urdu also boasts an impressive repertoire of poetry on Shia traditions, and Awadh has had a rich history of composing elegies called marsiya to commemorate the martyrdom of Imam Hussain, grandson of Prophet Muhammad, at the battle of Karbala. The most prominent poets of marsiya included Mir Hasan, Mir Babar Ali Anis (1802—1874) and Mirza Salaamat Ali Dabeer (1803—1875). Sauda, however, improvised the form and not only wrote some beautiful marsiyas but also composed their tunes set them to music himself. He is credited with reviving the marsiya as a folk tradition. He also immortalized two poetic forms, mukhammas and musaddas—the former is a poem consisting of stanzas of five lines each and the latter of six lines each. In fact, he was perhaps the first poet to compose marsiyas in the mukhammas and musaddas forms.[31] One of his well-known marsiyas in the musaddas form begins thus:

Haaye vo naati tumhaara, Ya Nabi
Fatima ke mann ka pyaara, Ya Nabi
Zaalimon ne kar bechaara, Ya Nabi
Kya kahoon kis tarah maara, Ya Nabi
Vaan mawa pyaasa tera lakht-e-jigar
Thay jahaan sairaab haivaan sar ba sar

(Alas! That grandson of yours, O Prophet
Whom Fatima adored from her heart, O Prophet
Oppressors made him so helpless, O Prophet
How do I describe how they killed him, O Prophet
Left to die thirsty there, your darling child
Where savage beasts were fully sated.)

Sauda was also a philosopher of sorts. With her unmatched grace and elegance, Zehra Nigah, the celebrated Urdu poet and one of the greatest connoisseurs of the works of Sauda and Mir, recited a poem to me, in which Sauda beautifully explains how a youngster, anxious to gain quick success, visited a wise man and asked him for Nuskha-e-Keemiya—

the fabled formula for the elixir which infuses eternal life in humans and makes them conquer death. The wise man told the youngster that he would give him the formula but the elixir would work only on one condition. When asked what that condition was, the wise man replied that the elixir-maker should never let the 'danger of a monkey' ('bandar ka khatra') cross his mind. This condition, of course, can never be fulfilled—the moment the elixir-maker is done with preparing the magical potion and is gleeful and relieved that he did not let the danger or fear of a monkey cross his mind all this while, the thought of that very danger actually enters his mind, and the elixir is rendered ineffective. The point of this story is that if you cannot conquer your fear, no magical formula will work. Sauda's poem runs like a conversation:

Kaha jaaye hai ek mahawwas ka haal, Ki rakhta tha nit keemiya ka khayaal
Ye sab kar ke dil beech apne qayaas, gaya ek vo mard-e-kaamil ke paas
Raha us ki khidmat mein vo chand saal, kiya mauqa pa ke phir aakhir sawaal
Ki agar nuskha-e-keemiya yaad ho, toh bande ko bhi apne irshaad ho
Kaha gar yahi tha tera mud'dua, toh deta hoon tujh ko, tu ja aur la
Ye ajzaan hain iske, ye le kar bana, magar is mein ek shart hai darmiyaan
Ye nuskha tu jis waqt le kar banaaye, kabhu dil mein bandar ka khatra na laaye
Kaha ab toh ye baat mumkin nahin, jo khatra ho dil mein vo jaaye kahin
Na samjha gharaz us ke ramz-o-nukaat, ke parde mein thi mard-e-aarif ki baat

Ki agar dil ko khatre ke qaabu kiya, yoh phir hech hai
nuskha-e-keemiya

(The story of a greedy man is thus narrated, he always
thought only of the fabled elixir
Having done everything, and with deep belief, he then
went to meet a wise man
And served him for some years, and finding an opportune
time, he asked,
If you recall the formula for the fabled elixir, be kind
enough to also recite it to me.

If this is what you want, [the wise man] replied, I give
you the formula, go bring these,
These are the ingredients, make it with them, but there's
one condition to make it work

Whenever you use this formula, the 'danger of a monkey'
should not enter your heart.
How is this possible, said he, that the fear which has
now entered my heart goes away?

He didn't understand the hidden hints, cloaked in the
wise man's advice
That if you let fear conquer your heart, then even the
fabled elixir is useless.)

Even in Awadh, Sauda never stopped thinking about his
beloved Delhi, and was pained by its desolation following
repeated invasions and assaults. Despite living in reasonable
comfort in Lucknow, Sauda, it is believed, longed for Delhi
till his last:

Sauda vatan ko taj kar gardish se aasmaan ke
Aawaara ghareebi hai itni muddaton se

(Having abandoned his homeland because of misfortune
Sauda is a pauper, wandering in penury for ages.)

In 'Veerani-e-Shahjanabad' (Desolation of Shahjanabad), his impassioned shehr-ashob, he laments:

> Jahaanabaad tu kab is sitam ke qaabil tha
> Magar kabhu kisi aashiq ka ye nagar dil tha
> Ke yoon mita diya goya ki naqsh-e-baatil tha
> Ajab tarah ka ye behr-e-jahaan mein saahil tha
> Ke jis ke khaak se leti thi falak moti rol

> Bas ab khamosh ho Sauda, ke aage taab nahin
> Vo dil nahin ke ab is gham se jo kabaab nahin
> Kisi ki chashm na hogi ki jo pur-aab nahin
> Siwaaye is ke teri baat ka jawaab nahin
> Ke ye zamaana hai be-tarah ka zyaada na bol.

> (Jahaanabad, you did not deserve this plight.
> Once this city was the heart of a lover
> It was erased as if it were only a false sign;
> It was once the magic shore of the sea of life
> With whose sands the sky would make pearls.

> Now be silent, Sauda, for there's no more endurance
> There isn't a heart that doesn't burn with sorrow
> There won't be an eye that isn't full of tears.
> There is no answer to your query but this—
> The world is hostile, that is all, don't speak anymore.)

Sauda died longing for Delhi, but Delhi has been cruel to him. The city seems to have completely forgotten its most celebrated satirist. There is no sign of Kabuli Darwaaza anywhere in the old city today. It is believed that the gate stood near a canal next to the Lahori Gate area. Now the place is only known for Khari Baoli, its neighbouring street which serves as Asia's largest wholesale spice market. Walking for hours all over the place, I could hardly find a soul who had heard of Kabuli Darwaaza, let alone of Mirza Mohammad Rafi Sauda. Even his memories are dead.

Books on Sauda are out of print and biographical sketches
are gathering dust in un-visited Urdu libraries.

It would seem that Sauda had a premonition of what
history had in store for him:

Kahiyo saba salaam hamaara bahaar se
Hum toh chaman ko chhor ke soo-e-qafas chaley

(O breeze, remember me to the spring
I now leave the garden and walk to exile.)

Or perhaps Sauda might yet defy history and the indifference
of generations. He may rise again to seize our imagination.
After all, he wasn't one to give up. He also wrote this:

Sauda ki jo baleen pe utha shor-e-qayaamat
Khuddaam-e-adab boley abhi aankh lagi hai

(When at Sauda's bedside rose the uproar of doomsday
The respectful attendants whispered, He's just gone to
sleep.)

III

SELECTED GHAZALS OF SAUDA

I

Gul pheinke hain auron ki taraf balki samar bhi
Ae khaana bar andaaz-e-chaman kuchh toh idhar bhi

Kya zid hai khuda jaane mere saath wagar na
Kaafi hai tasalli ko meri ek nazar bhi

Ae abr qasam hai tujhe rone ki hamaara
Tujh chashm se tapka hai kabhu lakht-e-jigar bhi

Ae naala sad-afsos jawaan marne pe tere
Paaya na tanik dekhne teein roo-e-asar bhi

Kis hasti-e-mauhoom pe nazaan hai tu, ae yaar

Kuchh apne shab-o-roz ki hai tujh ko khabar bhi

Sauda teri fariyaad se aankhon mein kati raat
Aayi hai seher hone ko tuk tu kahiin mar bhi

(You have showered flowers on others, even fruits
O guardian of the garden's charms, now something for
    me too!

God knows why you are so obstinate, for after all
Just a single glance from you is enough to satisfy me.

O Cloud, I ask you in the name of my sorrow
Tell me, have you ever cried tears of blood?

O lament, my sympathies on your untimely death
We barely saw your face, and you were gone.

What imaginary existence are you proud of, my friend?
Are you even aware of the realities of your life?

Sauda, your constant pleas kept me awake all night
It's almost morning now—go, get lost!)

2

Jab yaar ne utha kar zulfon ke baal baandhe
Tab maine apne dil mein, laakhon khayaal baandhe

Bosey ki toh hai khwaahish par kahiye kyon ki us se
Jis ka mizaaj lab par harf-e-sawaal baandhe

Sauda jo un ne baandha zulfon mein dil saza hai
Sheron mein us ke tu ne kyon khatt-o-khaal baandhe

(When she gathered her curls and tied them up
I wove together a million thoughts in my heart.

Yes, I yearn for a kiss, but why should I tell her
Whose temper only brings blame and questions to her
    lips?

Sauda, it's a curse to have my heart tied up in her curls
Why did you have to paint her figure and form in verse?)

3

Ve sooratein ilaahi, kis mulk bastiyaan hain
Ab dekhne ko jinke aankhein tarastiyaan hain

Kyon-kar na ho mushabbak sheesha sa dil hamaara
Us shokh ki nigaahein patthar mein dhanstiyaan hain

Barsaat ka toh mausam kab ka nikal gaya par
Mizhgaan ki ye ghataaein ab tak barastiyaan hain

Un ne kaha ye mujh se ab chhor dukht-e-raz ko
Peeri mein ae deewaane ye kaun mastiyaan hain

Jab mai'n kaha ye us se Sauda se apne mil ke
Is saal tu hai saaqi aur mai-parastiyaan hain

(Those lovely faces, Lord, which country are they from?
For just a glance of whom, my eyes yearn like this.

Why would my heart of glass, not be a nest of splinters?
That saucy beauty's gaze can bore a hole through stone.

The season of rains passed by so long ago, and yet
The clouds of her eyelashes are still pouring down.

She said to me, 'Old man, give up your love of wine
Enough, you love-mad fool, this is no age for mischief'—

When I said to her, 'Come and meet your Sauda
Come, be my cup-bearer, it's the season to worship wine.')

4

Aadam ka jism jab ki anaasir se mil bana
Kuchh aag bach rahi thi so aashiq ka dil bana

Sargarm-e-naala in dinon mai'n bhi hoon andaleeb
Mat aashiyaan chaman mein mere mutassil bana

Apna hunar dikha deinge hum tujhko sheeshagar
Toota hua kisi ka agar hum se dil bana

Sun sun ke arz-e-haal mera yaar ne kaha
Sauda na baatein baith ke yaan mutassil bana

(When Adam's body was created, of elements put together
Out of the spare fire, the lover's heart was made.

Even I sing the saddest songs these days, O nightingale
Don't build your nest in this garden next to me.

We'll show you our skills, too, O glassmaker
The day we mend someone's broken heart.

When I spoke of my condition to her, she said
'Sauda, stop making up such tales next to me.')

5

Jo guzri mujh pe mat us se kaho, hua so hua
Bala-kashaan-e-mohabbat mein jo hua so hua

Mabaada ho koi zaalim tera girebaan-geer
Mere lahu ko tu daaman se dho, hua so hua

Pahunch chuka hai sar-e-zakhm dil talak yaaron
Koi subu koi marham rakho, hua so hua*

Kahe hai sun ke meri sarguzisht wo be-rahm
Ye kaun zikr hai, jaane bhi do, hua so hua

Ye kaun haal hai ahwaal-e-dil pe, ae aankhon
Na photo-phoot ke itna baho, hua so hua

Diya usey dil-o-deen, ab ye jaan hai Sauda
Phir aage dekhiye jo ho so ho, hua so hua

(Don't share with her what I've gone through, what has
    happened has happened
With the lovelorn, what has happened has happened.

Lest some ruthless one seize you by the collar
Wash off my blood from your garment, what has
    happened has happened.

---

*In some collections, the second misra is written as 'koi siyo, koi marham karo, hua so hua' ('someone stitch it, someone tend to it, what has happened has happened'.)

The edge of my wound has reached my heart, my friends
Bring a goblet, bring a balm, what has happened has
  happened.

Upon hearing my story, the heartless one says,
'Why talk about this, let it be, what has happened has
  happened.'

What have you done to yourself, O eyes, seeing my
  ravaged heart!
Why these tears of grief, what has happened has
  happened.

Sauda, I've given up my heart and my faith, only my
  life remains

Now what will be will be, what has happened has
  happened.)

KHWAJA MIR DARD
Urdu's Dancing Dervish
(1721–1785)

Yahi paighaam Dard ka kehna
Gar saba koo-e-yaar mein guzre
Kaun si raat aan miliye ga?
Din bohot intezaar mein guzre

(Deliver only this message from Dard, O breeze
If you should pass through my beloved's lane:
Which night will you come to meet me?
I've spent too many days waiting.)

I

WHILE DELHI WAS BEING PLUNDERED BY REPEATED invasions and savagery was being unleashed on its people, in a quiet Sufi monastery in the city, removed from the uproar and mayhem, sat a dervish immersed in poetry. The man we know as Khwaja Mir 'Dard', though not as popular today as his contemporaries, is regarded by Urdu scholars as the second pillar in the triad of classical Urdu poets of eighteenth-century Delhi, the first being Sauda and the third, Mir Taqi Mir.

The tragedy of Dard, however, is that despite his verses being full of romance and sensuality, he has been regarded for long mainly as a Sufi poet. Literature on him and his work is thus found more in books on mysticism than in those on poetry. Scholars of Urdu poetry distinguish quite sharply between love for a fellow-human—ishq-e-majaazi; literally, 'metaphorical love'—and love for God—ishq-e-haqeeqi; 'real love'. The classical Urdu poets themselves made no such distinction. It was created much later by scholars and critics, who prefer neat divisions and hierarchies. Believers in this distinction have for long insisted that Dard's love and romance is haqeeqi and not majaazi. Their insistence is predicated on the family background and personality of Dard himself, and stems from the rather orthodox belief that viewing a mystic as an ordinary man who nurtures worldly desires is sacrilegious, that it demeans or belittles his spirituality. Those who persist with this belief forget an elementary fact brought out in this well-known couplet by an anonymous poet:

Haqeeqi ishq ki ishq-e-majaazi pehli manzil hai
Chalo soo-e-khuda ae zaahidon koo-e-bu'taan ho kar

(Metaphorical love is the first destination of divine love
O devout, walk through the lane of idols to reach God.)

Born in 1721 in Delhi, Khwaja Mir Dard belonged to a family of Sufi mystics, scholars and theologians. His grandfather, Nawab Zafrullah Khan (d. 1707), enjoyed a position of honour in the Mughal Court and army and traced his lineage to Baha-ud-Din Naqshband Bukhari (1318–1389), founder of the most influential Sufi order of the world—the Naqshbandi. One of Baha-ud-Din's great grandchildren, Khwaja Mohammad Tahir Naqshband, had travelled from Bukhara (now in Uzbekistan) to India during the reign of the sixth Mughal Emperor, Aurangzeb Alamgir, and was highly revered by him. Dard's father, Khwaja Mohammad Nasir, though a well-respected and acclaimed Sufi theologian of his time, was also a great poet who used the takhallus 'Andaleeb'. He was a disciple of the distinguished Sufi mystic and poet Shah Saadullah Gulshan (d. 1757). It was the fame of Shah Gulshan that had brought Wali Muhammad Wali Dakhni to Delhi in or around 1700, an event of enormous significance in the evolution of Urdu—it is believed Dakani's poetry, composed in Rekhta, an early form of Urdu, helped displace Persian as the favoured language of poets in Delhi and the rest of the Mughal Empire.

Since the word 'gulshan' means 'garden', and Mohammad Nasir considered himself his Sufi master's voice, he decided to call himself 'Andaleeb', which means 'nightingale'. Andaleeb married twice. His second marriage bore him three children—Khwaja Mir Dard, Syed Mir Muhammadi and Khwaja Mir Asar, author of the epic poem 'Khwaab-o-khayaal'.

The quintessence of Islam is equality and universal

brotherhood. However, even in Dard's India, like today, Muslims were divided into various ideological groups, sub-groups, sects and sub-sects which were always caught in *inter se* quarrels. Their disputes could range from issues as diverse as the correct method of burial to whether or not a Muslim could listen to music. Andaleeb was appalled by these continuous squabbles and believed that they were causing irreparable harm to the very idea of Islam. Disgusted with the atrocious debates between leaders of various sects, he decided to set up a new all-embracing spiritual order which did not discriminate on the basis of sect or school of jurisprudence. He called it Tareeqa Muhammadiya ('The Muhammadan Path'). Annemarie Schimmel, the renowned Orientalist, claims that when Mir Dard asked his father why he had named his order Tareeqa Muhammadiya, he clarified that the term 'Muhammadiya' referred to the Prophet Muhammad and not to him; he had not named the order after himself:

> But all of us are children, lost in the sea of identity and drowned in one ocean. Our name is the name of Muhammad, and our sign is the sign of Muhammad. Our love is the love of Muhammad and our claim is the claim of Muhammad. One must call this order 'Tareeqa Muhammadiya', the Muhamaddan path. It is exactly the path of Muhammad, and we have not added anything to it. Our conduct is the conduct of the Prophet, and our way the Muhammadan way.[32]

Dard was the first entrant to this new order and would later inherit his father's position and further the cause of a spiritual pan-Islamism.

Dard's grandfather lived in what is now known as the Barafkhana area in Delhi, just north of Paharganj, between

Pul Bangash and the Old Subzi Mandi. Back then the area was considered to be a suburb of the walled city of Shahjahanabad, and while there's no reliable information about what the area was called then, it certainly wasn't Barafkhana, which means 'ice-room'. The neighbourhood acquired this name much later, after an ice-factory was set up here, probably at the end of the nineteenth century. In *Twilight of the Mughals*, Percival Spear describes how ice used to be procured by the British in Delhi before the setting-up of the barafkhana:

> In Delhi the old Mughal custom of bringing ice from Srinagar in Garhwal by relays of runners (or in bullock carts) was too expensive for revival. It continued in Lahore for the supply of Ranjit Singh's Court. But the method of making ice in the cold weather by running water into shallow pans in the season of the cold winds and storing the ice in pits against the hot weather, was continued. Companies were formed whose members received ice regularly during the hot weather in proportion to the number of shares they held. The cutting off of the supply from the ice-pits was one of the hardships suffered by the (British) garrison during the siege of 1857. The ice-bed was divided into six-foot squares, each about 18 inches deep. In these were strewn straw of various kinds. Water-pots were provided for each square, and should the weather promise a cold clear night, water was poured into cloth-bottomed pans which were then fitted into the earthen squares or hollows. On a good night ice would form to the depth of one and a half inches on the pans. This was gathered by shivering coolies in the chill morning and stored in ice-pits. The pits were covered with a low mud house thickly thatched, drained by a well, and further protected from the air by layers of straw. The highest temperature at which ice

could be made was about forty-three degrees (F); the pits
were opened at the beginning of the hot weather and the
supply lasted as late as August. Each night in December
and January the old 'abdar'[33] would keep his watch. If
the winds were fresh and likely to increase, he wrapped
his blanket around him and retired to his bed, but if the
air was clear and frosty, a drum was beaten and from the
nearest bazaar came lines of muffled figures to fill the pans
and fix them in the beds. The ice-beds were between the
Delhi and Turkman Gates of the city and the ice-makers
lived in the village of Banskauli.[34]

The ice-makers seem to have been replaced by an ice-making
machine and deep-freezer—the baraf-khaana—after the
Revolt of 1857. The building that housed the baraf-khaana
still exists but the factory ceased to function long ago.
The grand old man of Delhi, R.V. Smith, claims that the
spot where the ice-factory was set up was once occupied
by an Armenian church that was destroyed during Nadir
Shah's invasion of Delhi in 1739.[35] Dard must have seen
that church as a young boy. The area is now inhabited by
transporters and shops selling agricultural produce and
junk, though a few ice-manufacturers can still be found.
A huge, but ill-managed mortuary is now the most well-
known landmark in the area.

But we have digressed. Coming back to Dard's story—
his grandfather's property, consisting of residential quarters
and stables, was later inherited by Dard's father and it
was in one of the quarters there that Dard was born.
It is believed that when Delhi was being ransacked by
Nadir Shah in 1739, Dard's family was offered shelter by
Mihrparwar Begum, widow of Emperor Bahadur Shah I,
but the offer was not accepted because, despite being a
member of the Mughal Court, Andaleeb firmly believed

that he was essentially a Sufi, and this did not permit him to accept favours from the high and mighty. Some years later, though, the family did agree to shift to a huge house specially built for them by the Begum in Kucha Chelan. The house was designed almost like a khanqaah, a Sufi monastery, and in addition to residential rooms for Dard's family, it consisted of a hall for spiritual retreat and an inn for visiting disciples and travellers. The house remained with Dard's descendants almost till Partition. Now no traces of the structure are found.

Dard obtained his elementary education at home. He took to poetry at an early age and adopted the takhallus 'Dard', which means 'pain' or 'anguish', perhaps to reflect the tumultuous times his city was going through. Some of his biographers maintain that he later became a disciple of Sirajuddin Ali Khan Aarzu (Khan-e-Aarzu), who was also Sauda's mentor. Besides mastering the Quran, Hadith (Prophet's teachings) and Fiqh (Islamic Jurisprudence), Dard formally trained in music, both vocal and instrumental. When he was about sixteen, he was married to a twelve-year-old girl. Nothing more is known about this marriage.

Like Sauda, Dard also saw, as we have noted before, the soul of Delhi being ravaged by one invader after another. He was not yet twenty when Nadir Shah invaded Delhi in 1739 and ordered the slaughter of thousands in the heart of the city. Some biographies claim that Dard initially enrolled himself in the Mughal army around this time but soon he was distraught with the bloodshed and violence that came with the military service.[36] In 1750, before he had turned thirty, he quit military service to spend the rest of his life as a mystic. Emperor Muhammad Shah Rangeela had died by then and his son Ahmad Shah Bahadur had succeeded him to the throne. Ahmad Shah, who ruled with the title Abu

Nasir Mujahid-ud-Din Ahmad Shah Ghazi, spent most of
his time in his harem. He appointed Abul Mansur Mirza
Muhammad Muqim Ali Khan Safdar Jung as the Nawab
of Awadh and gave a highly exalted position in his court
to Javed Khan, a transgender of Persian descent, conferring
upon him the title of Nawab Bahadur. Between them, Safdar
Jung and Javed Khan took all royal decisions. In fact, Javed
Khan gradually became the de facto regent, causing serious
hostility not only within the Royal family but also among
provincial rulers. The disintegration of the Mughal Empire,
which had begun soon after Aurangzeb's death, was now
clearly irreversible, with many provinces, including Deccan
and Awadh, refusing to accept the supremacy of Delhi's
Qila-e-Moalla. Politically, all was chaos. In the next few
years, Dard's cherished city would continue to be almost
uninterruptedly sacked by successive aggressors, while
he busied himself in spreading the message of love and
brotherhood through his works.

As a young man, Dard believed that more important
than bringing together different religions was to rid Islam
of external influences that were polluting its purity. He
became closely associated with the prominent Islamic
theologian, philosopher, reformer and Sufi scholar of his
time, Shah Waliullah Dehlavi (1703-1762) who had earned
the displeasure of the clergy by translating the Quran into
Persian—the language of the Mughal Court—to make it
more accessible and comprehensible to those who did not
understand Arabic. Like Shah Waliullah, Dard also wanted
to present undiluted faith to people in their own language.
Therefore, after quitting military service, he dedicated most
of his time to this cause through the Tareeqa Muhammadiya.
In 1759, in what came as a huge personal loss to him, Dard
lost his father. At the age of thirty-eight, he became the

head of the Tareeqa, and over the years made it even more popular and influential than it had been in his father's time.

Some Sufis believe in the integration of music with meditation to bring the believer closer to the creator. In keeping with this belief, they hold musical meditation sessions in the Persian tradition, called sama'a, where participants sing, chant and go into a trance, sometimes dancing or whirling. One of the most celebrated Islamic jurists and philosophers, Al-Ghazali (d. 1111) believed that sama'a is the best form of meditation and nothing brings man closer to his hidden powers than the sama'a:

> Know that hearts and consciences are treasuries of secrets and mines of jewels. Wrapped within them lie their jewels just as fire is enveloped in iron and stone and water is concealed in dust and loam. There is no way of extracting such hidden things save by the flint and steel of audition to poetry and music (sama'a), and there is no entrance to the heart save by the ante chamber of the ears.[37]

Some scholars of the Naqshbandi order of Sufism forbid sama'a. However, Dard, despite following the Naqshbandi path, not only participated in but also organized evenings of sama'a in his monastery where he would himself sing and sometimes dance. In *Maikhana-e-Dard*[38], Dard's biographer Nasir Nazir Firaq Dehlvi mentions that Emperor Muhammad Shah Rangeela had great fondness for Dard and would often visit him unannounced. The young Dard, it seems, was not favourably disposed to the Emperor's flamboyant disposition and once politely told him that he did not want to be disturbed while he was in the midst of a sama'a. The Emperor respectfully obliged and never again was Dard bothered during a sama'a. Such was the reverence that Dard commanded even in his youth. In later years, though, adds Dehlvi, he did not object to the presence of Emperor Shah Alam II in his sama'as.

Twice a month, Dard would also host mushairas at his house in which all the great poets of the time, whether devout or not, would participate, and where he, too, would recite his poetry. He appears to have made no distinction between people, just as he made none between the pursuit of art and the pursuit of his faith.

For thirty-five of his sixty-four years, Dard lived like an unassuming mystic, and in the last ten, hardly travelled out of his monastery, where he was visited by people from all walks of life, among them poets, scholars, merchants, peasants, artisans and aristocrats. While his well-read visitors revelled in debates and discussions with him on a diverse array of subjects, others sought his blessings or spiritual guidance. Though Dard was close to the Mughal royalty, he did not write a single ode or eulogy. Nor did he pay visits to the Court. On the contrary, it was royalty who would often visit Dard in his monastery.

Preaching love, compassion and brotherhood to the last—in his teachings and in his poetry—Dard died in 1785, during the reign of Shah Alam II. In a brilliant commentary on Urdu poets, Mirza Ghalib's contemporary and friend Nawab Mustafa Khan Shefta beautifully captures the entire personality of Dard and its varied dimensions in just one sentence:

> Mir Dard ek mard-e-faazil, darvesh-e-kaamil, jawaan-e-saalih, khush-zaat, nek safaat, arif, khuda-parast, jama-e-shariat-o-tareeqat, ahl-e-tasleem-o-tawakkul, jalal-o-jamaal ke maalik, haal-o-qaal ki raah ke saalik, sahib-e-dara-o-taqa, duniya se be-ta'alluq, tehzeeb-o-tazkiya nafs se aaraasta, girafta-dil, dil ba-rishta-e-jigar, khaleeq, mutwaaza'e o awaam se husn-e-sulook rakhne

waale, magar salateen-e-waqt se be-niyaaz, isteqaamat aur jamiat-khaatir mei*n* mumtaz thay.[39]

Mir Dard was a learned man, a complete dervish, a righteous person, sophisticated, virtuous, knowledgeable, God-fearing, faith and mysticism combined, a believer in submission and contentment, possessor of great beauty and dignity, debonair in words and deeds, continence and piety personified, unconcerned with the world, adorned with culture and self-respect, large-hearted, kind, courteous, hospitable, well-behaving with the common man but indifferent to rulers of the day, distinguished in steadfastness and sense of honour.

II

THE MUSHAIRAS THAT DARD ORGANIZED AT HIS FAMILY home, next to his monastery, were proof of his stature as a poet—participating poets included greats like Mir Taqi Mir. The mushairas were also proof of his refusal to subjugate poetry to any sombre or austere notion of mysticism— among those who attended the mushairas was the young poet Ghulam Hamdani Mushafi, a sensualist in life as in much of his poetry. Mushafi also tried his hand at humour:

Baal apne barhaate hain kis vaaste deewaane
Kya sheher-e-mohabbat mein hajjaam nahin hota?

(Why on earth do these crazy lovers grow their hair?
Is there no barber in the city of love?)

Dard also acted as ustaad, or teacher, to a large number of young poets, including Qayam Chandpuri, to whom this illustrious couplet is attributed:

Ahl-e-masjid ne jo kaafir mujhe samjha toh kya
Saakin-e-daiyr toh jaane hain musalmaan mujh ko

(If mosque-goers consider me an infidel, so be it
People in the temple consider me a Muslim.)

In the next century, Allama Iqbal would express the dilemma
of many Indian Muslims using the same allegory:

Zaahid-e-tang nazar ne mujhe kaafir jaana
Aur kaafir ye samajhta hai ki musalmaan hoon mai'n

(The narrow-minded devout considers me an infidel
And the infidel thinks I am a Muslim.[40])

Dard himself had no patience with the zealot or the puritan.
In his verses, he derides the clerics who usurp Islam by
forcing conformist practices down the throats of followers
and outlawing those who do not fall in line with their
version of Islam. In one of his most oft-quoted couplets,
in an unparalleled example of courage and audacity, Dard
takes on the mullah for arbitrarily judging people only by
their overt conduct. Admonishing the shaikh for ridiculing
his liquor-soaked clothes, he declares that his clothes are so
pure that if he squeezes the liquor out of them, even angels
would rush to cleanse themselves in it:

Tar-daamani pe shaikh hamaari na jaaiyo
Daaman nichod dein toh farishte wuzu karein

(Don't be deceived by my sodden clothes, O Shaikh
If I squeeze them, angels will cleanse themselves [in the
    wine].)

In Sufism, there is a long tradition of being formally
initiated as a disciple of a Sufi saint or holy man. A person
desirous of being enrolled as a disciple must accept the
saint as his master, swear allegiance to him and submit
to his commands. This formal act of initiation is done by
the disciple taking the hand of his master as a token of

his promise of allegiance and submission. The act is called 'bai'at karna' ('to make a pact'). Using this Sufi terminology, Dard advises the devout to swear allegiance to liquor:

Hai apni ye salaah ki sab zaahidaan-e-shehr
Ae Dard aa ke bai'at-e-dast-e-subu karein

(I advise that all the puritans of the city, O Dard!
Should come and swear allegiance to wine.)

Dard's poetic collection, containing 1499 couplets, is perhaps the smallest amongst those of the classical Urdu poets of Delhi. Nevertheless, his poetry has made a significant impact in the literary landscape of India. Its significance lies in the fact that it blazes with Dard's mastery over the Urdu ghazal. His language is simple and pellucid, his metre perfectly balanced, and love, in its many moods, is the theme of several of his ghazals.

Echoing countless poets and lovers—of mortal beings as of God—down the centuries, Dard writes—

Kabhu rona kabhu hansna kabhu hairaan ho jaana
Mohabbat kya bhale-changey ko deewana banaati hai

(Crying and laughing and bewildered, all at once
What's with love, driving even the sanest man mad!)

And yet, sometimes Dard's verses on love are gently playful:

Basa hai kaun tere dil mein gulbadan
Ke bu gulaab ki aayi tere paseene se

(Who's the pretty flower residing in your heart
That even your sweat smells of roses?)

At other times he writes of a love that is patient and constant, even in complaint, as in this ghazal:

Agar yoon hi ye dil sataata rahega
Toh ik din mera ji hi jaata rahega

Mai'n jaata hoon dil ko tere paas chhode
Meri yaad tujh ko dilaata rahega

Jafa se gharaz imtihaan-e-wafa hai
Tu keh kab talak aazmaata rahega

(If my heart keeps troubling me like this
It won't be long before I lose my mind.

I'm leaving, I give you this heart
It will keep reminding you of me.

My love will be tested by the heartless one—
Tell me, how long will you keep trying me?)

Love, for Dard, is a malady without a cure—a common
enough observation in Urdu poetry, but he makes it with
a lovely lightness of touch and understated humour:

Dekh mujhe tabeeb aaj poochha jo haalat-e-mizaaj
Kehne laga ki la-ilaaj, banda hoon mai'n khuda nahin

Chehra tera bhi zard hai aah labon pe sard hai
Ye toh miyaan vo dard hai jis ki koi dawa nahin

(The physician met me today to check how I was doing
And said, 'You are beyond cure, I am a man, not God.

'Your face is ashen, your sighs freeze on your lips
This, my friend, is a pain for which there is no potion.')

While the healer has no cure for this pain, the beloved who
has caused it denies there's any connection at all:

Naama-e-dard ko mere le kar
Paas jab yaar ke gaya qaasid

Parh ke kehne laga vo sarnaama
Kaun sa yaar hai, bata qaasid?

Jis ne bheja hai tere haath ye khat
Mai'n nahin us se aashna, qaasid

(With my message of pain when
The messenger went to my love

Reading my words that beloved said,
'Who, O Messenger, is this lover?

Who has sent this letter through you?
There is no love between us at all.')

There are also times when Dard, like Mir, believes that love
is a completely avoidable menace, an unnecessary nuisance.
And yet, the head is as much a fool as the heart:

Mujh ko tujh se jo kuchh mohabbat hai
Ye mohabbat nahin hai, aafat hai

Log kehte hain aashiqi jis ko
Mai'n jo dekha badi museebat hai

Bandd ahkaam-e-aql mein rehna
Ye bhi ek naua ki himaaqat hai

(That love which I have for you
It's not love, it's a nuisance

What people call love,
I've realized, is big trouble.

To remain locked in the commands of wisdom
This, too, is a foolishness of sorts.)

In another ghazal, Dard's haughty sense of superiority,
which is the reason behind his refusal to fall in love, has
been trampled underfoot by his beloved. He acknowledges
this as a crushing defeat and admits that pride goes before
a fall:

Hum ye kehte thay ki ahmaq ho jo dil ko deve
Dekhein toh chheen le dil hum se vo kaun aisa hai

So ab ek shakhs ke hai zer-e-qadam sar apna
Sach kaha hai ki badey bol ka sar neecha hai

(I used to say. 'Only a fool gives away his heart
Let's see if there's someone who can snatch mine.'
And so, my head is beneath someone's feet.
It's been rightly said, 'The proud will be brought low.')

In an article on Dard published in *Nayi Sadi* in 2008,[41] Shamsur Rehman Faruqi, though admitting that Dard has dealt with mysticism, refutes the popular claim that Dard was a Sufi poet. According to him, almost all poets of those days have written on mysticism and spirituality but that does not make them 'Sufi poets'. That Dard was a Sufi scholar and led a popular Sufi order founded by his father is not enough to treat him only, or even primarily, as a Sufi poet. On the contrary, calling him only a Sufi poet is a disservice to his poetic talent and erudition. In another piece on Dard, the legendary critic Majnun Gorakhpuri goes to the extent of saying that no mysticism whatsoever is found in Dard's poetry, not even in those couplets that are coloured by spirituality:

Dard ki shaayri ka agar kuchh andaaza karna hai toh hum ko iraada aur koshish ke saath is baat ko bhool jaana chaahiye ki vo Sajjada-nasheen Khwaja Nasir Andaleeb ke khalf-e-rasheed thay ya unka nasab-nama kayi vaaston se Khwaja Bahauddin Naqshband aur Imam Hasan Askari se ja milta tha. Ya vo khud khaasi jawaani ki umr mei*n* duniya aur us ki makroohaat se mu'*n*h mod kar sajjaade par baith gaye thay. Dard ke aashaar mei*n* kahi*n* se sajjaade ka rang ya khaanqaah ki mehek nahi*n* mehsoos hoti. Un aashaar mei*n* bhi nahi*n* jo darveshi aur ma'arfat ka andaaz liye hue hain.[42]

(To make an assessment of Dard's poetry, one needs to consciously make an effort to forget the fact that he was the inheritor of Sajjada-nasheen Khwaja Nasir Andaleeb or that he traced his lineage to Khwaja Bahauddin

Naqshband and Imam Hasan Askari. Or that, at a fairly
young age, he had himself bid farewell to the world
and its forbidden pleasures and taken to spiritualism. In
Dard's poetry neither can one see the colour of spirituality
nor smell the fragrance of the monastery, not even in
those couplets which have been composed in mystic or
metaphysical style.)

On the question of categorizing Dard's love as divine or
metaphoric, the leading Urdu critic and scholar Shamim
Hanfi does not mince his words. Interpretation, he says,
'is a strange thing'[43] as everyone is free to interpret a
verse as romantic or spiritual. A single verse may have
various connotations. It cannot be read in a vacuum or
without context. Now that the poet is dead, in most cases
one obviously does not know the context. In such a case,
to insist that a particular verse is only spiritual or only
romantic is foolish or presumptuous ('himaaqat hai'). One
should interpret it the way one understands it and let others
interpret it the way they do. Hanfi, in fact, advises that
readers should discard even this opinion and appreciate
every verse the way they understand it, without getting into
what scholars, including he, think. In a most meaningful
and rather profound couplet, Dard almost prophetically,
it seems, foresees the creation of this dichotomy by later
critics, and decides to obviate it. He places the logical
priority of faith in juxtaposition with the secondary concepts
of worship and practice. Dard claims that his identity is
predicated on faith—which does not follow any particular
structure—and not on worship or practice, which demand
protocol and decorum and are mere routes to that faith.
He eloquently beseeches his readers to judge him not by
his rituals but by his faith:

Ek imaan hai bisaat apni
Na ibaadat na kuchh riyaazat hai

(My being is Faith
Neither worship nor practice.)

That said, Dard did in fact produce some great poetry that
shines with his love for the omnipotent, omniscient God.
He believes that only heart and soul can reach you to God.
He is mesmerized by the magic of reason and knowledge
and cannot come out of its spell:

Qaasid nahin ye kaam tera apni raah le
Us ka payaam dil ke siva kaun la sakey

Ya rab ye kya tilism hai idraak-o-fehm yaan
Daude hazaar aap se baahar na ja sakey

(O messenger, this is not your job, go your way
Who but the heart can deliver His message?

O Lord, what is this magic of reason and knowledge
Though I tried so hard to run away, I couldn't leave you.)

Dard beautifully articulates the oneness of an unseen God
and claims that only his heart is vast enough to hold the
Lord in His full expanse; even earth and sky are insufficient
for that purpose:

Arz-o-sama kahaan teri vus'at ko pa sakey
Mera hi dil hai vo ke jahaan tu sama sakey

Wahdat mein teri harf-e-dui na aa sakey
Aaina kya majaal tujhe mu'nh dikha sakey

(How can the earth and sky contain your expanse?
My heart alone can hold all of you.

Not even a hint of duality can touch your Oneness,
The mirror doesn't dare face you.)

About a hundred years later, Ghalib would reiterate the same sentiment thus:

Usey kaun dekh sakta ke yagaana hai vo yakta
Jo dui ki boo bhi hoti toh kahin do-chaar hota

(Who can see Him, for He is unique and He is matchless
Had there been even a whiff of duality, He might have
been spotted somewhere.)

Having acknowledged the singularity of the unseen God, Dard finds Him everywhere:

Jag mein aa kar idhar-udhar dekha
Tu hi aaya nazar jidhar dekha

(Having come into this world, I looked here and there
I found You and only You, wherever I looked.)

And his heart longs only for the omnipresent God—or Love:

Mera ji hai jab tak teri justju hai
Zabaan jab talak hai yehi guftgoo hai

Tamanna hai teri agar hai tamanna
Teri aarzoo hai agar aarzoo hai

Nazar mere dil ki padi Dard kis par
Jidhar dekhta hoon vo hi ru-ba-ru hai

(My heart is alive till it longs for You
My speech, till it talks of You

If there is a yearning, it's the yearning for You
If there is a desire, it's the desire for You

Oh Dard, whom did my heart cast its eyes upon?
Whichever way I look, I am face to Face with Him.)

In love—whether metaphoric or divine—Dard believes in complete submission. Assuming different, and often opposing, roles for himself, he does not envisage a life for his beloved without his own presence in it:

Baagh-e-jahaan ke gul hain ya khaar hain toh hum hain
Gar yaar hain toh hum hain aghyaar hain toh hum hain

Waabasta hai hamin se gar jabr hai o gar qadr
Majboor hain toh hum hain mukhtaar hain toh hum hain

(In the garden of this world, I am the flower, I am the
    thorn
I am the friend, I am the stranger too.

Whether cruelty or kindness, they are both connected
    to me
I am the one who is helpless, and I am the one with
    power.)

And so, for Dard, the holiest place is where his beloved is present. He doesn't care about places of worship:

Hum jaante nahin hain, Kaaba-o-daiyr kya hai
Jidhar uthe vo abroo udhar namaaz karna

(I have nothing to do with the Kaaba or temple
I turn my face to pray wherever that gaze rests.)

—

Being contemporaries, both Mir and Dard dealt with many similar subjects. However, the peculiar language-play that Mir employs is missing in Dard's poetry. Both use simple language, but it is Mir's expertise in playing with syntax that often makes him far more effective than Dard. Here are two examples where both Mir and Dard deal with the same subject but Mir has a greater impact on the reader than Dard. In this couplet, Mir underlines the omnipresence of God:

Paaya na yoon ki kariye us ki taraf ishaara
Yoon toh jahaan mein hum ne usko kahaan na paaya

(I don't seem to have found Him; point Him out to me,
Although, there isn't a place on earth where I haven't
    found Him.)

The same thought is reflected in Dard's couplet:

Dhoonde hai tujhe tamaam aalam
Har-chand ki tu kahaan nahin hai

(The whole world looks for you
Although there's no place where you are not present.)

Again, Mir and Dard write not only on the same subject
but also in the same style and use the same phrases, pattern
and rhythm. Mir, in a widely quoted ghazal, says:

Faqeeraana aaye sada kar chaley
Miyaan khush raho hum dua kar chaley

Jo tujh bin na jeene ko kehte thay hum
So is ahd ko ab wafa kar chaley

Kahein kya jo poochhe koi hum se Mir
Jahaan mein tum aaye thay kya kar chaley

(Like a fakir I came, and with this cry I leave:
Stay happy, my friend, this is my prayer.

I won't live without you, I used to say
This promise, too, I redeem as I leave.

What should I say, if someone asks me, Mir
You came into this world, what did you achieve?)

On the same subject, Dard writes:

Tohmat-e-chand apne zimme dhar chaley
Jis liye aaye thay so hum kar chaley

Zindagi hai ya koi toofaan hai
Hum toh is jeene ke haathon mar chaley

Dosto dekha tamaasha yaan ka sab
Tum raho khush hum toh apne ghar chaley

(Some accusations I took upon myself
I've accomplished what I came for.

Is this life or is it a tempest?
I've died coping with this life.

Friends, I've had enough of this circus
You be happy, I'll just go back home.)

A bare reading of these couplets—even allowing for translations that cannot capture the music and word-play of the originals—makes it clear that Dard's verse does not have the same rhythm, emotion and power as Mir's.

While it is true that as a poet, whether of earthly or divine love, Dard may not always have reached the heights that his contemporary Mir did, his contribution as a philosopher compares with the best. He was a great thinker who wrote some crisp and profound poetry. In his collections, one finds sharp comments on a diverse array of themes: friendship, desire, disillusionment, human frailty— but also majesty—and the struggles of life in general.

Human prowess is boundless and Dard recognizes the innate ability of humans to do what angels cannot:

Bawujoode ki par-o-baal na thay Adam ke
Vahaan pahuncha ki farishte ko bhi maqdoor na tha

(Despite not having wings Adam [man]
Reached places where even angels could not tread.)

Dard believes that man is God's best product; it is to man that He has given the capacity for love and compassion— the real reason why man was created, for it wasn't mere obedience that God wanted:

Dard-e-dil ke vaaste paida kiya insaan ko
Varna taa'at ke liye kuchh kam na thay karr-o-bayaan

(It is for the compassion in his heart that man was created
Else, for the sake of obedience, there was no dearth of
　　pomp and rhetoric.)

Dard is aware that old age is a curse:

Raunde hai naqsh-e-pa ki tarah khalq yaan mujhe
Ae umr-e-rafta chhor gayi tu kahaan mujhe

(This mass of people tramples me into the earth like
　　footprints
O my past life, what have you left me to bear!)

And yet, though life is harsh and unsympathetic, Dard
compares it with a tavern which is about to close, but until
it does, he will carry on:

Saaqiya yahaan lag raha hai chal-chalaao
Jab talak bas chal sakey saaghar chaley

(O wine-bearer, I sense the time to depart is near
Till such time as they can, let the drinks flow.)

Dard has to his credit a collection of Urdu ghazals, a
Persian Diwaan, a prose discourse called *Ilm-ul Kitaab*,
a compilation of mystical sayings called *Chahaar Risaala*,
a book on the Tareeqa Muhammadiya and a number
of short pieces on various subjects, including music and
prayer rituals. Though he wasn't a prolific poet, he left
behind a formidable legacy which is a perfect example of
the pluralist tradition that Urdu poetry is legitimately
proud of:

Mai'n hoon gulcheen-e-gulistaan-e-khaleel
Aag mein hoon ya baagh-baagh hoon mai'n

(I am but the gardener of the garden of friends
Whether burning in fire or immersed in happiness.)

———

Dard lies buried in the centre of a ghetto named after him
on Asaf Ali Road. Between Delhi University's Zakir Husain
College and the Municipal Corporation's Shyama Prasad
Mukherjee Civic Centre, lies Basti Hazrat Khwaja Mir Dard.
Here, a badly-maintained, meandering lane full of tiny shops
selling everything from meat to stationery takes you to a
small, green-coloured circular enclosure housing Dard's
grave. It is maintained like a mausoleum. A signboard
reads: 'Dargah Hazrat Khawajah Meer Dard. Date of
Death 21 Safar 1199 Hijri.' The dargah is maintained by
a committee comprising locals who remember him only as
a great mystic and not as a poet. Every year they hold a
modest Urs (an annual festival held on the death anniversary
of a Sufi saint) to celebrate his spiritual prowess. After all,
Dard had wanted people to offer flowers on his grave with
a smile on their faces:

Hans qabr pe meri khilkhila kar
Ye phool charhaa kabhu toh aa kar

(Burst into laughter at my grave as trees burst into
    blossom
Come, offer these flowers here sometime.)

And did he want people to remember him as a poet or as
a mystic? Perhaps it did not matter in the end:

Vaa-e-nadaani ke waqt-e-marg ye saabit hua
Khwaab tha jo kuchh ke dekha jo suna afsaana tha

(Alas, my naivety! Only at the time of death was it proved
Whatever was seen was a dream, whatever was heard,
    a tale.)

III

SELECTED GHAZALS OF DARD

I

Hum tujh se kis havas ki falak justujoo karein
Dil hi nahin raha hai ke kuchh aarzoo karein

Tar-daamani pe shaikh hamaari na jaaiyo
Daaman nichod dein toh farishte wuzu karein

Sar-ta-qadam zabaan hain joon shama go ke ham
Par ye kahaan majaal jo kuchh guftgu karein

Har-chand aaina hoon par itna hoon na-qubool
Mu pher le vo jis ke mujhe roo-ba-roo karein

Hai apni ye salaah ki sab zaahidaan-e-shehr
Ae Dard aa ke bai'at-e-dast-e-subu karein

(What consuming passions should I ask you for,
     O heavens
I'm left with no heart any longer to make a wish.

Don't be deceived by my sodden clothes, O Shaikh
If I squeeze them, angels will cleanse themselves [in the
     wine].

Like a candle, from head to toe I burn to say something
But I don't dare speak [to her].

I am a perfect mirror, but such an unacceptable one
That every one made to face me turns his face away.

I advise that all the puritans of the city, O Dard!
Should come and swear allegiance to wine.)

2

Un ne qasdan bhi mere naale ko
Na suna hoga, gar suna hoga

Dil zamaane ke haath se saalim
Koi hoga jo reh gaya hoga

Dil ke phir zakhm taaza hote hain
Kahin guncha koi khila hoga

Yak-ba-yak naam le utha mera
Ji mein kya us ke aa gaya hoga

Qatl se mere vo jo baaz raha
Kisi bad-khwaah ne kaha hoga

Dil bhi ae Dard qatra-e-khooon tha
Aansuon mein kahin gira hoga

(She chose to ignore my lament
She heard me and yet she did not.

A heart left whole by this world
It must have survived by accident.

The wounds of my heart are fresh again
A bud must have blossomed somewhere.

Abruptly, she spoke my name
What thought stole into her heart?

She has abstained from killing me
Which ill-wisher of mine did she listen to?

My heart, O Dard, was but a drop of blood
I must have shed it with the tears that I've cried.)

3

Arz-o-sama kahaan teri vus'at ko pa sakey
Mera hi dil hai vo ke jahaan tu sama sakey

Wahdat mein teri harf-e-dui na aa sakey
Aaina kya majaal tujhe mu'nh dikha sakey

Qaasid nahin ye kaam tira apni raah le
us ka payaam dil ke siva kaun la sakey

Ya rab ye kya tilism hai idraak-o-fahm yaan
Daudey hazaar aap se baahar na ja sakey

Go behes kar ke baat bithaayi bhi kya husool
Dil se utha ghilaaf agar tu utha sakey

Itfaa-e-naar-e-ishq na ho aab-e-ashk se
Ye aag vo nahin jise paani bujha sakey

Mast-e-sharaab-e-ishq vo be-khud hai jis ko hashr
Ae Dard chaahe laaye ba-khud phir na laa sakey

(How can the earth and sky contain your expanse?
My heart alone can hold all of you.

Not even a hint of duality can touch your Oneness,
The mirror doesn't dare face you.

O messenger, this is not your job, go your away
Who but the heart can deliver His message?

O Lord, what is this magic of reason and knowledge
Though I tried so hard to run away, I couldn't leave you.

To argue and get your opinion accepted is no great feat
If you can, lift the dustcovers from their hearts.

The fire of love won't be put out with flowing tears
This is not the kind of fire that water can extinguish.

He, who is drunk on the wine of love
O Dard, not even the whole world can bring him back
    to his senses.)

4

Baagh-e-jahaan ke gul hain ya khaar hain toh hum hain
Gar yaar hain toh hum hain aghyaar hain toh hum hain

Dariya-e-ma'arifat ke dekha toh hum hain saahil
Gar vaar hain toh hum hain aur paar hain toh hum hain

Tera hi husn jag mein har-chand maujzan hai
Tis par bhi tishna-kaam-e-deedaar hain toh hum hain

Waabasta hai hamin se gar jabr hai o gar qadr
Majboor hain toh hum hain mukhtaar hain toh hum hain

(In the garden of this world, I am the flower, I am the
    thorn
I am the friend, I am the stranger too.

Of the river of mystic knowledge, I am the shore
It is only me on this bank and me alone on the other.

The magnificent storm of your beauty is spread across
    the world
And yet if there is someone who thirsts for a glimpse of
    you, it is me.

Whether cruelty or kindness, they are both connected
    to me
I am the one who is helpless, and I am the one with
    power.)

5

Agar yoon hi ye dil sataata rahega
Toh ik din mera ji hi jaata rahega

Mai'n jaata hoon dil ko tere paas chhode
Meri yaad tujh ko dilaata rahega

Jafa se gharaz imtihaan-e-wafa hai
Tu keh kab talak aazmaata rahega

Qafas mein koi tum se ae hum-safeeron
Khabar gul ki hum ko sunaata rahega

Khafa ho ke ae Dard mar toh chala tu
Kahaan tak gham apna chhupaata rahega

(If my heart keeps troubling me like this
It won't be long before I lose my mind.

I'm leaving now, I give you this heart
It will keep reminding you of me.

My love will be tested by the heartless one—
Tell me, how long will you keep trying me?

In prison, O fellow-travellers, someone will ask you
And keep me informed of the flower's well-being.

O Dard, disillusioned, you gave up your life
But how long will you keep hiding your sorrows?)

MIR TAQI MIR

The Incurable Romancer of Delhi
(1722–1810)

Paida kahaan hain aise paraganda-taba log
Afsos tum ko Mir se sohbat nahin rahi

(Such fragmented people are not born any longer
Alas! You did not have the pleasure of Mir's company.)

—

Dilli ke na thay kooche auraaq-e-musavvar thay
Jo shakl nazar aayi tasveer nazar aayi

(The streets of Delhi were like painted pages
Every sight I saw looked like a picture.)

I

IF YOU WANT TO RUBBISH WINSTON CHURCHILL'S CLAIM—
'History will be kind to me for I intend to write it'—you
must try to look for the relics and remnants of the life of Mir
Taqi Mir—that fiery romancer of Delhi, that fiercely self-
respecting poet, that passionate lover and that quintessential
Dilliwala, whom Urdu literature today knows as Khuda-e-
Sukhan (The God of Poetry). It was Mir who, in the words
of the noted critic Jamil Jalibi, 'brought the Urdu language
out of the royal court and made it stand on the staircases of
Delhi's Jama Masjid'.[44] It was for the same Mir that Mirza
Ghalib would later say:

> Rekhte ke tum hi ustaad nahin ho, Ghalib
> Kehte hain agley zamaane mein koi Mir bhi tha
>
> (You are not the lone master of Rekhta, Ghalib
> They say, in days gone by there was one Mir, too.)

And whom the Poet Laureate of the last Mughal Court,
Ustaad Zauq, would envy:

> Na hua, par na hua Mir ka andaaz naseeb
> Zauq, yaaron ne bohot zor ghazal mein maara
>
> (They couldn't, they just couldn't earn Mir's style
> Zauq, the fellows worked hard on their poetry.)

This was Mir. And he wrote history. But history treated
him rather shabbily.

Mir is the only pre-modern Urdu poet to have written
an autobiography[45]. But *Zikr-e-Mir*, his autobiography in
Persian[46], does not contain a detailed account of his life.
The book is in two parts. While the first part is dedicated
entirely to Mir's father and his personality, the second

mostly describes political developments of the time. The book does contain some personal accounts but these, too, contain hardly any facts about the poet's own life. It is Mir's poetry, especially his romantic masnavis[47] that reveal details about his life more than his autobiography.

Mir Taqi Mir was born in 1722 as Mohammad Taqi to Mir Ali Muttaqi, a religious scholar and mystic of Agra (then called Akbarabad). *Zikr-e-Mir* does not give his date of birth but some manuscripts found in the personal library of the Raja of Mahmudabad establish the year of his birth with reasonable accuracy. His father had married twice. Mir was his father's elder son by his second wife. By his first wife, Mir's father had a son called Muhammad Hasan who never accepted Mir as a brother. Mir was just a boy when his father died. If Mir's account of his early life in *Zikr-e-Mir* is to be believed, on his death bed, Mir's father called his sons and told them that he owned nothing more than 300 books, which they could divide amongst themselves. Mir's step brother objected to this division and insisted that he alone had the right to inherit all the 300 books. The helpless father had no choice but to give in to the demands of the elder son and, at a tender age of ten or eleven, Mir was left without any bequest. Penniless, he wanted to pay off his father's debts and bring him dignity in death. With immense difficulty he managed to repay the three hundred rupees that his father owed in total to various lenders and, having done so, left Agra for good.[48] The autobiography gives no details about how this was done by a boy who was barely twelve at the time.

A young Mir arrived in Delhi in or around 1733 and made the city his home. It is believed that in Delhi Mir lived at three different localities—Kucha Chelan, Chandni Mahal and Matia Mahal, all in the heart of Shahjanabad. All three localities exist to this day and are a short walk from each other. Kucha Chelan, which can now be approached from a lane next to Golcha Cinema on the main Netaji Subhash Marg, used to be a sought-after neighbourhood in the eighteenth and nineteenth centuries and many of the city's elite lived here. The area later became home to some distinguished scholars, including the renowned Persian academic Imam Bakhsh Sahbai, the noted Islamic scholar Mufti Kifayatullah and the legendary educationist Sir Syed Ahmed Khan. During India's freedom struggle it became a Muslim stronghold and was home to, among others, Asaf Ali, the prominent freedom fighter who would later become independent India's first Ambassador to the United States of America and after whom one of Delhi's major roads is named. Asaf Ali's house in Kucha Chelan was regularly visited by leaders across parties, including Mahatma Gandhi and Mohammad Ali Jinnah. It was in Kucha Chelan that Jinnah in 1941 launched *Dawn,* now Pakistan's most prominent daily, as a weekly publication of the Muslim League supervised by Nawabzada Liaqat Ali Khan, who would later serve as Pakistan's first Prime Minister.

The second neighbourhood where Mir lived, Chandni Mahal, is the locality just behind Delite Cinema on Asaf Ali Road and is believed to have been named after a mahal (palace) that once stood here. Today the most prominent landmark of the locality is its police station.

Matia Mahal, where Mir moved next, is the area facing Gate No. 1 of the great mosque Jama Masjid, and it, too, was named after a palace that stood here in the early seventeenth century. It is popularly believed that Matia Mahal served as Shah Jahan's residence while he was supervising the construction of the Red Fort, or Qila-e-Moalla. However, there is no concrete evidence to support this belief. Today the area is famous for its roadside eateries, and a few bookshops on the stretch known as Urdu Bazar, mostly selling Islamic religious literature.

When Mir reached Delhi, the reins of the Mughal Empire were in the hands of Muhammad Shah Rangeela and Delhi was overflowing with poetry and literature. Sauda was only twenty years old and had not yet gained recognition. Mir soon came in contact with a prominent nobleman, Khwaja Muhammad Basit, who in turn introduced him to Samsam-ud-Daula Shah Nawaz Khan, the Imperial Paymaster and Marshal of Nobility in the Mughal Empire. Samsam-ud-Daula had known Mir's father and had immense respect for him. Out of sympathy for Mir, he made provision for a daily stipend for him from his own treasury. In *Three Mughal Poets*[49], Khurshidul Islam and Ralph Russell have recorded an interesting story relating to this stipend which not only reveals the young Mir's forthrightness but also his straight thinking. It is believed that when Mir asked Samsam-ud-Daula to issue written orders for payment of the stipend, Basit, who thought the request would annoy Samsam-ud-Daula, intervened and said: 'Ye qalamdaan ke liye munaasib waqt nahin hai' ('This is not the proper time for the inkstand'). Mir laughed. Samsam-ud-Daula, visibly irritated by now, asked him why he was laughing. Mir replied:

Iska kya matlab hua—ye qalamdaan ke liye munaasib waqt nahin hai? Agar inhone kaha hota ke 'Nawab saheb abhi dastakhat nahin kar sakte' toh mujhe samajh aata. Par ye ek ajeeb baat hai. Qalamdaan koi zinda insaan hai jo waqt aur mauqe ki paabandi karega? Vo toh ek lakdi ka tukda hai jisko aap ke khaadim, jab aap hukm farmaaein, le aaeinge.

(Whatever does this mean—not the proper time for the inkstand? If he had said 'Nawab sahib cannot sign now,' I could have understood it. But this is a curious statement. The inkstand is not a living thing that can observe time and occasions; it is a piece of wood, which your servants will fetch whenever you order them to.)

Samsam-ud-Daula laughed at this and immediately issued a written order for Mir's stipend. Now that he was assured of a daily income, Mir first found quarters for himself in Kucha Chelan. Awe-struck by the sheer splendour of the place, he would later marvel at its grandeur:

Haft-aqleem har gali hai kahin
Dilli se bhi dayaar hote hain

(No lane opens into seven climes anywhere else
Places like Delhi do exist.)

Thus began Mir's poetic journey in Delhi—a place he remained passionately in love with till he breathed his last.

Mir seems to have initially stayed in the city for about six years. In 1739, the year which marked the invasion of Delhi by Nadir Shah, Samsam-ud-Daula was killed in the Battle of Karnal and Mir was, once again, left without any financial support. He returned to Agra but the decision proved to be disastrous. In Agra, Mir, who was eighteen now, saw a girl who was already married and fell in love with her. He started meeting her discreetly and she reciprocated his love. Mir started dreaming of a life with her and when he was not with her, he would spend all his time thinking about her. He was consumed by love. One day the girl met him and told him that she did not see a future with him and that it would be best that they parted ways. Mir was heartbroken. When his family came to know of the affair, they mistreated him so badly that the already dejected and disconsolate Mir lost his mental balance. At night, he would be scared to look at the moon, for whenever he looked at it, he would imagine the girl sitting inside the moon. Her image would haunt him. His mental state deteriorated. His family resorted to spiritual cures, and when they did not succeed, they locked him up in a tiny cell and starved him. When even this did not improve his condition, a healer advised them to drain the 'bad blood' out of his body. The already starved, confined and psychologically fragile young man was made to bleed until he fell unconscious.[50] When he got a little better and regained some strength and mental balance, somehow, miraculously, he escaped his family and made his way back to Delhi. However, this incident, which is narrated by Mir in one of his long poems—'Masnavi Maamlaat-e-Ishq' ('Affairs of Love')—had a lasting effect on his mind and he would experience occasional bouts of madness till the end of his life.

Having returned to Delhi, Mir stayed with Khan-e-Aarzu, whose deep influence on the poetry of Sauda and Dard was already being recognized. Khan-e-Aarzu, who lived in Kucha Chelan, was the uncle of Mir's step-brother, Muhammad Hasan. Hasan was soon reprimanding his uncle for offering shelter to his estranged and good-for-nothing step-brother and Khan-e-Aarzu, to avoid bad blood, asked Mir to leave forthwith. Mir left, and suffered another, more serious bout of insanity which lasted some months. Mir's biographers believe that:

> [I]t was the cumulative effect of all this that drove him mad. Thus Mir had indeed suffered 'pain and grief more than you know' when he began to make his name as a poet; and it took him only a few years after he recovered his sanity to establish a reputation.[51]

Thrown out by Aarzu, Mir decided not to return to Agra but to somehow make ends meet in Shahjahanabad. He stayed in Delhi till 1782 and, during this long period of more than forty years, remained under the patronage of several noblemen. His first patron was Riayat Khan, a nephew of Qamaruddin Itimad-ud-Daula II, a powerful Mughal vazir (minister) who used to live in Hauz Qazi. By the time he was in his early twenties, Mir's poetry was becoming the talk of the town, as were his eccentric ways—for he often seemed to inhabit a world of his own, deep in the throes of passion for poetry or beautiful people. News about this curious and talented young poet also reached Riayat Khan. One evening, Mir, in his usual distracted fashion, lost his way and reached Hauz Qazi. While he was drinking water, a man arrived and asked him if he was Mir Taqi. Mir replied in the affirmative and asked the man how he knew him. The man replied that it was Mir's eccentricity that identified him. He told Mir that Riayat Khan wanted to meet him and requested Mir to accompany him to the haveli. Mir agreed. Soon he had befriended Riayat, who began to support him, but the friendship did not last long.[52] Mir, it appears, took offence to something Riayat said in jest and parted ways with him. After Riayat, Mir was patronized first by Nawab Bahadur Javed Khan and then by Imad-ul-Mulk.

Javed Khan, the darogha (police chief) of the Mughal Court during the reign of Muhammad Shah Rangeela, had risen rapidly through the ranks after Rangeela died, in 1748, and was succeeded by his pleasure-loving son Ahmad Shah Bahadur. Javed, who was a handsome transgender, grew close to Ahmad Shah and was soon so powerful that he was said to be the de facto Emperor. As long as Javed was alive Mir did not have to fend for himself. But Javed soon overreached himself and, on a couple of serious state matters his advice proved calamitous for the Emperor. When Ahmad Shah Abdali began his regular invasions of North India, around 1749, Abul Mansur Mirza Muhammad Muqim Ali Khan Safdar Jung, who was the Nawab Vazir (Prime Minister) of the Mughal Court and Subedar of Awadh, decided to take on Abdali, as the Emperor clearly seemed incapable of organizing an effective defence. Fearing this would undermine his position, Javed, who did not like Safdar Jung, hatched a conspiracy to kill him. The conspiracy failed but led to grave hostility between the two. To make matters worse, on Javed's advice, the Emperor ended up ceding territory to Abdali, which led to further enmity between Javed and Safdar Jung. In September 1752, Javed was killed by Safdar Jung's men, and Mir again lost all patronage.

However, as before, his patron-less days did not last long. By killing Javed, Safdar Jung had made enemies in the Mughal Court and soon a rival faction led by Imad-ul-Mulk, a prominent minister, started to become powerful. Imad-ul-Mulk was himself a poet of sorts and occasionally invited Mir to 'mend' his poetry. In him, Mir found not only a wealthy but also a very powerful patron. In 1754, Imad-ul-Mulk oversaw the dethronement of Ahmad Shah Bahadur and his replacement on the Mughal throne by Azizuddin Alamgir II. In the meanwhile, Mir had also come in touch with Raja Jugal Kishore, who served as the agent of Alivardi Khan Mahabbat Jung, Nawab of Bengal, in the Mughal Court. Raja Jugal Kishore was fond of poetry too, and, in fact, considered himself a poet. He requested Mir to be his ustaad and help him improve his poetic skills, but Mir did not think much of his verses and, not finding them worthy of improvement, is said to have 'scratched a line across most of them'[53]. Remarkably, this didn't seem to ruin his chances with Jugal Kishore, who did Mir the favour of introducing him to Raja Nagar Mal, Deputy Minister in the Mughal Court, who took a shine to the poet. Soon Mir became a close confidant of the Raja and remained in his patronage for almost fourteen years.

It says something for Mir's stature as a poet, or perhaps for the decency of many of the nobles and other elite of his time, that he managed to find generous patrons through much of his life. After all, Mir did not make it easy for himself or for his admirers. He was very touchy, perhaps a little too conscious of his pride and honour. With several nobles, he broke ties on issues of self-respect and principles—he was so sensitive that many people considered him disagreeably haughty and kept their distance.

Mir was aware of the superiority of his work compared with that of his contemporaries and made no secret of it, insisting that, on merit, he was entitled to a far more exalted stature than any of them. He was once asked: 'Aaj ke zamaane ke shaayar kaun kaun hain?' ('Who are the poets of today?'),

He replied, 'Pehle Sauda phir khaaksaar.' ('First, Sauda; then yours truly.') After a pause, he added, 'Aur Mir Dard aadha shaayar hai.' ('And Mir Dard is half a poet.')

He was then asked, 'Aur Mir Soz?' ('And Mir Soz?')

To which he said, 'Kya vo bhi shaayar hai?' ('Is he a poet too?')

The man responded: 'Aakhir vo Nawab Asaf-ud-Daula ke ustaad hain.' ('After all, he is the ustaad of Nawab Asaf-ud-Daula.')

'Waqayi?' (Really?), said Mir, then added, 'Theek hai, toh phir kul mila ke do aur teen chauthaayi kar leejiye.' ('Ok, then make that a total of two and three quarters.')[54]

Sauda himself, though senior to Mir in age and poetic experience, acknowledged him as a greater poet:

Sauda, tu is ghazal ko ghazal-dar-ghazal hi keh
Hona hai tujh ko Mir se ustaad ki taraf

(Sauda, go on perfecting your art of ghazal-writing
You have to be on the side of a master like Mir.)

Mir, not an immodest man, would have considered such regard as mere statement of fact. He was utterly certain of the beauty of his own verse:

Na dekho kabhi motiyon ki ladi
Jo dekho meri guftgu ki taraf

(You will never look at a string of pearls
Once you've looked at the manner of my expression.)

Convinced of his genius, and fortunate in a string of patrons who allowed him to be disdainful of work to earn a living, Mir was vocal about the fact that he did not care about the high and mighty. He was a mystic, a fakir who needed no favours:

Ho koi baadshaah, koi yahaan vazeer ho
Apni bala se, baith rahe jab faqeer ho

(Someone may be a king or a minister here
I don't give a damn, I'm a carefree fakir.)

—

It is not known in which year Mir got married or to whom, but he did marry, sometime after he was thrown out by Aarzu. He had two children—a daughter and a son. His daughter, it seems, was a poet herself, though none of her work was published. Miraji (d. 1949)—the bohemian poet and pioneer of free verse in Urdu poetry—is believed to have once attributed this couplet to her[55]:

Abr chhaaya hai, mih barasta hai
Baat karne ko ji tarasta hai

(Dark clouds are gathered, it's raining;
The heart longs to speak to someone.)

In an age when it was almost criminal for women to express
themselves at all, for a young woman to reveal her romantic
desires in poetry was quite a courageous feat.

During one of Abdali's invasions, Raja Nagar Mal
moved to Kumber, a Jat province outside Delhi, and Mir,
with his wife and children, moved with the Raja. It is
believed that while they were at Kumber, the Raja requested
Mir to help him facilitate a political deal and also compose
some verses which would impress the Raja's opponent. Mir
did so and the deal was negotiated. In 1760, Shah Alam
II ascended to the throne of Delhi and some semblance of
peace and civilization was restored. Mir returned to Delhi
with Nagar Mal. However, when he realized that the Raja
had changed his mind about the deal that was negotiated
with Mir's poetic intervention, he decided to part ways with
him. Nagar Mal's son, Bahadur Singh, though, continued
to maintain his ties with Mir for some more time.

After Nagar Mahal and Bahadur Singh, Mir did not
find another patron in Delhi. By the mid-1760s, he was in
dire straits. Even though the position of Shah Alam II was
not as precarious as that of his predecessors', this wasn't
saying much. Delhi continued to be vulnerable to further
attacks, it was always on edge, and the exodus of the city's
elite and its poets and artists continued unabated. Mir's
friends and companions had either been killed or had fled
the city for the fear of being killed:

Dilli mein ab ke aa kar un yaaron ko na dekha
Kuchh ve gaye shataabi kuchh hum bhi der aaye

(Having come to Delhi this time, I don't see those friends
They went away a bit too soon and I arrived a bit too
   late.)

It wasn't only the loss of friends and compatriots that haunted Mir. Through his youth and early middle age— over just a couple of decades—Mir had seen the city of his dreams lose its soul and character:

Tab thay sipaahi ab hain jogi
Aah jawaani yoon kaati
Is thodi si raat mein humne
Kya-kya svaang rachaaye

(I was a soldier then, I'm an ascetic now
Alas, this is how I spent my youth,
In such a short night, I have
Played so many deceptive roles.)

The rich rulers and nobles had lost their wealth and estates and the Mughal Empire seemed to be on death-row. Mir was grief-stricken at this unimaginable shift in power:

Hamaare dekhte zer-e-nageen tha mulk sab jin ke
Koi ab naam bhi leta nahin un mulk-geeron ka

(They, whose rule we witnessed across the country
No one even speaks the names of those rulers now.)

Narrating the plight of the inhabitants of his now frequently-ransacked city, he lamented:

Chor-uchakke, Sikh, Maratthey, Shah-o-gada az
    khwaahaan hain
Chaiyn mein hain jo kuchh nahin rakhtey faqr hi ek
    daulat hai ab

(Thieves, pickpockets, Sikhs, Marathas, king and
    beggar—all are in need
In peace are those alone who own nothing, poverty is
    now the only wealth.)

The story of Delhi and its people being incessantly plundered and pillaged is a heart-breaking one, and no one tells it more evocatively than Mir:

> Ab kharaaba hua Jahanabad
> Varna har ek qadam pe yaan ghar tha
>
> (Jahanabad is now a ruin
> At every step, there was once a home here.)

And to this broken and battered city, he compares his heart:

> Deeda-e-giryaan hamaara neher hai
> Dil-e-kharaaba jaise Dilli sheher hai
>
> (My weeping eyes are like a canal
> My ruined heart like the city of Delhi.)

Providing a valuable insight into Mir's verse that connects the individual to his world, personal emotion to public experience, the eminent literary critic and poet Majnun Gorakhpuri remarks: 'Mir's time was one of sorrow and had he not been a poet of sorrow, he would have betrayed his times.'[56]

With no patronage, Mir was forced to fend for himself—in the only way he knew. Right outside the Qila-e-Moalla, the Jama Masjid was a great tourist attraction for visitors. With its lively surroundings, it had also become a favourite haunt for locals who spent their evenings relishing the delicious kebabs sold by its wide, sweeping steps. And around the mosque had come up shops selling various necessities. Mir would sit on the steps of the Jama Masjid and compose verses not only for visitors but also for traders. If he needed medicines, he would compose a verse or two for the pharmacist who would offer him the required medicines in lieu of his verse. If he wanted to buy clothes, he would pay the cloth-merchant in poetry.

Tourists and shopkeepers would buy him food in exchange for his couplets. In this pursuit, he wrote a number of verses praising the physical appearance of men he wanted to buy from. These and other verses have led to a debate about Mir's sexual orientation. There is no doubt, though, that Mir did write homoerotic verses. He also wrote verses which, by current standards, would probably qualify as obscene. But scholars, including Shamsur Rahman Faruqi, believe that in those days homosexuality and pornography were not frowned upon.

So Mir had created a barter system of sorts and made poetry his currency. But how long could such an arrangement go on? Soon he sank into penury. On the one hand, life in Delhi was becoming unbearable on account of this woeful financial condition and, on the other, he could not bear his beloved city being repeatedly plundered. He eventually went into seclusion.

The only way out of this wretchedness, it seemed, was migration to Lucknow, where the ruler, Nawab Asaf-ud-Daula, was known to be a great lover of Urdu poetry and a generous patron of Urdu poets. Sauda had already migrated to Lucknow and later died there. So had Aarzu. Finally, in 1782, a year after Sauda's death, with a heavy heart and tearful eyes, Mir bid adieu to Delhi for good and migrated to Lucknow:

Ab toh jaate hain bu'tkade se Mir[57]
Phir mileinge agar khuda laaya

(And so we depart from this house of idols, Mir
Perhaps we'll meet again, if God brings us back.)

Though Mir lived in Lucknow for the rest of his days, Delhi remained his first love. For him, those streets that he had left behind were no less than an artist's paintings:

Dilli ke na thay kooche auraaq-e-musavvar thay
Jo shakl nazar aayi tasveer nazar aayi

(The streets of Delhi were like painted pages
Every sight I saw looked like a picture.)

Popular accounts of Mir's arrival in Lucknow also reveal his robust sense of pride in being a Dilliwala. It is said that the day he arrived in Lucknow, there was a mushaira he wanted to attend. New to the city of the flamboyant nawabs, he reached the elitist gathering alone in an old-fashioned and modest dress. Not recognizing him, people made fun of his clothes and questioned him on his origins. It was then that Mir recited one of his most famous poems:

Kya bood-o-baash poochho ho poorab ke saakino
Hum ko ghareeb jaan ke hans-hans pukaar ke

Dilli jo ek sheher tha aalam mein intekhaab
Rehte thay muntakhab hi jahaan rozgaar ke

Us ko falak ne loot ke veeraan kar diya
Hum rehne waale hain usi ujde dayaar ke[58]

(You ask about my origins, O people of the East,
Mocking my poverty and laughing at me?

Delhi, which was the favoured city of the world
Where dwelt only the chosen from every walk of life

Now plundered by Fate and reduced to a wilderness,
I am a resident of that ruined place.)

Discovering who he was, the highbrow attendees embraced him, and Mir made Lucknow his new home.

And yet, though he spent the remaining twenty-eight years of his life in Lucknow, Mir, much to the chagrin of Lucknow-waalas, would often compare it unfavourably with Delhi. Once some leading noblemen of Lucknow called upon Mir and, after exchanging pleasantries, requested him to recite his poetry. Initially Mir was evasive but when the gentlemen insisted, he told them that his poetry was beyond their comprehension. Surprised, one of them remarked: 'But we understand the poetry of Anvari and Khaqani—the greatest of Persian poets!'

Mir retorted: 'I'm sure you do. But to get my poetry you need to understand the language that is spoken at the steps of Delhi's Jama Masjid, and that you do not.'[59]

Mir soon caught the attention of Asaf-ud-Daula, Nawab of Lucknow, and became a frequent visitor to his court. But the good fortune did not last long. Mir had a fallout with the Nawab, too. Once again, it was Mir's lack of tolerance for what he considered discourteous behaviour. One afternoon, the Nawab asked Mir to recite a ghazal for him when they were sitting by a fish pond in the Nawab's palace. As Mir began reciting, the Nawab continued to play with the fish. Mir stopped but the Nawab asked him to carry on. Mir replied: 'Gar huzoor tawajjo dein toh mai'n parhoon.' ('If your honour pays attention, I will recite.')

The Nawab saheb said airily, 'Har achha misra meri tawajjo ka mustahiq hoga.' ('Every worthwhile line shall receive my unreserved attention.')

The Nawab did not mean to belittle Mir's poetry, but the touchy genius took offence and walked off. Some days later, the Nawab was returning to his palace on an elephant after offering Friday prayers at the main mosque. He saw Mir sitting at a small shop in a corner of the street and asked his men to stop. While still seated on his elephant, the Nawab asked Mir why he had not visited the court for so long. Since the Nawab was seated atop an elephant, he had to almost shout in order to be heard. Instead of explaining the reason for his long absence, Mir said: 'Hamaare yahaan

shurafa oonchi aawaaz mein sadak par baatein nahin karte.'
('In our society gentlemen do not speak in raised voices on
the streets.')

Though Mir had been contemptuous of the Nawab's
majesty, the Nawab let it pass and did not stop paying
Mir his stipend. His successor, Nawab Sa'adat Ali Khan,
continued the tradition. But Mir cared two hoots for him,
too. Once he even refused to accept robes and money sent
to him by Sa'adat Ali Khan, asking the messenger to remind
the Nawab of the impermanence of his position and advise
him to give the gifts away in charity:

> Jis sar ko ghuroor aaj hai yaan taajwari ka
> Kal us pe yahin shor hai phir nauhagari ka

> (The head that takes such pride in wearing the crown
>   today
> Tomorrow cries of mourning will crown it in this very
>   place.)

This time Mir had gone too far. Shortly afterwards, his
stipend was stopped. Mir fell into penury again, and began
to regret ever having come to Lucknow:

> Kharaaba Dilli ka vo chand behtar Lucknow se tha
> Vahin mai'n kaash mar jaata, sara-seema na aata yahaan

> (The desolation of Delhi was far better than Lucknow
> I wish I had died there and not come running here.)

Mir's last years were difficult and lonely. Even as he
struggled with illness himself, he lost his daughter, son and
wife. Friendless and lonely in a city where he no longer felt
welcome, or even wanted to call home, he breathed his last
on 21 September 1810.

In his eighty-eight years, Mir lived many different lives.

He witnessed battles and invasions, saw his city being repeatedly razed to the ground, experienced the aristocratic ways of nobility closely and suffered hunger and starvation. No one explains this as beautifully as Zehra Nigah[60]:

Mir ka ye maan'na tha ki jab tak zindagi hai, ishq karo. Insaanon se insaanon ka ishq, jo zeest karne ka hunar sikhaata hai. Jo qalandari ka taj pehnaata hai. Aur is ishq ki inteha ye hoti hai ki khaaliq-o-makhlooq ek jaan ho jaate hain. Is raah-e-ishq pe chalne waala is tarah chalta hai kin na aabley phoot'te hain aur na khaar toot'te hain. Ba qaul T.S. Eliot, bada shaayar ek zindagi mein kayi zindagiyaan ji leta hai. Mir bhi kayi zindagiyaan jiye aur har zindagi mein ishq karte rahe. Pehli zindagi mein ek mehbooba mili jis ki jhalak parde ya chilman ke peechhe se nazar aayi, aur jab vo na mil paayi toh unhone usey chaand mein bitha liya. Doosra ishq faaqe aur usrat se kiya. Teesri zindagi mein Nawab ki mulaazimat ki. Bawujood apni bad-dimaaghi ke, nawab ki mulaazimat se ishq kiya aur usko is tarah chhora ki phir apne aap se surkhru bhi hue. Chauthi zindagi mein Jama Masjid ki seerhiyon pe baithe baithe, aate jaate, Allah ke sab bandon se ishq kiya aur aakhir-e-kaar ye hi ishq, ishq-e-mukammal kehlaaya aur aisa misra phir zubaan se nikla:

'Har shaey jo yahaan paida hui hai, mauzoon kar laaya hai ishq.'

(Mir believed that as long as you are alive, you must love. The love that exists between humans, which teaches man the art of living; which makes you wear the crown of the wandering ascetic. And the ultimate state of this love is reached when the creator and the creature become one. Those who walk on this path of love walk so finely that neither do the boils on their feet burst, nor do the thorns on their path break. As T.S. Eliot has said, a great poet lives many a life in a single life. Mir also lived many a life, and in every life, he loved. In his first life, he found a beloved; he caught a glimpse of her behind the drape of a curtain and when he could not have her, he put her in the moon. His second love was for starvation and poverty. In his third life, he found employment with the Nawab. Despite his ill-temper, he loved the Nawab's employment but when he left it he felt victorious. In his fourth life, sitting on the steps of the Jama Masjid, he loved every creature of God who passed by and ultimately it was this love that came to be known as 'complete love' and what words then fell from his lips:

'Every single thing born here has been perfected by love.')

II

MIR SYMBOLIZES AN AGE WHEN URDU AS A LANGUAGE of structured poetry was still in its infancy. Poets were experimenting with the still evolving Rekhta, and chief among those who contributed to its development as a language that was both refined and accessible, supple and formal, was Mir. In his ghazals he creates a distinct syntax and style, best seen in his poems of love and romance, poems about matters of the heart.

Columbia University Professor, Frances W Pritchett describes Mir as a 'true chronicler not of the events of his life, but of his inner moods, feelings, and susceptibilities'. She maintains that 'his verse is felt, even by an unsympathetic critic, as moving and powerful, a kind of poetry which at its best, comes from the heart and goes to the heart. He can express moods of melancholy, futility, pain, and despair with such simple dignity that his ghazals are evocative even in translation.'[61]

It is widely believed that no Urdu poet has written with greater feeling and beauty about the tragedy of love than Mir. In one of his most moving verses, he compares his ruined heart to the state of Delhi in his time which was repeatedly sacked by invaders:

Dil-o-Dilli donon agar hain kharaab
Pa kuchh lutf is ujde ghar mein bhi hain

(My heart and my Delhi may both be in ruins
There are still some delights in this ravaged home.)

He also believes that it is this very miserable condition and sense of helplessness that keeps him going:

Rah-e-talab mein girey hote munh ke bal hum bhi[62]
Shikasta-paayi ne apni hamein sambhaal liya

(On the path of desire, I too would have fallen badly
But my broken feet kept me steady.)

The pain of love is the pain of existence, neither God nor Love shows mercy; one is the other, and their ways are mysterious. Mir's beloved is unmoved by his agonies. The whole world is aware of his miserable condition, only his beloved ignores it, and deliberately chooses not to soothe him:

Patta patta, boota boota haal hamaara jaane hai
Jaane na jaane gul hi na jaane baagh toh saara jaane hai

Chaaragari beemaari-e-dil ki rasm-e-shehr-e-husn nahin
Varna dilbar-e-naadaan bhi is dard ka chaara jaane hai

Mehr-o-wafa-o-lutf-o-inaayat ek se waaqif in mein nahin
Aur toh sab kuchh tanz-o-kanaaya ramz-o-ishaara jaane
    hai

(Every leaf and every plant knows of my state
Only the flower does not know, all the garden knows.

Tending the afflicted heart is not the custom in the city
　　of the beautiful
Else even the naïve beloved knows well the cure for this
　　pain.

Mercy, loyalty, kindness and favour—no one knows of
　　them here
Taunts and gestures, signs and allusions—these are all
　　they know.)

Mir's poetry is a poetry of unfulfilled love; it is a poetry
of yearning, of desire and longing—of the heart and soul:

Faqeeraana aaye sada kar chaley
Miyaan khush raho hum dua kar chaley

Dikhaayi diye yoon ke be-khud kiya
Hamein aap se bhi juda kar chaley

Bohot aarzoo thi gali ki teri
So yaan se lahu mein naha kar chaley

(Like a fakir I came, and with this cry I leave:
Stay happy, my friend, this is my prayer.

Just a glimpse of you has put me in a trance
You've left me detached from my own self.

I had a great desire to visit your lane
And now I return, soaked in blood.)

But the lover's passion is undimmed, it will make God of
the beloved:

Jabeen sajda karte hi karte gayi
Haq-e-bandagi hum ada kar chaley

Parastish ki yaan tak ki ae bu't tujhe
Nazar mein sabon ki khuda kar chaley

(I have worn out my brow in prostration
I have paid my debt of obeisance.

I have worshipped you to such an extent, O idol
I have made you God in the eyes of all.)

Mir's passion also yields less lofty, more conventionally romantic images that are employed to describe the beloved's beauty:

Naazuki us ke lab ki kya kahiye
Pankhari ek gulaab ki si hai

Mir in neem-baaz aankhon mein
Saari masti sharaab ki si hai

(Ah! The tenderness of her lips
Is like the petal of a rose.

Mir, in these half-open dreamy eyes
There is the intoxication of aged wine.)

And, just as conventionally, he also grumbles that falling in love is a headache:

Kya kahoon tum se mai'n ke kya hai ishq
Jaan ka rog hai bala hai ishq

Mir ji zard hotey jaate hain
Kya kahin tum ne bhi kiya hai ishq

(How should I tell you what love is?
It's a disease of the soul, it's a curse, this love.

Mir, I see you're turning pale
Tell me, have you also fallen in love?)

Sometimes, though, Mir can't be bothered with the rituals of love. His legendary self-regard, his pride, makes him deliberately insensitive:

Gul ne bohot kaha ki chaman se na jaaiye
Gulgasht ko jo aaiye aankhon pe aaiye
Mai'n be-dimaagh kar ke taghaaful chala gaya
Fursat kahaan ke naaz kisi ke uthaaiye

(The flower begged me not to leave:
'If you've come for a stroll in the garden, be my valued
    guest.'
I thoughtlessly ignored it and came away—
Where, really, is the time to indulge anyone?)

And it isn't clear if he deplores such insensitivity or applauds
it:

Kya kahiye dimaagh us ka ki gulgasht mein, ae Mir
Gul shaakhon se jhuk aaye thay par munh na lagaaya

(What can one say of his mood, O Mir, he was strolling
    in the garden
And flowers bowed down from the branches, but he
    cared two hoots.)

At other times, Mir is so mesmerized by his beloved that he
does not dare to utter a single word in her presence. What
then gives her cause to be annoyed, he wonders:

Apne toh honth bhi na hiley unke ru-ba-ru
Ranjish ki wajeh Mir vo kya baat ho gayi

(In her presence, I was struck dumb.
Mir, what did she take offence to, then?)

Whether playful or full of pain, earthy or mystical, Mir's
poetry of love is perhaps his greatest gift to us. The centrality
of love in his worldview is best realized in the following
two couplets:

Ishq hi ishq hai jahaan dekho
Saare aalam mein bhar raha hai ishq

Ishq maashooq, ishq aashiq hai
Yaani apna hi mubtala hai ishq

(There is love and only love wherever you look
All of creation is overflowing with love.

Love is the beloved, love is the lover, too
As if love is involved in an affair with itself.)

In a powerful couplet that defies any single interpretation, Mir equates lovers—in a world where love is all that can mean anything—with a fistful of dust:

Aawaargaan-e-ishq ka poochha jo mai'n nishaan
Musht-e-ghubaar le ke saba ne uda diya

(When I asked how the wanderers of love were doing
The morning breeze took a fistful of dust and blew it
    away.)

Mir spoke to his readers in their own language—the colloquial language of Shahjahanabad—and not the Persianized language of the Mughal Court or the Qila-e-Moalla. Even ideas and emotions of great intensity and depth are conveyed with stunning simplicity and have an immediate impact:

Bekhudi le gayi kahaan hum ko
Der se intezaar hai apna

(Where has my delirium taken me?
I've been waiting for myself for so long.)

The bitter realities of life stare him in his face, but he expresses his desolation with an effortless elegance that would resonate with anyone, high or low, young or old:

Shaam hi se bujha sa rehta hai
Dil hua hai chiraagh muflis ka

(All but extinguished since evening
My heart, like a poor man's lamp.)

Mir wrote poetry day and night, and sometimes even, as we have seen, in exchange for everyday necessities like groceries. Obviously, we can neither expect the same flair and panache in all his verses nor the same depth and meaning. No poet who earns a living by writing poetry can claim to write with equal excellence all the time. Mir's collection too is full of frivolous, run-of-the-mill poetry. Called 'bharti ke sher' (couplets written for the heck of it), they were composed just to fill up pages. However, even in such pages, every once in a while, a perfect jewel will emerge. Zehra Nigah points out one such couplet in an otherwise ordinary ghazal which begins with:

> Aankhon mein ji mera hai idhar yaar dekhna
> Aashiq ka apne aakhiri deedaar dekhna

> (My heart is in my eyes, look here, my love
> Look at your lover just one last time.)

An incredible couplet finds its way into this ghazal[63]:

> Kaisi bahaar hum se aseeron ko mana hai
> Chaak-e-qafas se baagh ki deewaar dekhna

In its ordinary meaning, the couplet would be translated thus:

> What springtime? For us prisoners, it is prohibited
> To even see the garden-wall through a crevice in our cell.

However, Zehra Nigah's son, Nomaan Majid, a distinguished connoisseur of poetry, an economist at work and an artist at heart, explains that the beauty of this couplet is in its play on the duality of things:

> The first line could be interpreted variously, with respect to the word 'kaisi'. But let us take it in the sense of a statement of curiosity and not a literal question. Mir is saying, 'Incredible, is it not, this view of springtime from my space of separation (incarceration and wilderness),

because I can only see the wall of the garden.' Now he is an 'aseer' (a prisoner), but of what kind? The kind who is trapped in a wilderness; like a lover—a Majnun—and 'qafas' is the space that the lover inhabits. Similarly, 'baagh' and 'bahaar' are associated with the space of 'husn' (beauty), the space of the beloved. The couplet is a discovery of the fact that both 'ishq' (passion) and 'husn' (beauty, signified by 'bahaar' or springtime) are trapped. Mir is saying that I wonder if you realize that if you tore through the space of wilderness, the abode for lovers, you would come closer to the space of union, but you will still not encounter it. For Mir this situation is cause for amused wonderment. Another poet would identify it as a fundamental condition of man.[64]

It is fascinating to note that two centuries later, first Faiz Ahmed Faiz and then Nida Fazli used a similar semantic metre for their ghazals containing couplets ending with words like 'deewaar dekhna' and 'rukhsaar dekhna'. One of Faiz's well-known ghazals begins with this couplet:

Toofaan ba-dil hai har koi dildaar dekhna
Gul ho na jaaye mish'al-e-rukhsaar dekhna

(A storm is brewing in every heart, look, sweetheart
The glow on your face may just be blown out, take care.)

And Nida Fazli opens a ghazal with:

Do-chaar gaam raah ko humvaar dekhna
Phir har qadam pe ek nayi deewaar dekhna

(For a step or two your journey will be smooth
Then at every step you will find a new wall.)

In a sense, the 'fundamental condition of man' that Nomaan Majid spoke of is at the heart of Mir's poetry. Humanity is Mir's only true subject and muse. For him, it is the temporal, mortal, questing man who brings grace and glory to the otherwise unbearable, worthless world. Mir elevates the stature of man to an almost divine level:

Aadam-e-khaaki se aalam ko jila hai varna
Aaina tha toh magar qaabil-e-deedaar na tha

(It is earthly man who glorifies the world, else
The mirror was there but not worth looking into.)

Profound philosophy, however, is never at the expense of simplicity. Mir's verse is powerful but his language is unpretentious. After all, his real intention was to speak to the man on Delhi's streets, to the public at large, and not to the elite:

Sher mere hain sab khawaas-pasand
Par mujhe guftgu awaam se hai

(All my verses are liked by the elite
But I speak to the public at large.)

Mir's syntax is natural and effortless. More often than not, he writes as if he is speaking to his readers. His characteristic language that inspired even Ghalib and Zauq continues to enthuse modern poets and even lyricists who emulate his semantic style. In a recent Bollywood film, *Dedh Ishqiya*, Gulzar made his protagonist Naseeruddin Shah open a mushaira recitation with these lines:

Na boloon mai'n toh kaleja phunke jo bol doon toh
    zubaan jaley hai
Sulag na jaave agar sune vo jo baat meri zubaan taley hai

(If I don't speak, my heart burns; if I do, my tongue is
    singed.
She may catch fire if she hears the words I want to say.)

One of the greatest masters of the Urdu ghazal in the twentieth century, Firaq Gorakhpuri, revels in Mir's glory when he opens and ends one of his most delightful ghazals with these couplets:

Ab aksar chup-chup se rahe hain yoon hi kabhu lab
    kholey hain
Pehle Firaq ko dekha hota ab toh bohot kam boley hain

Sadqe Firaq aijaaz-e-sukhan ke udaayi kahaan se ye
    aawaaz
In ghazlon ke parde mein toh Mir ki ghazlein bolein hain

(Now I'm usually quiet, I hardly open my mouth
You should have seen Firaq before, now he barely speaks.

This miracle of poetry, Firaq, is to die for; where did you
    snatch this voice from?
In the cloak of these ghazals, you're reciting the ghazals
    of Mir.)

—

Mir, like Sauda, does not hesitate to audaciously announce his disbelief in formal, orthodox religion and its rituals. One of his most well-known ghazals, beautifully sung by the incomparable Begum Akhtar, begins with this couplet:

Ulti ho gayin sab tadbeerein kuchh na dawa ne kaam kiya
Dekha is beemaari-e-dil ne aakhir kaam tamaam kiya

(All my plans were turned upside down, the medicine
    didn't work at all.
Have you not seen how this sickness of the heart has
    finally killed me?)

Later in this ghazal, Mir first lights into the mullah, exposing his debauchery and hypocrisy, and then proclaims that he, Mir, has already shunned religious formalism and now believes in the oneness of creation:

Shaikh jo hai masjid mein nanga, raat ko tha maikhaane
    mein
Jubba, khurqa, kurta, topi, masti mein inaam kiya

Kis ka Kaaba kaisa qibla kaun haram hai kya ehraam
Kooche ke us ke baashindon ne sab ko yahin se salaam
    kiya

Mir ke deen-o-mazhab ko ab poochhte kya ho un ne toh
Qashqa kheincha daiyr mein baitha kab ka tark Islam
    kiya

(The Shaikh who stands naked in the mosque today, was
    in the tavern last night
His cloak, gown, shirt and cap—drunk out of his wits,
    he gave them all away.

Whose Kaaba, what prayer-direction, what holy mosque,
    what pilgrim robes?
We, the inhabitants of her lane, bid farewell to these
    from a distance.

What is it that you want to know about Mir's faith and
    religion?
With a tilak on his forehead he sits in a temple, he
    renounced Islam long ago.)

This ghazal, in fact, has some marvelous couplets. In a
couplet that could be addressed to both God and the
beloved, Mir complains that the poor lover or devotee
exercises no power upon himself. He is a helpless soul and
simply accepts, without questioning, what is done to him
or what he is made to do. Why then should he be accused
of having authority over his own affairs?

Na-haq hum majbooron par ye tohmat hai mukhtaari ki
Chaahte hain so aap kare hain hum ko abas badnaam
    kiya

(We helpless ones are accused of being in authority for
    no reason
You do whatever you like and we are unjustly defamed.)

He then goes on to clarify that he is a mere spectator in
this world:

Yaan ke saphed-o-siyaah mein hum ko dakhl jo hai so
    itna hai
Raat ko ro-ro subaha kiya aur din ko joon-toon shaam
    kiya

Literally translated, the couplet would mean:

In the white and black of this world my only role is this:
I weep the night into morning and somehow pass the
    day into evening.

But Mir is making a larger, perhaps 'heretic' observation.
If there is a design to Creation, he doesn't know what it is.
He has no role to play, much less any power, in the affairs
of this world and over the cosmic cycle of day and night.

Mir believes that the involvement of the Shaikh and
Brahmin—Muslim and Hindu holy men—pollutes faith, and
for purity of faith it is imperative to stay away from them:

Shirkat-e-Shaikh-o-Barahman se Mir Kaaba-o-daiyr se
    bhi jaaye ga
Apni derh eent ki judi masjid kisi veeraane mein banaaye
    ga[65]

(With the involvement of Shaikh and Brahmin, Mir will
    lose both Kaaba and temple
He will then make a separate tiny mosque for himself,
    in some secluded corner.)

Love is his only creed and conviction. He claims to belong
to a religion where the loving and compassionate heart
alone is the prophet, prayer and God:

Hamaara khaas maslak ishq jis mein
Payambar dil hai qibla dil khuda dil

(My precise religion is love, in which
The heart is the prophet, the heart is the prayer-direction,
    the heart is God.)

The One Creator is the origin of everything; the same divine
light illuminates the mosque and the temple:

Uske farogh-e-husn se jhamke hai sab mein noor
Shamm-e-haram ho ya ke diya Somnaat ka

(It is His beauty that illuminates all
Be it the candle of the mosque or the lamp of Somnath.)

Owing to his pluralist beliefs, neither Muslims accept Mir as
their own nor do the Hindus, and he expresses his dilemma
so simply and so well:

Daiyr-o-haram mein kyon ki qadam rakh sakega Mir
Idhar is se bu't phirey udhar khuda phirey

(How will Mir be able to step into temple or mosque?
Idols turn away from him here, and God there.)

—

Mir was a man of traditional values and was aghast at
the changing values of his times. He could not bear the
thought that he was living amongst people who had no
time for the old principles, traditions and morals which
were quintessential to his very existence. His disillusionment
with such social transformation became more intense with
time and this is reflected in his later poetry:

Rasm uth gayi duniya se ik baar murawwat ki
Kya log zameen par hain kaisa ye sama aaya

(Kindness as a custom has disappeared from the world
Strange people inhabit the earth now, strange are the
   times.)

In an era where people don't think twice before harming
even good men, he is aware of his own vulnerability and
defencelessness:

Mir Saheb zamaana naazuk hai
Donon haathon se thaamiye dastaar

(Mir sahib! These are delicate times,
Hold your turban with both your hands.)

⸺

Mir's collection of poetry is more voluminous than that of
any other classical Urdu poet. His poetry is spread over six
diwaans. Till his fifth diwaan, composed in an advanced age,
his ghazals make it clear that he hoped to find refuge in a
more cultured and agreeable place than Lucknow. The city
seemed gloomy to him and he found it hard to live there.
By the time the last diwaan was penned, the sourness had
receded; not because his views on the city had changed,
but because he had no more strength left to criticize. He
had already lost his daughter, son and wife one after the
other in a short span of time. His friends were dying one
by one. Back in Delhi, Shah Alam II had died and his son,
Akbar Shah, has occupied the Mughal throne in November
1806, albeit only as a titular figurehead. It was the British
East India Company that was actually in power. Mir could
not bear the thought of his beloved Delhi having become
a mere British protectorate. He had neither the will nor
the strength to go on. Penniless and seriously ill with a
painful gastrointestinal disease, he continued to write, but
only out of habit:

Aur kuchh mashghala nahin hai hamein
Gaah-o-begah ghazal saraayi hai

(I have no other work to occupy me now
In and out of season, I recite my ghazals.)

This was how the days of the proud, prolific and troubled genius ended. He was buried in his neighbourhood graveyard of Bheem Ka Akhaara, located north of what is now called the City Station. Until half a century ago, a grave situated just before the Chhatte Waala Pul near the City Station railway tracks was believed to be that of Mir. Sometime in the 1960s or early 1970s, a railway line was laid there and the grave was covered by a track. It seems that some years later, the track was moved to the side to make way for housing but the land was later illegally acquired. Today, there stands a humungous slum on the spot where the grave once existed and where Mir spent the last three decades of his life. My friend Kanishka Prasad and I walked all over the area for hours one day, enquiring about the remnants and relics of the poet's life. There was hardly a soul in the vicinity who had even heard of the poet. An old resident of the area, one Baqai saheb, who runs a printing press right in front of the spot where Mir's grave is said to have once existed, was kind enough to offer us cups of tea and tell us that the area had been usurped by land-grabbers long ago.

A lone broken stone erected in a park calls itself 'Nishaan-e-Mir' ('Mark of Mir') and, if someone can search for it, an almost invisible and decrepit road-sign at the end of the street reads 'Mir Taqi Mir Marg'. These are the only visible (with effort) signs of this 'God of Poetry' that exist in Lucknow today. Mir has written:

Baad marne ke meri qabr pe aaya vo Mir
Yaad aayi merey Eesa ko dawa merey baad

(Mir, he came to my grave after I died
My Messiah thought of a cure after I was gone.)

But no one comes.

Back in Delhi, where Mir's heart lived even after he had migrated to Lucknow, the situation is even more pitiable. Hardly any resident of Kucha Chelan, Chandni Mahal and Matia Mahal—neighbourhoods which Mir had once described as 'auraaq-e-musavva' ('painted pages') and whose lanes once echoed with his poetry—knows who Mir was, much less where he lived. My recitation of Mir's well-known couplet which aptly describes this harrowing state of affairs was also lost on them:

Deedni hai shikastgi dil ki
Kya imaarat ghamon ne dhaayi hai

(My heart's rubble is quite a sight
What a citadel have sorrows razed.)

And why should it not have been? After all, Mir had himself prophesied:

Baatein hamaari yaad rahein phir baatein aisi na suniye ga
Parhte kisi ko suniye ga toh der talak sar dhuniye ga

(Remember my words, for you won't hear such words
    again
If you hear someone narrating them, you'll bang your
    head in regret.)

It is heart-breaking that in our mad race for survival, we forget that souls like Mir are not born twice. Delhi will never see another Khuda-e-Sukhan. There will never be another Mir Taqi Mir:

Mat sehel hamein jaano phirta hai falak barson
Phir khaak ke parde se insaan nikalte hain

(Don't consider me commonplace; heavens wander for
　　years
Only then, from the cloak of dust, is a human born.)

III

SELECTED POETRY OF MIR

I

Ulti ho gayin sab tadbeerein kuchh na dawa ne kaam kiya
Dekha is beemaari-e-dil ne aakhir kaam tamaam kiya

Na-haq hum majbooron par ye tohmat hai mukhtaari ki
Chaahte hain so aap kare hain hum ko abas badnaam
　　kiya

Yaan ke saphed-o-siyaah mein hum ko dakhl jo hai so
　　itna hai
Raat ko ro-ro subaha kiya aur din ko joon-toon shaam
　　kiya

Shaikh jo hai masjid mein nanga, raat ko tha maikhaane
　　mein
Jubba, khurqa, kurta, topi, masti mein inaam kiya

Kis ka Kaaba kaisa qibla kaun haram hai kya ehraam
Kooche ke us ke baashindon ne sab ko yahin se salaam
　　kiya

Mir ke deen-o-mazhab ko ab poochhte kya ho un ne toh
Qashqa kheincha daiyr mein baitha kab ka tark Islam
　　kiya

(All my plans were turned upside down, the medicine
　　didn't work at all.
Have you not seen how this sickness of the heart has
　　finally killed me?

We helpless ones are accused of being in authority for
　　no reason
You do whatever you like and we are unjustly defamed.

In the white and black of this world my only role is this:
I weep the night into morning and somehow pass the
day into evening.

The Shaikh who stands naked in the mosque today, was
in the tavern last night
His cloak, gown, shirt and cap—drunk out of his wits,
he gave them all away.

Whose Kaaba, what prayer-direction, what holy mosque,
what pilgrim robes?
We, the inhabitants of her lane, bid farewell to these
from a distance.

What is it that you want to know about Mir's faith and
religion?
With a tilak on his forehead he sits in a temple, he
renounced Islam long ago.)

2

Faqeeraana aaye sada kar chaley
Miyaan khush raho hum dua kar chaley

Dikhaayi diye yoon ke be-khud kiya
Hamein aap se bhi juda kar chaley

Bohot aarzoo thi gali ki teri
So yaan se lahu mein naha kar chaley

Jabeen sajda karte hi karte gayi
Haq-e-bandagi hum ada kar chaley

Parastish ki yaan tak ki ae bu't tujhe
Nazar mein sabon ki khuda kar chaley

Kahein kya jo poochhe koi hum se Mir
Jahaan mein tum aaye thay, kya kar chaley

(Like a fakir I came, and with this cry I left:
Stay happy, my friend, this is my prayer.

Just a glimpse of you has put me in a trance
You've left me detached from my own self.

I had a great desire to visit your lane
And now I return, soaked in blood.

I have worn out my brow in prostration
I have paid my debt of obeisance.

I have worshipped you to such an extent, O idol
I have made you God in the eyes of all.

What should I say, if someone asks me, Mir
You came into this world, what did you achieve?)

3

Dekh toh dil ke jaan se uthta hai
Ye dhuaan sa kahaan se uthta hai

Gor kis dil-jaley ki hai ye falak
Shola ik subaha yaan se uthta hai

Naala sar kheinchta hai jab mera
Shor ek aasmaan se uthta hai

Ladti hai us ki chashm-e-shokh jahaan
Ek aashob vaan se uthta hai

Sudh le ghar ki bhi shola-e-aawaaz
Dood kuchh aashiyaan se uthta hai

Baithne kaun de hai phir us ko
Jo tere aastaan se uthta hai

Yoon uthe aah us gali se hum
Jaise koi jahaan se uthta hai

Ishq ik Mir bhaari paththar hai
Bojh kab natavaan se uthta hai

(Do you see this, does it rise from my heart or my soul?
This thing like smoke, where does it rise from?

O sky, which broken-heart lies in this grave?
A flame rises from here every morning.

When cries of complaint start hurting my head
An outcry rises up in the skies.

Wherever her playful gaze comes to rest
A turbulence rises from that spot.

O flaming voice, spare a thought for your own house too
A cloud of smoke rises from your nest.

Who will let him sit anywhere again
He, who rises once from your doorstep?

Oh, how we rose to leave that lane
As one rises from this world upon death.

Mir, love is a heavy rock
What weakling can rise with that weight?)

4

Hasti apni habaab ki si hai
Ye numaaish saraab ki si hai

Naazuki us ke lab ki kya kahiye
Pankhari ek gulaab ki si hai

Chashm-e-dil khol is bhi aalam par
yaan ki auqaat khvaab ki si hai.

Baar-baar uske dar pe jaata hoon
Haalat ab izteraab ki si hai

Mai'n jo bola kaha ke ye aawaaz
Usi khaana-kharaab ki si hai

Mir in neem-baaz aankhon mein
Saari masti sharaab ki si hai

(My existence is like a bubble
This show is like a mirage.

Ah! The tenderness of her lips
Is like the petal of a rose.

Open your heart's eye now
All the world is just a dream.

I visit her door again and again
I am in a state of restlessness now.

As I spoke, they said, this voice
Belongs to that ruined man.

Mir, in these half-open dreamy eyes
There is the intoxication of aged wine.)

5

Patta patta, boota boota haal hamaara jaane hai
Jaane na jaane gul hi na jaane baagh toh saara jaane hai

Chaaragari beemaari-e-dil ki rasm-e-shehr-e-husn nahin
Varna dilbar-e-naadaan bhi is dard ka chaara jaane hai

Mehr-o-wafa-o-lutf-o-inaayat ek se waaqif in mein nahin
Aur toh sab kuchh tanz-o-kanaaya ramz-o-ishaara jaane
    hai

Aashiq sa toh saada koi aur na hoga duniya mein
Ji ke ziyaan ko ishq mein us ke apna vaara jaane hai

Tishna-e-khoon hai apna kitna Mir bhi nadaan talkhi-
    kash
Dum-daar aab-e-tegh ko us ke aab-e-gavaara jaane hai

(Every leaf and every plant knows of my state
Only the flower does not know, all the garden knows.

Tending the afflicted heart is not the custom in the city
    of the beautiful
Else even the naïve beloved knows well the cure for this pain.

Mercy, loyalty, kindness and favour—no one knows of
    them here
Taunts and gestures, signs and allusions—these are all
    they know.

No one in this world would be as simple as a lover
Losing his heart in love he thinks is gain.

Mir, the bitter simpleton, thirsts so much for his own blood
He thinks her heavy sword-blade is the elixir of life.)

MIRZA ASADULLAH KHAN GHALIB
The Master of Masters
(1797–1869)

Poochhte hain vo ki Ghalib kaun hai
Koi batlaao ke hum batlaaein kya

(They ask, 'Who is Ghalib?'
Someone tell us, what should we say!)

—

Baazeecha-e-atfaal hai duniya mere aagey
Hota hai shab-o-roz tamaasha mere aagey

(The world is but the playground of children before me
A spectacle unfolds night and day before me.)

I

By THE END OF THE 1820s, DELHI HAD BECOME QUITE a tourist destination for foreign visitors. With the British slowly consolidating their hold over the Mughal capital, the city had not only seen demographical changes but also cultural transformations. Emma Roberts, the celebrated travel writer from England, visited the city in the early 1830s. About Chandni Chowk, she writes:

> The shops are crowded with all sorts of European products and manufactures, and many of them display signboards, on which the names and occupations of the inhabitants are emblazoned in Roman characters—a novel circumstance in a native city. The introduction of this useful custom is attributed to Burruddeen Khan, an ingenious person patronized by the reigning emperor, Akbar the second...The English placards have a very curious appearance, mingled with the striped purdahs or curtains which shade the windows.[66]

C.M. Naim adds that the big attractions for tourists were the Jama Masjid, the Red Fort (the Qila-e-Moalla) and the Emperor himself. One of the main sources of income for Akbar Shah II was receipts from foreign visitors. An audience with him would cost an ordinary foreign visitor four gold coins. If the Emperor agreed to receive a khilat (robe of honour), the price would be more. The 'must-see places' for tourists outside Shahjahanabad were the Qutub Minar, the tombs of Humayun and Safdar Jung and the Jantar Mantar observatory. Some also visited Tughluqabad and the Dargah of Hazrat Nizamuddin.[67]

Despite the changing demography and political balance of power and somewhat new culture, the light of Urdu poetry continued to shine brightly in Delhi. The city was bristling with Urdu poetry and remained the seat of Urdu literature. Urdu had matured into a language of structured poetry and its syntax and semantics were changing to suit the literary needs of the time. Some of the most well-known poets known to Urdu literature, including Shaikh Mohammad Ibrahim Zauq, Hakim Momin Khan Momin, Mufti Sadruddin Azurdah, Nawab Mustafa Khan Shefta and Imam Bakhsh Sahbai had made Delhi their home. The last Mughal, Bahadur Shah Zafar, was not only a connoisseur of Urdu poetry but a poet himself. Towering high over all of them—and also his predecessors—was Mirza Asadullah Khan Ghalib.

Ghalib is today regarded as the loftiest poet Urdu has ever produced. His greatness prompted one of his biographers, the remarkable scholar Abdur Rehman Bijnori, to proclaim that his poetry is nothing short of being divine. In fact, in a rather audacious statement, Bijnori says: 'There are only two divinely revealed books in India—the Holy Vedas and the *Diwaan-e-Ghalib*.'[68]

But what is it about Ghalib that makes him different from all others? In a longish poem titled '*Ghalib ko Bura kyon kaho?*' ('Why Call Ghalib Bad?') the renowned satirist Dilawar Figaar (d. 1988) has made an attempt to answer this question in his inimitable style. The poem begins with a humorous touch, making fun of Ghalib and his universal fame, and then takes a serious turn expounding the core character of a poet whose mind beats like the heart:

> Kal ek naaqid-e-Ghalib ne mujh se ye poochha
> Ke qadr-e-Ghalib-e-marhoom ka sabab kya hai
> Mujhe bataao ki diwaan-e-Hazrat-e-Ghalib
> Kalaam-e-paak hai, Injeel hai, ki Geeta hai

Suna hai Shahr Karachi mein bhi ek sahib hain
Kalaam unka bhi Ghalib se milta julta hai
Toh phir ye Ghalib-e-Marhoom hi ki barsi kyon
Mujhe bataao ki un mein khusoosiyat kya hai

Kabhi hai mahv haseenon se dhaul-dhappe mein
Kabhi kisi ka vo sotey mein bosa leta hai
Jo keh rahe hain ki Ghalib hai falsafi shaayar
Mujhe bataaein ki bosey mein falsafa kya hai

Barhi jo baat, toh phir maine un ko samjhaaya
Adab mein Hazrat-e-Ghalib ka martaba kya hai
Bataaya usko ki vo zindagi ka hai shaayar
Bohot qareeb se duniya ko usne dekha hai

Ajab tazaad ki haamil hai us ki shakhsiyat
Ajeeb shakhs hai, barbaad ho ke hansta hai

Vo likh raha hai hikaayat e khoon-chakaan
Jabhi toh uske qalam se lahu tapakta hai

Pahunch gaya hai vo us manzil-e-tafakkur par
Jahaan dimaagh bhi dil ki tarah dharakta hai

(Yesterday, a Ghalib-critic asked me
'Why is the dear departed Ghalib so revered?
Tell me, is his collection
The Holy Quran, the Bible, the Geeta?

Even in Karachi, we hear, there's a gentleman
Whose poetry is similar to Ghalib's
Then why celebrate Ghalib's anniversary alone?
What's so special about him, tell me?

Sometimes he's in a tug of war with beautiful women
Sometimes he's kissing someone in her sleep.[69]
They who claim Ghalib is a philosopher-poet should
	tell me:
What's so philosophical about a kiss?'

When things got worse, I explained to him

What stature Ghalib holds in literature.
I told him, Ghalib is a poet of life
He has seen the world up close.

His personality is fraught with strange contradictions
What an odd man he is—he laughs when he's ruined!

He writes tales of those bathed in blood[70]
Which is why blood drips from his pen;

He has reached that final stage of reflection
Where even the mind beats like the heart.)

Ghalib's mind did beat like a heart; a heart that derives pleasure in being pierced by the dagger of knowledge and experience; a dagger that seeks its target repeatedly, and each time plunges deeper than before. These were the deep wounds that produced Ghalib's immortal poetry, which has seeped through the literary and cultural landscape not only of the country that produced him but, indeed, of the entire world. Even a century and a half after his death, Ghalib haunts millions of restless minds with his articulation of desire and despair, and yet exudes peace and tranquillity with his wisdom.

To understand Ghalib, we need to take at least a broad overview of his social, economic and political circumstances. Ghalib was born in Agra on 27 December 1797 as Mirza Asadullah Beg Khan to parents of Turkish lineage who traced their roots to the Aibak Turks of Samarkand. Ghalib's grandfather, Mirza Quqan Beg Khan, a Turk warrior, had travelled to India from Samarkand and joined, one after the other, the armed forces of the Governor of Punjab, the Mughal Emperor Shah Alam and the Maharaja of Jaipur.[71] Ghalib's father, Mirza Abdullah Beg Khan, was Quqan Beg's eldest son and, like his father, also joined various armed forces as a soldier. (Some biographers claim that he and his younger brother, Mirza Nasrullah Beg Khan, were, in fact, professional mercenaries employed by various rulers to carry out political killings.[72]) Abdullah's wife, Izzat-un-Nisa Begum, belonged to a well-heeled family of Agra. Her father, Khwaja Ghulam Husain Khan 'Kamidaan' (Commandant), had a huge estate in the city and while Abdullah was on military expeditions, which was almost all the time, she lived in her father's house. It was in this house in Agra that Ghalib was born in 1797. He had a younger brother, Yusuf, and a sister whom everyone called Chhoti Begum.

Abdullah Beg died in a battle in 1803 in Alwar when Ghalib was only five. For a few years after his father's death, his uncle, Nasrullah—who by then had risen to the position of Commander of Agra Fort under the Marathas—took care of him and his two siblings. But he too died in 1806. Ghalib and his siblings were, therefore, raised by their mother and her parents and spent most of their childhood years with their maternal grandparents. Psychoanalyzing Ghalib, the eminent psychologist Narendra Nath Wig concludes that the trauma that Ghalib went through as a child, having lost his father and uncle when not yet nine, found its way into his poetry.[73] Many other scholars and biographers, however, are of the opinion that Ghalib had a carefree childhood, a sheltered and privileged one, since his mother's family was among Agra's wealthiest. It is believed that Ghalib's almost regal pride, his love of the good life and his near complete obsession with material advancement through his entire adult life had their origins in his childhood, which was clearly one of great material comfort.

In Agra, one of Ghalib's childhood friends was a neighbour's son, Bansi Dhar, who remained his closest

friend, in thick and thin, till the very end and finds mention
in almost all works on Ghalib's life. Much later in life,
Ghalib recounted his association with Bansi Dhar, and
some of the circumstances of his boyhood, in a letter to
Bansi Dhar's grandson, Shiv Narain Aram, one of his young
patrons:

> Be it known to you, dear young friend Munshi Shiv
> Narain, that I had no idea that you were who you truly
> are. Now that I discover that you are the grandson of
> Nazir Bansi Dhar, I recognize you as my beloved son.
> Thus, from now on, if I address you in my letters as
> 'Benevolent and Honoured Friend', it will be a sin...
> Listen. In the days of Najaf Khan and Hamadani, the
> father of your paternal grandfather [Munshi Bansi Dhar]
> was a constant companion of my maternal grandfather,
> the late Khwaja Ghulam Husain Khan...Munshi Sahib
> and I were about the same age—he may have been a year
> or so older or younger. We played chess together and
> became fast and loving friends. It was not unusual for
> us to be together until midnight. Since his house was not
> far, I went there whenever I liked. Between their house
> and ours, the only intervening buildings were the home
> of Machhya Randi [Courtesan] and two blocks of rented
> homes owned by my family. Our larger mansion is the one
> which is now owned by Lakhi Chand Seth. The baradari
> of stone which is joined to the main entrance of this
> mansion was my sitting-room and lounge. Then there was
> the mansion known as Ghatya-vali haveli and near Salim
> Shah's hovel, another mansion and another adjoining the
> Kala Mahal, and beyond that there was another block of
> rented houses called the Gadaryon-vala Katra and then
> another similar block called the Kashmirion-vala Katra.
> On the roof of one of the houses in this last block, I
> used to fly kites and we used to have kite matches with

Raja Balvan Singh. There was a veteran soldier named Vasil Khan in your family's employ who used to collect the rents from the tenants of the block of rented houses which belonged to your grandfather.

Your grandfather became very wealthy. He purchased extensive farmlands and established himself as a zamindar. He paid between ten and twelve thousand rupees as revenue to the government annually. Did his holdings come into your possession? Write to me in detail telling me what happened to those estates.

Asadullah

Tuesday, October 19, 1858[74]

Ghalib was initially home-tutored by one Maulvi Mohammad Muazzam, a highly-respected scholar of Agra and, perhaps, for some months, also attended a madrassa. But the history of his later education is unclear. Ghalib himself used to claim that, around 1811-12, he was taught by a Persian scholar from Iran, Mulla Abdus Samad, who was then visiting Agra and lived in Ghalib's grandfather's house for almost two years. He was originally a Zoraoastrian named Hurmuzd, who had converted to Islam and taken the name Abdus Samad. But many biographers have disputed this claim. In fact, Maulana Altaf Hussain Hali has quoted Ghalib himself to refute this claim. He writes:

> From time to time I heard Mirza say that 'the source of my learning is Providence as such and Abdus Samad is nothing but a made-up name because people teased me as "one without a teacher". To silence these people, I had no choice but to concoct a story and carve up the persona of an imaginary teacher'.[75]

In a slim but delightful volume explaining twenty-one select ghazals of Ghalib, Azra Raza and Sara Suleri Goodyear call the teacher a 'ghostly presence whom the poet can conjure up...to satisfy the traditional tastes of his contemporaries as well as to shield his prolific genius'.[76]

In 1810, at age thirteen, Ghalib was married to Umrao Begum, niece of the first Nawab of Loharu and Firozepur Jhirka, Ahmad Bakhsh Khan. Umrao was only eleven or twelve then. Umrao's father, Mirza Ilahi Bakhsh Khan, was a wealthy jagirdaar and the Nawab's younger brother. He was himself a poet and had acquired the takhallus 'Maroof'. Ilahi Bakhsh was an influential man, and enjoyed a high status in Delhi's elite society. The word 'nausha' in Urdu means bridegroom and it is customary for newly married young men to be referred to as Nausha Mian. Having become a bridegroom now, Ghalib began to be called Mirza Nausha, an epithet that remained with him for life. A year or more into their marriage, the couple shifted to Delhi and made it their home. Ghalib had already begun writing by then. In fact, some of his best works are believed to have been completed by 1816, when he was just nineteen.

Ghalib, it appears, had an easy, informal relationship with his father-in-law. He was once handed over a copy of the Loharu family tree by by his father-in-law and asked to make more copies of the document. Ghalib made the copies but omitted some names, perhaps to make his job easier. When the copies reached his father-in-law, he asked Ghalib why he had omitted some names. Ghalib replied: 'Sir, this family tree is like a staircase that takes you to God. So if we remove one step no harm will be done. Rather, people can jump a step and reach God faster!'[77]

When Ghalib arrived in Delhi, the city was brimming with action. While Chandni Chowk was teeming as the centre of trade and commerce, stories of the glories of Jama Masjid and the enchanting evenings on its steps had already beguiled hundreds of prospective visitors across the world. In his classic book on the monuments and history of Delhi, *Asar-al-Sanadid*, Sir Syed Ahmed Khan draws a beautiful image of the activities around the mosque:

> The South Gate has its trinket-sellers (bisati), faluda-makers, kabab-sellers and poultry-dealers. The East Gate is where cloth-hawkers sit and bird-sellers gather. While the North Gate not only has its own kababis (kebab-sellers), it is also the place to find storytellers and jugglers. Likewise, after detailing the glories of the royal mosque, Syed Ahmad feels it necessary to point out, with obvious pleasure, a far humbler structure close by—the shop of Ghazi, the grain-roaster (bharbhunja).[78]

In the heart of Shahjahanabad, next to Chandni Chowk, was the mohalla of Ballimaran inhabited by aristocrats, nobles and high-ranking hakims (Unani physicians) of the day. The Loharu family also owned an estate in Ballimaran. The estate occupied a fairly large area on the street called Gali Qasimjan, almost at the end of the street, where it goes towards Lal Kuan. The gali was named after the Nawab's uncle, Qasim Jan, a prominent courtier during the reign of Shah Alam II. Ghalib and Umrao, it seems, temporarily lodged themselves in a mansion in the Loharu estate. The building still exists in Gali Qasim Jan. In one part of the estate now runs the junior division of Rabea Girls' Public School, founded in 1973 by the great educationist and owner of the Hamdard Group, Hakim Abdul Hamid, who named it after his mother.

Ghalib and Umrao soon found a rented house for themselves—Haveli Shabban Khan—near a locality called Phatak Habbash Khan next to the Chandni Chowk area. Today, the locality can be found behind what used to be the Novelty Cinema on Shyama Prasad Mukherjee Marg. The length of Ghalib's stay at this haveli is not known but it is certain that, after moving out from here, till his death, Ghalib lived in one or the other house in Ballimaran. The last house in which he lived was also in Gali Qasimjan, were the gali today meets the optical market on the main Ballimaran Road leading towards Bazar Chandni Chowk.

Ghalib wrote both in Urdu and Persian. As his takhallus, he initially adopted the word 'Asad', already part of his first name, which means 'lion' but later also began using Ghalib, which translates as 'dominant'. Some of Ghalib's initial Urdu verse, composed in his teens, is highly Persianized, sometimes even complicated, making his poetry far too complex and difficult to understand both in terms of language and meaning. In that early phase, his poetry seems to have been influenced, both in language and style, by the renowned Persian poet of the eighteenth century, Mirza Abdul Qadir Bedil. Ghalib himself admits:

Tarz-e-Bedil mein Rekhta likhna
Asadullah Khan qayaamat hai

(To write Rekhta in Bedil's style
O Asadullah Khan, is a hell of a job.)

Ghalib's first Persian collection was ready by 1816. But his first Urdu diwaan was published only in 1841, although most of the poems included in it would have been originally written between the ages of sixteen and twenty or twenty-one. There is credible evidence that before this first diwaan was published, on the advice of some friends, he discarded more than half of his Urdu poetry for being obscure.

Ghalib and Umrao were an odd couple. He was a good-looking man of the world, non-comformist, free-spirited, bohemian, with the gift of the gab and a deep understanding of literature and philosophy; she a deeply religious, homely woman who could hardly satisfy his intellectual needs. She bore him seven children, none of whom survived the first two years. All their children having died in infancy, the couple informally adopted Umrao's nephew, Zainul Abedin, alias Arif, and treated him like their own child. Ghalib's younger brother, Mirza Yousuf Khan, had developed schizophrenia at a young age and Ghalib was also expected to take care of him and his family. Despite such serious responsibilities, Ghalib never took up any formal employment in Delhi. He would survive on occasional honorariums and sporadic grants from patrons of poetry and frequent loans from friends and professional lenders. Through his in-laws, he soon found easy access to the Capital's elite and also befriended some British officers fond of poetry. However, in 1825, Ghalib's father-in-law died and Ghalib could no longer receive favours as easily. He, therefore, decided to fight for his family pension.

—

In the late eighteenth century, Ghalib's paternal uncle, Mirza Nasrullah Beg, had been appointed as an officer of 400 cavalrymen in the British Armed Forces by its Commander-in-Chief, Lord Lake, at a handsome salary of Rs 1700 per month. When he died in 1806, his family pension was fixed at Rs 10,000 per annum, to be paid by the British East India Company, but linked, for reasons not entirely clear, to the Estate of Firozepur Jhirka. So even before Ghalib came to be associated with the Loharu family through marriage, his uncle's family pension was being paid by the Loharus. In 1822, Ahmad Baksh Khan, the Nawab of Luharu and Firozepur Jhirka, had abdicated in favour of his eldest son, Nawab Shamsuddin Khan, who had reduced the Begs' family pension to Rs 3000 per year, out of which Ghalib's share was Rs 62.50 per month. For half his life, Ghalib unsuccessfully litigated for this amount. Having failed to have the matter resolved through the intervention of his influential friends, he decided to seek recourse to the legal remedies available to him. For years, this would remain the central concern and activity of his life, apart from writing poetry. A psychological study of this strange and bafflingly persistent preoccupation should be a fascinating study.

By 1803, the British East India Company had firmly established its presence in Delhi and had posted Sir Charles Metcalfe as their Resident in the Mughal Capital. Metcalfe is best known for the house built by him for the Residents—himself and those who followed—and their families on the right bank of the River Yamuna, now called Metcalfe House, situated near Civil Lines just below the Kamla Nehru Ridge, adjoining the main Ring Road. Ghalib approached the Resident in Delhi with a claim for his pension but could not meet him personally. He was told that only the Governor General-in-Council sitting in Calcutta—the highest officer of the British establishment in India—could help him. Deeply convinced of the strength of his claim, in late 1826 Ghalib set out on a journey to Calcutta to meet Governor-General William Amherst.

The fastest way to reach Calcutta in those days was to travel by boat for most of the journey. However, with his limited finances, Ghalib could not afford a boat trip up to Calcutta. He, therefore, travelled on horseback, bullock-carts and even in a palanquin, making the journey unduly long. On his way, he stopped at Kanpur, Lucknow, Banda, Allahabad, Benaras and Murshidabad. The rough journey to Lucknow made him sick and he decided to stay there for a few months to recuperate. Awadh was being ruled by

Nawab Nasiruddin Haider Shah and its capital, Lucknow, was one of the significant centres of literature and art. Ghalib expressed his desire to meet the Nawab. But he put two conditions—he would not present a nazraana, or customary offering, and the Nawab would accord him due honour by rising from his seat to receive him personally. The Nawab's emissaries told him that while his first condition could be accepted, albeit with some difficulty, the second was far too outrageous to even be conveyed to the Nawab. Therefore, in May 1827, Ghalib left Lucknow for Banda without meeting the Nawab.

In Banda, the presiding ruler, Nawab Zulfiqar Ali Bahadur, was known to Ghalib and offered some financial assistance for his remaining travel. Ghalib stayed with him for a few days before proceeding to Benaras through Allahabad. It is said that when the Nawab was seeing him off, in a customary manner, he said to Ghalib: 'Achha Mirza, Khuda Hafiz. Tumhein Allah ke supurd kiya.' ('Ok, Mirza, Khuda Hafiz. I entrust you to God.') Ghalib quipped: 'Wah, Nawab saheb. Usne toh aap ke supurd kiya tha. Aap phir us hi supurd kiye de rahe hain!' ('Come on, Nawab saheb. He had entrusted me to you and you're sending me back to him!'). The Nawab laughed and bid Ghalib adieu.

Ghalib reached Benaras in August 1827 and fell in love with the ancient city. He stayed there for almost a month and wrote an ode in the form of a masnavi in Persian extolling the glories of the city. The masnavi, which Ghalib called *Chiragh-e-Dair* (Lamp of the Temple), shows Ghalib's deep understanding of the Hindu religion and beliefs. He compares the city to the holiest and most sacred site for Muslims, the Kaaba, and refers to Benaras as the 'Kaaba of Hindustan'—a description that would have led to his excommunication from Islam, had he been alive today:

It's the worship-house of the conch-blowers
The Kaaba of Hindustan
Whose idols radiate with the same light
That once gleamed from Mount Sinai.

The masnavi has generated immense interest in scholars and artists alike. It has been translated into Urdu by, among others, the leading progressive poet Ali Sardar Jafri. Some years ago, Kathak exponent Shovana Narayan based one of her major choreographic works on *Chiragh-e-Dair.*

From Benaras, Ghalib was able to buy a boat trip to Calcutta. On the boat ride, he befriended some Englishmen who shared their favourite drink with him. Ghalib, who had known only whiskey (or rum), was amused by the colourless drink. He was even more amused to learn that the liquor was called 'gin', which he thought was 'jinn'—the supernatural creature in Arab and Islamic mythology. In a letter to a friend, he told him how impressed he was with the drink and how apt its name was, for it did bring about a jinn-like influence on the drinker!

Ghalib arrived in Calcutta on 21 February 1828 and stayed there for about a year and a half. He rented decent quarters in the haveli of Mirza Ali Saudagar in Simla Bazar for a monthly rent of ten rupees. (At the spot where he lived in Calcutta, stands House No. 133 of Bethune Row today.)

Ghalib soon managed to secure an audience with the Brirtish Chief Secretary, Andrew Sterling, and his deputy, Simon Fraser. They placed his case before the Governor General-in-Council, who refused to hear him personally unless the matter was brought to the Council through the British Resident in Delhi. By this time, Charles Metcalfe had been replaced by Edward Colebrook, whom Ghalib knew personally. Ghalib immediately decided to engage the services of Pandit Hira Nand, a prominent lawyer of Delhi, to represent him before the Resident. He sold some of his belongings and sent his case papers by post to the lawyer. But as luck would have it, Colebrook was transferred out of Delhi and William Fraser succeeded him as the Resident, and hopes of an early settlement of Ghalib's claim receded. At one point, Ghalib also approached the Sadar Diwani Adalat in Calcutta—the Chief Revenue Court, established by the British in 1772—only to be told that it had no jurisdiction in the case. When the matter remained pending with William Fraser in Delhi for more than a year, a dejected and demoralized Ghalib returned to Delhi in August 1829, cursing his time in Calcutta as one of the most painful periods of his life:

Kalkatte ka jo zikr kiya tu ne hum-nasheen
Ek teer mere seene mein maara ke haaye-haaye

(When you mentioned Calcutta, my friend
You pierced my heart with an arrow!)

Back in Delhi, the Resident rejected his claim. Ghalib submitted an appeal before the Court of Directors of the East India Company in London, which was also summarily dismissed.

The saga of the elusive pension wasn't yet over. Shortly after the Company had dismissed Ghalib's claim, Nawab Mirza Shamsuddin Ahmed Khan, Umrao's cousin, who had succeeded his father as Nawab of Loharu and Firozepur Jhirka, approached Ghalib and told him that he could convince William Fraser to decide the case in his favour but it would cost him some money. Ghalib, it is believed, again borrowed money from lenders and gave it to Shamsuddin. But in a near-incredible twist of fate, the Nawab fell foul of the British. Shamsuddin had recently married Wazir Khanum—a remarkable woman of independent spirit and enterprise—who had earlier caught Fraser's attention, but had refused to reciprocate it fully. On 22 March 1835, Fraser was assassinated and Shamsuddin was charged with conspiracy to kill him. He was sentenced to death and hanged on 3 October 1835. With Shamsuddin's death, Ghalib lost all hopes of getting any pension.

—

Despite not having a regular source of income, Ghalib was fond of the finer things in life—expensive liquor, delectable kebabs, the best mangoes from across the country, and the company of aesthetes, the most refined among them being Delhi's famed courtesans. In an interesting letter to a friend much later, Ghalib wrote that he did not fear death but did fear being deprived of these indulgences. He would spend a major portion of his money in buying stocks of 'Old Tom' which, probably, was a whiskey or rum available only at select cantonments and ports. The nearest place where Ghalib could buy it from was the British cantonment at Meerut and he used his British connections to ensure a regular supply. His household was managed by a small staff co-headed by a manservant called Kallu and a maid named Wafadar. Ghalib was very particular about how he would have his drink, and Kallu was trained to make it to his satisfaction. Mixed with rosewater, the spirit would be poured into a bowl of clay called aabkhora. The aabkhora would then be covered and buried in earth or kept afloat in a pool of water for a couple of hours before it was time for Ghalib to have the drink.

Among Ghalib's favourite young poets was Altaf Husain Hali, who hailed from Panipat and later earned global fame for his epic poem *Madd-o-Jazr-e-Islam* (The Ebb and Tide of Islam), popularly known as *Musaddas-e-Hali*[79]. In 1897, Maulana Hali, as he came to be called, wrote a biography of Ghalib titled *Yaadgar-e-Ghalib* (Commemoration of Ghalib)[80]. The Maulana used to narrate an amusing incident. Once, soon after the month of Ramzan, when Ghalib visited the Red Fort, addressing him by his epithet Mirza, Emperor Zafar asked him: 'Mirza Nausha, kitne rozey rakkhey?' ('Mirza, how many days did you fast?')

Pat came the reply: 'Bas huzoor, ek nahin rakkha.' (My Lord, I did not fast for a day.')

On another occasion during Ramzan, Ghalib's close friend Mufti Sadruddin Azurdah visited him and found him drinking and gambling in a kothri (a secret cell) in his house. Mufti saheb taunted: 'Mirza Nausha, humne toh suna tha ke Ramzan mein shaitaan qaid kar diya jaata hai.' ('Mirza Nausha, I had heard that Satan is locked up during Ramzan.')

Ghalib shot back: 'Ji, Mufti saheb, aap ne sahi suna tha. Par yahi toh vo kothri hai jahaan shaitaan qaid kiya jaata hai.' ('Yes, Mufti saheb, you've heard right. But this is the very cell where Satan is locked up.')

In yet another incident, when told that a wine-drinker's prayers are not accepted, Ghalib is believed to have replied: 'Jis ke paas sharaab ho, usey kis cheez ke liye dua karne ki zaroorat hai? ('When a man has liquor, what else does he need to pray for?)

After the 1857 revolt, when the British were rounding up people across Shahjahanabad, especially if they were Muslim and had any connection with the Mughal royalty, Ghalib was arrested and brought before the Presiding Officer of the forces, one Colonel Burn (or Brun). When in the course of routine questioning, the colonel asked Ghalib if he was

Muslim, Ghalib is said to have famously replied: 'Ji, aadha Musalmaan hoon.' ('Yes, I'm half a Muslim.')

When the amused colonel asked him what he meant by 'half a Muslim', Ghalib explained, 'Sharaab peeta hoon, suar ka gosht nahin khaata.' ('I consume alcohol but don't eat pork.')

The colonel burst into laughter and let him go.

Ghalib had borrowed money from friends and lenders for his travel to Calcutta. After he returned to Delhi, he continued to borrow to meet his needs. He would borrow money, fail to repay and then borrow more. He was addicted not just to fine liquor and food but also to playing the game of chausar, which was a form of gambling. At first, this was easy because the kotwal, the police chief of Delhi, was a friend. But when he was replaced by a man called Faizul Hasan Khan, who disliked Ghalib intensely, things became difficult. Ghalib, however, continued to indulge in chausar in his house and outside. Soon he was sinking in debt and creditors began pressing him for recovery. In 1837, an English wine-merchant sued him for recovery of Rs 5000 and a money-decree for recovery of the amount was passed against Ghalib. It is believed that a friend paid the money on his behalf.

In the meanwhile, his reputation as a poet had soared in Delhi. His ghazals were being sung by courtesans in their quarters and by fakirs in the streets. Shopkeepers quoted his verse and men whiling away their time at teashops would discuss his poetry. He had also had occasion to recite at a couple of mushairas in the Qila-e-Moalla. Of this fame, Ghalib is believed to have said: 'Jis shaayar ki ghazal baalakhaane mein domni aur sadak par faqeer gaaye, usey kaun maat kar sakta hai.' ('Who can beat a poet whose ghazals are sung by courtesans in salons and faqirs on the street alike?')

It is believed that a popular courtesan of the time, Nawab Jan, had fallen for Ghalib's poetry and, perhaps, for the poet, too. The affair seems to have been shortlived, though, as she died young. In a letter addressed to one of his friends, Hatim Ali Baig Mehr, in 1860, Ghalib writes:

> Mughal bachchey bhi ajab hote hain. Jis pe martey hain, us hi ko maar rakhtey hain. Mai'n bhi Mughal hoon. Ek badi sitam-pesh domni ko maine bhi maar rakkha tha.[81]

> (Mughal boys are strange. Those that they fall for, they love with a vengeance and kill. I too am a Mughal. I too had killed a cruel courtesan.)

Ghalib's fame had reached such proportions that when once someone asked him for his postal address, he replied, 'Just write "Asadullah Khan Ghalib, Delhi". It will reach me.' Literary historian Rakhshanda Jalil calls him 'Delhi's truest metaphor' and writes:

> Just as the Delhi of Ghalib was a metaphor for many things—change, survival, growth, modernism, a catholic worldview, the end of an era and the beginning of a new one which rises phoenix-like from the ashes of the old—Ghalib himself was man of many moods. From rhapsodizing on the charms of the beloved, in the best tradition of Urdu poetry, to ruing the insignificance of all human endeavour, from displaying a delightful sense of humour to wallowing in self-pity, all the myriad shades of life and living are reflected in this one man's vast and varied oeuvre.[82]

While Ghalib's fame as a poet was growing by the day, his notoriety, too, had soared, mainly due to his more than occasional brush with the law. In his own words:

Hoga koi aisa bhi ki Ghalib ko na jaane
Shaayar to vo achha hai pe badnaam bohot hai

(Would there be anyone who wouldn't know of Ghalib?
He is a good poet, but also just as notorious.)

Ghalib had also forged close friendships with leading poets and scholars of his time. Among them was Shah Naseeruddin Naseer, alias Kaale Saheb, a highly revered spiritualist. Interestingly, Shah Naseer had been a pupil of Shah Mehdi Maail who, in turn, had been tutored by Sauda's disciple and Mir's friend, Qayam Chandpuri. Other friends and admirers of Ghalib included the Nawab of Jehangirabad, Mustafa Khan Shefta, and Delhi's Grand Mufti, the highest ranking Indian judicial officer of the day, Sadruddin Azurdah. Ghalib's childhood friend and frequent visitor from Agra, Lala Bansi Dhar, and Azurdah remained his pillars of support till their last.

Another close friend was Delhi's best-known physician, the suave and charming Hakim Momin Khan Momin, a distinguished poet himself. In the early 1840s, one of Momin's friends, the British Secretary Thompson,[83] was heading the capital's most prestigious educational institution, Government College, Delhi (popularly called Delhi College, which still exists, though at a different site). The College was looking for Persian teachers and Thompson asked Momin if he would be interested. Momin declined the offer but, concerned about Ghalib's financial situation, quietly recommended his friend's candidature to Thompson. He asked Thompson not to disclose his role in the recommendation, for Ghalib was a proud man and would often refuse favours from all but a few friends, even if he frequently borrowed money from them. Thompson was himself one of Ghalib's ardent admirers. He would often

invite Ghalib to his house and, in keeping with the culture
of Mughal Delhi, would always receive him in person at the
entrance. On Momin's recommendation, Thompson called
Ghalib for an interview to the College, which was then
housed in the campus of the Madrasa Ghaziuddin Khan
at Ajmeri Gate. Riding a palanquin, Ghalib arrived at the
college-gate and asked to be announced to Thompson. He
waited for the sahib to come out and receive him. Thompson
did not do so, and sent word that he was bound by official
protocol, as Ghalib had come to his office as a candidate
for an employment interview and not as a guest. Ghalib's
sensibility was so wounded by this explanation that he
returned from the gate itself, saying that he had thought that
an academic appointment in a British institution would be
a 'reason for additional honour, not something in which I
would lose my ancestral honour as well!'[84] The experience
inspired a defiant couplet:

Bandagi mein bhi vo azaadah-o-khudbeen hain ki hum
Ultey phir aae dar-e-kaaba gar vaa na hua

(Even in servitude I am so independent and self-regarding
I turn and walk away if the door of the Kaaba does not
    open [for me].)

In 1841 Ghalib's house was raided and a fine of hundred
rupees was imposed on him for gambling. After another
raid six years later, he was arrested and sentenced to six
months' rigorous imprisonment and fined two hundred
rupees. Ghalib accused the kotwal of excessive punishment,
which was probably true. However, in appeal, the sentence
was confirmed. Bahadur Shah Zafar, who had become
Emperor by this time, sought to intervene and request
the British authorities to grant Ghalib reprieve but his

intervention bore no fruit—he was, after all, Emperor only of his extended household. After he had served about half his sentence, Ghalib was released on the advice of the Civil Surgeon, Dr. Ross, who, it seems, had been approached by Momin for this personal favour. After his release, for some time, Ghalib lived with his friend Kaale Saheb, the popular mystic and spiritual guide, a few houses away from his own in Gali Qasimjan. Not being a religious man, Ghalib didn't particularly enjoy the experience, deprived as he would have been of Old Tom and chausar. The word 'kaale' literally means 'the black one' in Urdu. When someone asked him how he was feeling on his release from a British prison, Ghalib is believed to have said: 'Bas, pehle gorey ki qaid mein tha, ab kaale ki qaid me hoon.' ('Well, earlier I was in the white man's prison, now I am in the black man's prison.')

But at least the 'incarceration' in the house of a spiritual man kept Ghalib out of trouble, and debt, for a short time. Though fragmented and split into many small houses and shops, the building which was once Kaale Saheb's house can still be found in Gali Qasimjan and is called 'Ahaata Kaale Saheb' (The Enclosure of Kaale Saheb). One portion of the mansion is now the Aminia Muslim Girls School.

—

The new Emperor, Bahadur Shah Zafar, who had ascended to the Mughal throne in 1837, admired Ghalib's poetry and appears to have been fond of him too, although there are also some accounts that suggest he didn't entirely approve of the poet's lifestyle. Yet, despite Ghalib's poor financial condition, the Royal admirer could not offer him a Court position for many years. The reasons were well known— Zafar's ustaad and Poet Laureate of the Mughal Court,

Shaikh Mohammad Ibrahim Zauq, disliked Ghalib, and
Ghalib's 'unsavoury' social reputation was the perfect excuse
he needed to limit, if not prevent altogether, his access to the
Qila-e-Moalla. There was a continuing war of sorts between
the two poets. Despite his ustaad's antipathy, in 1850,
persuaded by some of his advisors, including his personal
physician Hakim Ahsanullah Khan as well as Kaale Saheb,
Zafar commissioned Ghalib to compose the history of the
Mughal Empire in Persian verse and conferred upon him
the titles of Dabir-ul-Mulk and Najm-ud-Daulah[85]. Along
with the titles came an annual honorarium of six hundred
rupees, payable bi-annually. This was done, obviously, to
offer financial assistance to Ghalib and not because the
Emperor was in need of a Persian chronicler. The laid-back
poet, however, could hardly go beyond the second Mughal,
Humayun.

It was only in 1854, when Zauq died, that Ghalib was
appointed the Emperor's ustaad and Malik-ul-Shoara (Poet
Laureate). Although he soon developed a good personal
rapport with Zafar and would often take liberties with him,
Ghalib did have a complaint—as part of his duties at the
Mughal Court, he was required to be present at the Qila-
e-Moalla every day, and he thought it a nuisance:

> Ghalib vazeefakhvaar ho, do Shah ko dua
> Vo din gaye jo kehte thay naukar nahin hoon mai'n

> (Ghalib, you're now a salaried man, pray for the King,
> Gone are the days when you could say, 'I'm not a
>   servant.')

In 1852, Ghalib suffered a personal bereavement. Umrao's
nephew Arif, who by now was treated as their own child,
died suddenly, leaving Ghalib and Umrao devastated. Ghalib
had to now fend not only for his brother's family but also

for Arif's young children, Baqar and Husain. He wrote a highly evocative eulogy which began with these couplets:

> Laazim tha ke dekho mera rasta koi din aur
> Tanha gaye kyon ab raho tanha koi din aur
>
> Jaate hue kehte ho qayamaat ko mileinge
> Kya khoob qayaamat ka hai goya koi din aur
>
> (You should've waited for me a little longer
> Why did you leave alone? Now stay alone a little longer.
>
> While leaving you say, 'See you on the day of judgment.'
> As if the day of judgment is not already upon us.)

His art and the many difficulties he faced did not detach Ghalib from the realities of the world he inhabited, a world that was in flux and confusion reigned. Ghalib was a forward-looking man. He believed in change and reform. In 1855, the great educational reformer and founder of what is now Aligarh Muslim University, Sir Syed Ahmed Khan, translated into Urdu Abul Fazal's magnum opus, *Ain-e-Akbari*, documenting the rules of governance in Emperor Akbar's Court. He approached Ghalib to write a foreword to his translation. A few years before this, in *Asar-ul-Sanadid*, Sir Syed had named Ghalib as one of the most prominent poets of Delhi, so Ghalib obliged. But it was not the kind of foreword Sir Syed would have expected—Ghalib wrote a masnavi in Persian disapproving of the original *Ain-e-Akbari* itself and telling Sir Syed, in no uncertain terms, that there was no use celebrating a 300-year-old document when the British were writing their own modern laws for the country. It is believed that even though this event soured relations between Ghalib and Sir Syed, it was this poem that had a transforming effect on Sir Syed and made him shift his loyalties to modern education.

Perhaps this disillusionment with the tendency of the intellectuals of Mughal India to wallow in the past, their inability to offer an alternative to the increasingly dominant Western thought, science and administrative and mercantile skills represented by the British, also explains Ghalib's ambivalent reactions to the revolt of 1857 and its aftermath. That, and, it must be said, Ghalib's fear of ending up on the wrong side of the new and all-powerful dispensation. The prospect of losing financial security, of losing the comforts and pleasures he cherished—a fate he once described as worse than death—haunted him all his life.

After the Ghadar of 1857, Delhi fell prey to a wholesale massacre at the hands of the British who wanted to stamp out every last remnant of resistance, but also to terrorize the people into complete submission to their rule. Manuscripts of Ghalib's collection were lost in the turmoil. He also lost his schizophrenic brother to a bloodbath in his neighbourhood. The city fell to the British within four months. By then, most of Ghalib's friends had died. Some were killed, others had fled for fear of being killed. His regal patron, Bahadur Shah Zafar, was imprisoned and deported to Rangoon for life. Zafar's sons were executed and beheaded. Ghalib remained confined to his house where, in a corner, he would sit and write his account of the revolt and its bloody aftermath. For some time, he took refuge in Sharif Manzil, the haveli of his next-door neighbour, Hakim Mahmood Khan (father of the well-known freedom-fighter Hakim Ajmal Khan), guarded by the soldiers of the Maharaja of Patiala, who had sided with the British, and to whom the Hakim was the State Physician. Sharif Manzil still exists at the same spot and continues to be occupied by the family of Hakim Ajmal Khan.

The mutiny was a turning point in Delhi's history and

its aftermath changed the city forever. In a letter to one Maulvi Azizuddin, Ghalib laments:

> Saheb, kaisi sahebzaadon waali baatein karte ho! Dilli ko vaisa hi aabaad jaante ho jaise aage thi? Qasimjan ki gali Mir Khairaati ki phaatak se Fatehullah Beg ke phaatak tak be-chiraagh hai. Haan agar aabaadi hai toh ye hai ke Ghulam Husain Khan ki haveli aspataal hai aur Ziauddin Khan ke kamre mein ek doctor sahib rehte hain aur Kaale saheb ke makaanon mein ek aur sahib-e-aalishaan Inglistaan tashreef rakhte hain...Lal kuein ke mohalle mein khaak udti hai, aadmi ka naam nahin...Mohalle ke mohalle tabaah-o-barbaad ho gaye. Ahl-e-sheher ki jamiyat mein farq aa gaya aur vo haalat hui—'sab kuchh baha kar le gaya, aaya tha ek sailaab sa.'[86]

(Sahib, you talk like a teenager! You think Delhi survives as it was? From the gate of Mir Khairaati to that of Fatehullah Beg, Gali Qasimjan is in complete darkness. If there are any inhabitants, they are these—Ghulam Husain Khan's haveli, which has been turned into a hospital, and in Ziauddin Khan's room lives a doctor, and Kaale saheb's houses have been taken over by a grand Englishman... The Lal Kuan locality is deserted, with no trace of men... Localities after localities have been wrecked and ruined. Structures of the city's dwellers have changed and the situation is as such—'It has torn down and washed away everything, the tempest that visited us.')

Ghalib was an extraordinary letter-writer. He wrote to his friends and disciples in conversational Urdu as if he was talking to the person he was writing to. His letters to his student Munshi Hargopal Tufta, to Munshi Nabi Baqsh Haqeer and to Husain Mirza are fine examples of written conversations. Scholars are unanimous that had Ghalib not been a poet, he would still have had the same literary stature because of the contribution he made to Urdu literature in the form of his letters. He relied heavily on the British postal system and was distraught when the system came to a temporary halt after the 1857 revolt. At least in his letters he appears not to have held back in his descriptions of the horrors the British forces perpetrated in Shahjahanabad.

By October 1858, Ghalib had completed *Dastanbu*, his Persian diary recording accounts of the revolt, which the British referred to as a 'mutiny'. Most of *Dastanbu* gives a pro-British version of the 'mutiny' and its aftermath, even though there runs a macabre undercurrent through its pages. Rakhshanda Jalil says that the reason for this is that Ghalib 'was dependent on the pension he received from the British. He was, in his own words, a *namak-khvaar-e-sarkaar-e-angrez*, or an eater of the salt of the British government on account of his hereditary pension'. However, she adds, 'there is much in his oeuvre that is in the nature of a testimony to his times'.[87]

In July 1859, Yusuf Ali Khan, the Nawab of Rampur, who was a great admirer of Ghalib, fixed for him a monthly pension of one hundred rupees, to be paid from the Rampur Estate. The very next year, in January 1860, Ghalib travelled to Rampur and stayed there for about three months. In March, he returned to Delhi. On his way back, his boat met with an accident and he had to break journey in Moradabad. It is believed that Sir Syed, who was then the Collector of Moradabad, despite the bad blood between them (after the unflattering foreword that Ghalib wrote to Syed's translation of *Ain-e-Akbari*), offered him hospitality in this hour of need. An interesting incident relating to this reunion of the two greats is narrated by the eminent scholar Gopi Chand Narang, though he does not cite any source:

During 1860, Ghalib visited Rampur at the invitation of Nawab Yusuf Ali Khan. On his return trip he had to pass through Moradabad where Sir Syed was posted as a collector. Although there was still some bitterness left in the relationship, Sir Syed acted as a gracious host and he received Mirza at the outpost of the town and brought him to the comfort of his bungalow. A relaxed Mirza took out his bottle of wine, wrapped it in an old newspaper, and placed it on the central table. After a while, when the evening approached, he noticed that the bottle had disappeared. He got worried and asked his host, 'What happened to the bottle which I had left here?' Sir Syed took Mirza to a small room where the bottle was safely stored, away from the glare of ascetic visitors. Mirza picked up the bottle, looked at it suspiciously. While smiling naughtily, he told Sir Syed, 'I sense something here. Tell me, who took a sip?' Sir Syed smiled but remained silent. Ghalib recited Hafiz's (Persian) couplet:

Vaa'ezaan kiin jalva bar mehraab-o-mimbar mikunad
Chuun b khilvat mi ravand aan kaar-e-diigar mikunad

Preachers, when they adorn the pulpit, say lofty things
But in the privacy of their quarters, they do things
    differently.

The tension that had prevailed between the two came to an end. Ghalib laughed and embraced Sir Syed.[88]

Ghalib returned to Delhi in March 1860. By now, he had seen the worst of times. He was disillusioned with life and saw no light at the end of the tunnel. He spent his time waiting for death to claim him:

Koi ummeed bar nahin aati
Koi soorat nazar nahin aati

Maut ka ek din muaiyyin hai
Neend kyon raat bhar nahin aati

Aage aati thi haal-e dil pe hansi
Ab kisi baat par nahin aati

Hai kuchh aisi hi baat jo chup hoon
Varna kya baat kar nahin aati

Hum vahaan hain jahaan se hum ko bhi
Kuchh hamaari khabar nahin aati

Marte hain aarzoo mein marne ki
Maut aati hai par nahin aati

(No hope is fulfilled
No reprieve comes to sight.

The day of death is appointed
Why am I sleepless all night?

I would laugh at the state of my heart once
Now I cannot laugh at anything.

There is a reason for my silence
Otherwise, don't I know how to speak?

I've reached a place where even I know
Nothing at all about my well-being.

In the desire for death I die
Death comes, but it evades me.)

But despite his poor health and old age, despite his disillusionment, Ghalib refused to give up the pleasures of life till his last breath:

Go haath ko jumbish nahin aankhon mein toh dum hai
Rehne do abhi saaghar-o-meena mere aagey

(My hands may have no movement, my eyes still have life
Let the wine-glass and pitcher remain before me.)

In October 1868 was published *Ood-i-Hindi* (Fragrance of Hindi[89]), the first collection of his letters. Ghalib was quite frail then, having suffered a severe attack of 'Delhi Sore', a disease common at the time, which had led to eruption of painful boils on his limbs. Four months after the publication of *Ood-i-Hindi*, on 15 February 1869, Ghalib died. He was buried the same day in the family graveyard of the Nawab of Loharu in Delhi, next to the dargah of the Sufi saint Hazrat Nizamuddin Auliya. His wife died on the same date a year later, and was buried next to him.

II

PRIVATIONS AND HARDSHIPS — SOCIAL, ECONOMIC, LEGAL, financial and personal—constituted the core of Ghalib's life and resound in his poetry. However, what has also found its way into his poetry, and in equal measure, is his audacity, belligerence, chutzpa and a deep sense of pride and self-respect that would remain uncompromised till the very end.

Ghalib can appear arrogant and egoistical. But his pride is not unfounded or artificial. It stems from his personal experiences, and his profound understanding of our life as mortals coupled with, almost paradoxically, his equally profound self-belief. One of his oft-quoted ghazals begins with this couplet:

Baazeecha-e-atfaal hai duniya mere aagey
Hota hai shab-o-roz tamaasha mere aagey

(The world is but the playground of children before me
A spectacle unfolds night and day before me.)

The entire ghazal echoes with Ghalib's disdain for the frivolous world in which he lives:

Ek khel hai aurang-e-Sulemaan mere nazdeek
Ek baat hai aijaaz-e-Maseeha mere aagey

Juz naam nahin surat-e-aalam mujhe manzoor
Juz vehem nahin hasti-e-ashia mere aagey

Hota hai nihaan gard mein sehra mere hotey
Ghista hai jabeen khaak pe dariya mere aagey

(To me, the throne of Solomon is just a game
Before me, the miracles of Christ are mere talk.

I accept the face of the universe merely as a name
Before me, the status of reality is but a superstition.

In my presence, even the wilderness hides in dust
Before me, even the river rubs its forehead on earth.)

Raza and Goodyear argue:

> The great refrain 'mere aagey' states the poet's presence
> even when he claims the diminishment of all that
> surrounds him: he is there as an integral poetic voice
> while scorning the significance of all beings other than
> himself.[90]

Even in the face of hostility, upheaval and neglect, Ghalib is
sure that the world will be at a loss if it does not understand
that he is irreplaceable:

Daayam pada hua tere dar par nahin hoon mai'n
Khaak aisi zindagi ki paththar nahin hoon mai'n

Ya rab zamaana mujh ko mitaata hai kis liye
Lauh-e-jahaan pe harf-e-mukarrar nahin hoon mai'n

(I am not one to lie forever at your doorstep
To hell with such a life, I am not stone.

Oh Lord, why is the world so determined to erase me?
On the slate of the world, I'm not an alphabet written
   inadvertently twice.)

In the same ghazal, in a classic couplet, on the one hand
Ghalib boldly demands his right to be treated with dignity

because he is a mere sinner and not an infidel, and, on the other, he skilfully sums up the doctrine of proportionality of punishment in criminology:

Hadd chaahiye saza mein uqoobat ke vaastey
Aakhir gunehgaar hoon kaafir nahin hoon mai'n

(There ought to be a limit to the punishment for an
   offence
After all, I am only a sinner, not an infidel.)

Ghalib believes that he is meant for higher things than engaging in petty worldly affairs. He is above the here and now of this sorry business that we call existence:

Fikr-e-duniya mein sar khapaata hoon
Mai'n kahaan aur ye vabaal kahaan

(I break my head over worldly worries
Whither me, whither this wretched affair?)

He does not deserve the chaos, the turmoil and the bedlam that surround him. He wants peace:

Rahiye ab aisi jagah chal kar jahaan koi na ho
Hum-sukhan koi na ho aur hum-zubaan koi na ho

Be-dar-o-deewaar sa ek ghar banaaya chaahiye
Koi humsaaya na ho aur paasbaan koi na ho

Padiye gar beemaar toh koi na ho teemaardaar
Aur agar marr jaaiye toh nauha-khvaan koi na ho

(Let us go and live somewhere where there's no one
No one to speak to, no one to share our language

Let us make a house without doors and walls
No neighbour next door, and no one to guard it

If we fall sick, no one to tend to us
And if we die, no one to mourn us.)

Ghalib is not an agnostic, but his hostility towards structured religion and religious formalism is well-known. He makes no bones about his religious beliefs, or the lack of them. He ridicules both the Hindu tradition of idolatry and the Islamic belief in life hereafter. The idea of a paradise is juvenile fiction:

> Dekhiye paate hain ushhaaq bu'ton se kya faiz
> Ek barahman ne kaha hai ki ye saal achha hai

> Hum ko maaloom hai jannat ki haqeeqat, lekin
> Dil ke khush rakhne ko Ghalib ye khayaal achha hai

> (Let's see how lovers benefit from idol-worship
> A brahmin has predicted this to be a prosperous year

> We know the reality of Paradise, but
> To keep the heart happy, it is a good idea.)

There may be divine rewards for worship and piety, but he can't bring himself to follow religious protocol:

> Jaanta hoon sawaab e taa'at-o-zuhd
> Par tabiyat idhar nahin aati

> (I am aware of the reward of obedience and piety
> But my temperament doesn't tilt that way.)

When he finds a mosque next to his rented accommodation at Gali Qasimjan, he is flustered. He decides to first declare himself God's neighbour:

> Masjid ke zer-e-saaya ek ghar banaa liya hai
> Ye banda-e-kameena hamsaaya-e-khuda hai

> (In the shadow of a mosque, he has made his home
> This rascal is now a neighbour of God!)

He then demands a place for debauchery right next to the mosque. He needs to drink not for pleasure but to reach a state of oblivion:

Masjid ke zer-e-saaya kharaabaat chaahiye
Bhon paas aankh qibla—e-haajaat chaahiye

Maiy se gharaz nishaat hai, kis rooh siyaah ko
Ik goona be-khudi mujhe din-raat chaahiye

(In the shadow of the mosque is required a tavern—
Like the brow above the eye—the altar of life's necessities.

Which wretched fellow wants pleasure out of drinking
A means to attain oblivion is all I need day and night.)

Ghalib refuses to change his ways even in captivity and wonders what the preacher will have to say to him:

Gar kiya naaseh ne hum ko qaid, achha yoon sahi
Ye junoon-e ishq ke andaaz chhut jaaweinge kya

Hazrat-e-naaseh gar aavein, deeda-o-dil, farsh-e-raah
Koi hum ko ye toh samjha do, ke samjhaaveinge kya

(If the preacher imprisons me, so be it
Will that rid the world of my wild and passionate ways?

If the preacher comes, I'll lay out my eyes and heart to
welcome him
But will someone please explain to me what he will
explain?)

Ghalib's personal experiences in courts as a litigant resonate in the form of legal terminology married to verse in many of his ghazals. *Diwaan-e-Ghalib* is full of terms such as adaalat (court), faujdaari (criminal law), sarishtedaar (court master), gawaah (witness), talab (summon), hukm (order), muqaddama (lawsuit), daim al-habs (life imprisonment), giraftaari (arrest), muddai (plaintiff or petitioner), mudda'a alaih (defendant), roobakaari (hearing), etc. Even though Ghalib has used most of these terms metaphorically more

often than in their literal sense, such use itself shows the
poet's familiarity with the legal system of his day. The
distinguished jurist Tahir Mahmood has drawn a list of some
verses from the *Diwaan-e-Ghalib* where legal metaphor has
been freely used[91]:

> Jaan dar hawa-e yak nigaah-e-garm hai Asad
> Parwaana hai vakeel tere daad-khvaah ka

> (Your soul, Asad, beseeches one burning glance
> Your petitioner has engaged the moth as advocate for
>   her cause.)

> Dil mudda'i o deeda bana mudda'a alaih
> Nazzaare ka muqaddama phir roobakaar hai

> (The heart is the plaintiff and the eye, the defendant
> The case of gazing is being heard again.)

In a five-verse set found in one of his most beautiful ghazals
which begins with the words 'Phir kuchh ek dil ko beqaraari
hai' ('One again, the heart is somewhat restless'), Ghalib
tries a delightful use of legal metaphor:

> Phir khula hai dar-e-adaalat-e-naaz
> Garm bazaar-e-faujdaari hai

> Ho raha hai jahaan mein andher
> Zulf ki phir sarishte-daari hai

> Phir diya paara-e-jigar ne sawaal
> Ek faryaad-e aah-o-zaari hai

> Phir hue hain gawaah-e-ishq talab
> Ashkbaari ka hukm jaari hai

> Dil-o-mizhgaan ka jo muqaddama tha
> Aaj phir us ki roobakaari hai

> (The court of beauty's games is open again
> There is a bazaar-like briskness about the criminal case.

The world is covered in darkness
Her curls have been appointed the court's record-keepers.

A piece of the heart has filed a petition
The complaint is full of sighs and moans.

The witnesses of love have been summoned again
An order has been passed to shed tears.

That old dispute between the heart and the eyelashes
It has come for a hearing yet again.)

Ghalib's life as a litigant surely influenced his poetry. But there is also a fascinating instance where his poetry decided his fate as a litigant. It is said that once a wine-merchant sued Ghalib for recovery of debt. The case came up before Ghalib's old friend Mufti Sadruddin Aazurdah. Those were the days when judges were not so sensitive that they would not hear cases of people known to them. They would hear all cases before them and decide in accordance with law without being influenced by the parties. When Ghalib appeared before the Mufti in response to the court summons, the Mufti asked him if he admitted the claim. Ghalib recited his now oft-quoted couplet:

Qarz ki peete thay mai, aur samajhte thay, ki haan
Rang laave gi hamaari faaqa-masti ek din

(I used to drink on borrowed money and think—
Surely, making merry in penury will bear fruit some day.)

Mufti sahib treated this as an admission of liability, ruled in favour of the wine-merchant's claim and paid the decretal amount to the plaintiff out of his own pocket, leaving Ghalib free to go home.

The above incident is not only an example, one of many, of Ghalib's sangfroid but also his wit. Ghalib was as well known for his quick wit as for his twitchy temper.

One evening, in an open space just outside his house in Ballimaran, Ghalib was treating his friends to some mangoes gifted by his childhood friend from Agra, Lala Bansi Dhar. Ghalib loved his mangoes. His friend Hakim Razi-ud-Din Khan did not; he was the only man in the group that evening who wasn't eating the fruit. A man carrying a load on a donkey passed by the lane where Ghalib and others had been throwing the mango-skins. The donkey sniffed the mango skins, rejected them and walked on. At this, Hakim Sahib taunted: 'Mirza aapne dekha, gadhe bhi aam nahin khaate.' ('Mirza, did you see that? Even donkeys don't eat mangoes.')

Ghalib continued devouring his mango and, without looking at Hakim Saheb, said: 'Ji haan, gadhey aam nahin khaate.' ('You're right, donkeys don't eat mangoes.')

Once, in the course of a serious debate on the question of the correct use of gender in Urdu grammar, poets and scholars were discussing whether the word 'taanga' (tonga) is masculine or feminine. The house asked Ghalib for his opinion, for that would be decisive. Ghalib replied: 'Bhai mera toh ye khayaal hai ki agar taange mein aurat baithi ho toh muannas hai, aur agar mard baitha ho toh muzakkar.' ('Well, in my opinion, if a woman is seated in the tonga, it would be feminine and if a man, it would be masculine.')

The house burst into laughter, which had not even subsided when a friend asked Ghalib for his opinion on the correct gender for the word 'jooti' (a kind of footwear). At this, another friend quipped: 'Inse kya poochhna? Ye toh ye hi kaheinge ki agar aurat pehne toh muannas aur mard pehne toh muzakkar.' ('Why ask him? He will only say if a woman wears it, it would be feminine and if a man, it would be masculine.')

Ghalib let him finish and then said calmly: 'Ji nahin.

Agar dheere padey toh muannas, aur Agar zor se padey toh muzakkar.' ('Not at all. If it strikes softly, it would be feminine and if it strikes hard, it would be masculine.')

The debate was promptly brought to an end.

—

Ghalib is a profound philosopher who transcends time, cultures and geographies. He is a spiritualist who first celebrates God's manifest presence and then immediately pitches it against the need for His unmanifest, all-pervading form. He mourns loss but only to tell us that pain is as much a part of a full life as pleasure. He is a powerful visionary but also aware of the inevitability of being hopelessly caught up in the exigencies of everyday existence. Like all geniuses, Ghalib is a mystery:

> Hoon garmi-e-nishaat-e-tasavvur se naghma-sanj
> Mai'n andaleeb-e-gulshan-e-na-aafreeda hoon

> (The heat of the joy of imagination fuels my songs
> I'm the nightingale of a garden not yet created.)

And then:

> Aate hain ghaiyb se ye mazaameen khayaal mein
> Ghalib sareer-e-khaama nawa-e-sarosh hai

> (These subjects come to me from some hidden cosmos
> Ghalib, the scratching of my pen is the voice of angels.)

One of the key distinguishing characters of Ghalib's verse is that the same verse can be understood in many different ways. In one of his most well-known couplets, interpreted in more than a dozen ways, Ghalib deals with the issue of man's existential crisis. He talks about human existence and juxtaposes it with non-existence, seemingly giving priority to the latter:

Na tha kuchh toh khuda tha, kuchh na hota toh khuda
   hota
Duboya mujh ko hone ne, na hota mai'n toh kya hota

Professor Frances W Pritchett, who has compiled Ghalib's
complete works with translaions and commentary on
Columbia University's website ('A Desertful of Roses')[92]
finds this couplet 'honestly awe-inspiring in its tangle of
complexities of meaning', a couplet which 'will repay any
amount of thought'. At first, it may seem that in the first
line, Ghalib is simply alluding to the Abrahamic belief that
God is infinite, was always present and shall always be:

Na tha kuchh toh khuda tha, kuchh na hota toh khuda
   hota

(When there was nothing, God existed, had there been
   nothing, He would have existed)

And in the second line he appears to be cursing his own
existence and wondering if his non-existence would have
made any difference to the world:

Duboya mujh ko hone ne, na hota mai'n toh kya hota

(Existence has ruined me, had I not existed, what
   difference would it have made?)

However, another way of looking at the couplet—an
interpretation supported by numerous scholars, including
Ghalib's disciple, Altaf Husain Hali—is that in the first line,
the word 'mai'*n*' ('I') is hidden in four places and what
Ghalib is really saying is:

Jab [mai'n] kuchh na tha, tab [mai'n] khuda tha, agar
   [mai'n] kuchh na hota toh [mai'n] khuda hota

(When I was nothing, I was God, if I were nothing, I
   would be God)

Consequently, in the second line, when he says:

Na hota mai'n toh kya hota

he is really asking:

Had I not existed, what would I have been?

And the answer is found in the first line:

Kuchh na hota toh khuda hota

(If I were nothing, I would be God)

If read this way, the couplet would mean:

When I was nothing, I was God, if I were nothing, I
would be God
Existence has ruined me, had I not existed, I would have
been God

In this interpretation of the couplet, Ghalib is emphasizing that God is really an individual experience. There is no duality.

In another incomparable couplet, while dealing with the physical manifestation of beauty vis-à-vis beauty that has not revealed itself but is nevertheless present, Ghalib plays with the words 'numaayaa*n*' (manifest) and 'pinha' (hidden). Dust, he says, has a thousand faces but only a few get manifested in physical form, for instance, a flower. Others remain hidden and become food for the same dust that hides them.

Sab kahaan kuchh laala-o-gul mein numaayaan ho gayin
Khaak mein kya sooratein hongi ke pinha ho gayin

(Not all, only a few, manifest themselves in tulips and
roses;
What faces they must be, that stay hidden in dust!)

In the following sher, Ghalib pronounces that it is impossible
to describe the state of people who nurture passion, for they
become the fuel of their own fire:

> Poochhe hai kya wujood-o-adam ahl-e-shauq ka
> Aap apni aag ke khas-o-khaashaak ho gaye
>
> (What do want to know of the being or non-being of the
>   people of passion?
> They become the straw and woodchips of their own fire.)

He then questions the Earth, death's ally, in which are
interred the bones of the people he loved—people who
ignited his passion:

> Maqdoor ho toh khaak se poochhon ke ae laeem
> Tu ne vo ganj-haaye gira-maaya kya kiye
>
> (If I were given the power, I would ask the Earth, 'O
>   miser!
> What have you done to those precious treasures [that
> were buried in you]?)

Unlike Mir who finds material signs on earth, Ghalib is
metaphysical in his approach. He looks for signs somewhere
else. His sense of loss is not materialistic but has to do
with the silence that befalls life. The goal is to attain a
state of oblivion, like a tiny drop that gets obliterated in
the enormity of the river:

> Ishrat-e-qatra hai dariya mein fana ho jaana
> Dard ka hadd se guzarna hai dawa ho jaana
>
> (The ecstasy of a drop is in being obliterated in the river
> When pain crosses its limits, it becomes its own cure.)

In the end he remains restless. His discontent is eternal. He
has a lot to say. His mind is bursting with things he wants
to express but no medium is enough:

Ba-qadr-e-shauq nahin zarf-e-tangnaa-e-ghazal
Kuchh aur chaahiye vus'at mere bayaan ke liye

(The narrow limits of my ghazal will not satisfy my desire
My expression needs a vaster space.)

A voice for eternity, Ghalib is particularly relevant in the twenty-first century, when bigotry and parochialism appear to have popular support in every other country, and the world is rife with communal hate and violence. Ghalib is above religious, sectarian and communal factionalism. Islam rejects idol-worship. But Ghalib believes that if a devout Hindu, who has been worshipping idols all his life and has been resolute in his faith in idolatory, dies in the temple, his loyalty to his faith makes him a true believer and entitles him to be buried in the Kaaba, the holiest place in Islam, even though the Kaaba, to many, is the very antithesis of the temple where he has died and vice versa:

Wafadaari ba-shart-e-ustuvaari asl-e imaan hai
Marey bu'tkhaane mein toh kaabe mein gaarho barahman
    ko

(Steadfast loyalty is the quintessence of faith
If the Brahmin dies in his temple, bury him in the Kaaba.)

—

Like all great poets, Ghalib writes with sublime skill and feeling about love. More often than not, he is a submissive romantic, yearning for his beloved and complaining of her indifference (or, sometimes, of God's indifference):

Ye na thi hamaari qismat ki visaal-e-yaar hota
Agar aur jeete rehte ye hi intezaar hota

Terey vaade par jiye hum toh ye jaan jhooth jaana
Ke khushi se mar na jaate agar aitbaar hota

(It was not my destiny to be united with my beloved
Had I lived any longer, it would have been the same
      long wait.

Had I lived on your promise, it would have been a sham
Wouldn't I have died of happiness if I had trusted you?)

And yet, love's pleasures may be greater in memory and dreaming:

Muddat hui hai yaar ko mehmaan kiye hue
Josh-e-qadah se bazm charaaghaan kiye hue

Jee dhoondta hai phir vahi fursat, ke raat-din
Baithe rahein tasavvur-e-jaanaan kiye hue

(It's been such a long time since I hosted my friend
Since the gathering was illuminated with a sizzling glass
      of wine.

The heart looks for that time of leisure when, all day
      and night
I would sit and dream only of the beloved.)

Interestingly, in 1975, the last couplet was borrowed by the Bollywood director and lyricist Gulzar in one of his songs composed as the title-track for the Sanjeev Kumar-Sharmila Tagore starrer, *Mausam*. Gulzar, however, substituted the word 'jee' with 'dil' and also removed the implied punctuation after the word fursat, consequently changing the meaning of the entire couplet. Gulzar's couplet reads:

Dil dhoondta hai phir vahi fursat ke raat-din
Baithe rahein tasavvur-e-jaanaan kiye hue

(The heart looks for those leisurely days and nights when
I would sit and dream only of the beloved.)

Ghalib's desires are limitless. Each one of his longings is worth dying for:

Hazaaron khwaahishein aisi ki har khwaahish pe dum
  nikley
Bohot nikley mere armaan lekin phir bhi kam nikley

(Thousands of desires have I nurtured, and each one to
  die for
Many wishes were fulfilled; but they were few and far
  between.)

This ghazal then progresses into a complaint of a different
sort. In a classic example of poetic hyperbole, he compares
his beloved's apathy with that of God when he expelled
Adam from the Garden of Eden:

Nikalna khuld se Aadam ka sunte aaye hain lekin
Bohot be-aabru ho kar tere kooche se hum nikley

(We've heard all our lives of Adam's expulsion from
  Eden, but
With far greater disgrace we've made our exit from your
  street.)

But the beloved who subjects him to such indignity is also
the reason for his very existence. She is the one who not
only infuses life in him but also the desire to live:

Mohabbat mein nahin hai farq jeene aur marne ka
Usi ko dekh kar jeete hain jis kaafir pe dum nikley

(In love, there's no difference between life and death
I live gazing upon that unfaithful one whom I die for.)

In the maqta of the ghazal, Ghalib skewers the preacher,
accusing him of secretly visiting the tavern after everyone
else leaves:

Kahaan maikhaane ka darwaaza Ghalib, aur kahaan vaaiz
Par itna jaante hain kal vo jaata tha ke hum nikley

(Whither the tavern-door, whither the preacher.
But I know this—last night, as I was leaving, he tiptoed
　　in!)

Another couplet has, for long, been atrributed to Ghalib,
often quoted by many lovers of Urdu poetry and sung by
many singers as part of this ghazal:

Khuda ke vaaste parda na kaabe se utha zaalim
Kahin aisa na ho yaan bhi vo hi kaafir sanam nikley

(For God's sake, don't lift the curtain off the Kaaba,
　　O oppressor
What if we find the same infidel idol here as well?)

Various scholars have disputed the claim that this couplet
was written by Ghalib. Pritchett emphatically denies its
connection to Ghalib:

This verse is NOT by Ghalib. Even if you have heard
it recited as such, even if in your heart you think it is,
it's just not. Ghalib published his own divan four times,
and we do know what he composed, and this verse is
not his...In fact, I think Ghalib would have shuddered at
the thought of having this verse attached to his name.[93]

She cites a letter written by Ghalib to his printer where he
not only denies authorship of this couplet but also squarely
abuses the interloper who has fraudulently inserted this
couplet in his ghazal.

Ghalib is but human. In one of his best-known
ghazals, he acknowledges that, despite his vanity and high-
headedness, his heart still aches when subjected to grief
and torment. He then, somewhat piquantly, wonders why
a lover like him, sitting peacably by the road, should be
a threat to anyone. After all, he isn't usurping a religious
ground or sitting by someone's door—places from where he

has already been expelled. His beloved is a self-confessed infidel and, as if speaking on her behalf, he says that one who cares about fidelity and the like should not meet her if he is not willing to risk his faith. Finally, he admits the stark reality that no one is indispensable, not even he, and that the world will go on without him. People, after all, move on:

> Dil hi toh hai na sang-o-khisht dard se bhar na aaye kyon
> Roeinge hum hazaar baar koi hamein sataaye kyon
>
> Daiyr nahin haram nahin dar nahin aastaan nahin
> Baithe hain rah-guzar pe hum ghair hamein uthaaye kyon
>
> Haan vo nahin khuda-parast jaao vo bewafa sahi
> Jis ko ho deen-o-dil azeez us ki gali mein jaaye kyon
>
> Ghalib-e-khasta ke baghair kaun-se kaam bandd hain
> Roiye zaar-zaar kya kijiye haaye-haaye kyon

> (It's only a heart, after all, not stone or brick. Why won't
> it fill with pain?
> A thousand times over will I cry, why should anyone
> trouble me?
>
> Not a temple or a mosque, not someone's door or
> doorway
> I sit at the roadside, why should anyone remove me?
>
> Yes, she's not a believer. Fine, she's unfaithful,
> If he cares so much for faith and heart, why should he
> even go to her?
>
> What worldly tasks have stopped without Ghalib, the
> broken, the wounded?
> Why weep so bitterly, then, why moan and wail like this?)

Ghalib was not only conscious but also proud of his unsurpassable brilliance, and wasn't loath to boasting about it. In this sher, he declares, and perhaps with good reason, that no one can write like him:

> Hain aur bhi duniya mein sukhanwar bohot achhe
> Kehte hain ki Ghalib ka hai andaaz-e-bayaan aur

> (Indeed, there are many other good poets in this world
> But they say Ghalib's style of expression is in a class of
>   its own.)

In Mughal India, Persian was considered to be a language far superior to Urdu and, consequently, Persian literature had an exalted position. Ghalib enters and changes the rules of the game. He claims that Rekhta, the Urdu that the classical poets used, when used by him, becomes a language that even Persian would be envious of:

> Jo ye kahe ke Rekhta kyon-kar ho rashk-e-faarsi
> Gufta-e-Ghalib ek baar parh kar usey suna ke yoon

> (Whoever asks why Persian would be envious of Rekhta
> Recite to him Ghalib's poetry once, and say, 'This is why.')

However, despite his strong belief in his excellence, he appreciates other poets too. He is reported to have offered to trade his whole diwaan for just this one couplet of Momin's:

> Tum mere paas hotey ho goya
> Jab koi doosra nahin hota

> (You are with me, as if
> When there is no one else.)

And comparing himself with Mir, he says:

> Rekhte ke tum hi ustaad nahin ho Ghalib
> Kehte hain agley zamaane mein koi Mir bhi tha

> (You are not the lone master of Rekhta, Ghalib
> They say, in days gone by there was also a Mir.)

But for the most part, Ghalib was an admirer of his own work. Even in suffering and grief, his supreme pride remains intact, almost as a weapon against the demon of despondency:

> Yoon hi gar rota raha Ghalib toh ae ahl-e-jahaan
> Dekhna in bastiyon ko tum ki veeraan ho gayin
>
> (If Ghalib keeps sobbing like this, O people of the world
> You'll see that these habitats will soon be desolate.)

He knows he is the last of the literary wizards of his time and wonders who, after him, will inherit his unwavering devotion to the idea of love, his burdens and his suffering:

> Husn ghamze ki kashaakash se chhuta mere baad
> Baar-e-aaraam se hain ahl-e jafa mere baad
>
> Shama bujhti hai toh us mein se dhuan uthta hai
> Shola-e-ishq siyah-posh hua mere baad
>
> Gham se marta hoon ki itna nahin duniya mein koi
> Ke kare taaziyat-e-mehr-o-wafa mere baad
>
> Aaye hai bekasi-e-ishq pe rona Ghalib
> Kis ke ghar jaayega sailaab-e bala mere baad
>
> (Beauty will no longer need to tease when I'm gone
> Those tyrants will finally be at ease when I'm gone.
>
> Smoke rises from a candle when it goes out,
> Passion will be smothered in black when I'm gone.
>
> I die of grief for there's no one in the world who
> Will mourn for love and loyalty when I'm gone.
>
> The destitution of love makes me cry, Ghalib
> Whose home will the flood of ordeals drown when I'm
> gone?)

In the same ghazal is found a mindboggling couplet:

Kaun hota hai hareef-e-mai-e-mard-afgan-e-ishq
Hai mukarrar lab-e-aaqi mein sala mere baad

A literal translation of this couplet would be:

'Who will accept the challenge to drink the poison-wine
of love?'
The wine-bearer keeps calling out when I'm gone.

However, what Ghalib seems to be really saying is that he is the last one to have the gall to love fiercely and to submit without fear of pain. Delhi's finest storyteller and heritage activist, Sohail Hashmi, once narrated that his cousin, the well-known thespian and activist Mansoor Saeed, who later migrated to Pakistan, had a fascinating take on this couplet. When asked by Hashmi what the couplet really meant, Saeed explained:

Have you seen an akhara (wrestling pit)? That's what it is. The successful wrestler, after having knocked down every other player, takes a round of the arena challenging the ones who are left—'Is there anyone left to take my challenge?' This is what Ghalib is suggesting. There's no one to accept his challenge.[94]

Ghalib is sure that even years after his death, people will remember him for his unmatched intellect and inquisitive nature that seeks—and finds—wisdom:

Hui muddat ki Ghalib mar gaya par yaad aata hai
Vo har ek baat par kehna ki yoon hota toh kya hota

(Ghalib has been dead for long, but we still remember
how
He questioned everything—'If it were so, how would it
have been?')

In one of his Persian couplets, Ghalib had prophesied that the world would recognize his worth only after his death. The prediction did come true, and how! Ghalib is today, undoubtedly, the most well-known and quoted Urdu poet, so much so that even frivolous nonsense masquerading as poetry is often atrributed to him, for there is hardly a name other than his in the popular imagination when it comes to Urdu poetry. Though much of his work was lost, he did compile and leave behind sizeable collections of his Persian and Urdu verses. His ghazals have been sung by almost every ghazal singer. Commercial and documentary films have been made on him. Hundreds of books in various languages have been written on him. Scholars have been awarded doctorates for research done on him and Ghalibiyaat—Ghalib Studies—is today an established branch of Urdu literature, not only in the Indian subcontinent but in universities all over the world. Streets, schools, academies of research and even eating joints have been named after Ghalib. In 1969, when the Government of India, which had otherwise hardly done anything to preserve, much less promote, the Urdu language, decided to celebrate 100 years of Ghalib's death, an agitated Sahir Ludhianvi, a famous Urdu poet himself, taunted:

Ghalib jisey kehte hain Urdu ka hi shaayar tha
Urdu pe sitam kar ke Ghalib pe karam kyon hai

(The one whom we call Ghalib was a poet of Urdu
Having crushed Urdu, why be kind to Ghalib?)

Ghalib spent a lifetime litigating. However, little did he know that even after his death, he would have to continue to litigate for his rights. In response to a Public Interest Petition filed in the High Court of Delhi in the year 1996, the court directed the Government of Delhi to restore Ghalib's haveli at Gali Qasimjan, where he breathed his last. Most parts of the haveli had been acquired by different people by then and in a part of the property a Public Call Office (PCO) was being run. Following the judicial order, the state made feeble attempts at a cosmetic conservation of some parts of the building. Some years later, in a laudable yet shoddy endeavour to 'infuse new life' into the haveli, the Indian Council for Cultural Relations and the Government of Delhi created a museum of sorts in a portion of the property. The restored portion of the haveli looks more like a page from the *Illustrated Arabian Nights* than a tribute to Ghalib.

Ghalib's relationship with law and judiciary still continues in curious ways. In a 2011 ruling, an eminent judge of the High Court of Delhi, rejecting the argument of a former law minister that expenses incurred on his heart treatment were deductible while computing income tax, began his judgment with one of Ghalib's most well-known couplets[95]:

Dil-e-naadaan tujhe hua kya hai
Aakhir is dard ki dawa kya hai

(O naive heart, what has happened to you?
Whatever could be the cure for this pain?)

Following landscaping and conservation work by the Aga Khan Trust for Culture and the Archaeological Survey of India, the surroundings of Ghalib's grave in Nizamuddin have been restored with stone screens and marble. However, there is little effort made to encourage tourists or even Dilliwalas to visit the mausoleum. A lone guard appointed to take care of the place is ususally absconding.

Ghalib's legacy, however, endures. He requires neither

judicial intervention nor State patronage. He continues to live in the hearts of millions and is a part of the lives of thousands who would quote his own sher for their deep connection with him:

Hum-pesha-o-hum-mashrab-o-humraaz hai mera
Ghalib ko bura kyon kaho, achha merey aagey

(He shares my vocation, my drinks and my secrets
Don't condemn Ghalib, he's good enough for me.)

III

SELECTED GHAZALS OF GHALIB

I

Dil-e-naadaan tujhe hua kya hai
Aakhir is dard ki dawa kya hai

Hum hain mushtaaq aur vo bezaar
Ya Ilaahi ye maajra kya hai

Mai'n bhi munh mein zubaan rakhta hoon
Kaash poochho ke mud'd'a kya hai

Jab ke tujh bin nahin koi maujood
Phir ye hungaama, ae Khuda, kya hai

Humko un se wafa ki hai ummeed
Jo nahin jaante wafa kya hai

Jaan tum par nisaar karta hoon
Mai'n nahin jaanta dua kya hai

Maine maana ke kuchh nahin Ghalib
Muft haath aaye tou bura kya hai

(O naive heart, what has happened to you?
Whatever could be the cure for this pain?

I'm consumed by desire, and she's indifferent
O Lord, what a state is this!

Even I have a tongue to speak with
How I wish you'd ask me what the matter is.

When there is no one else but you
What, O God, is all this commotion then?

We expect fidelity from those
Who don't know what fidelity is.

I just offer my life to you
I don't know what prayer is.

I admit, Ghalib is nothing at all
But if you get him for free, where's the harm?

2

Dil hi toh hai na sang-o-khisht dard se bhar na aaye kyon
Roeinge hum hazaar baar koi hamein sataaye kyon

Daiyr nahin, haram nahin, dar nahin aastaan nahin
Baithe hain rah-guzar pe hum, ghair hamein uthaaye kyon

Haan vo nahin khuda-parast, jaao vo bewafa sahi
Jis ko ho deen-o-dil azeez, us ki gali mein jaaye kyon

Qaid-e-hayaat o band-e-gham, asl mein dono ek hain
Maut se pehle aadmi gham se nijaat paaye kyon

Vaan vo ghuroor-e-izz-o-naaz, yaan ye hijab-e-paas-e-
    waz'a
Raah mein hum milein kahaan, bazm mein vo bulaaye
    kyon

Ghalib-e-khasta ke baghair kaun-se kaam bandd hain
Roiye zaar-zaar kya, kijiye haaye-haaye kyon

(It's only a heart, after all, not stone or brick. Why won't
    it fill with pain?
A thousand times over will I cry, why should anyone
    trouble me?

Not a temple or a mosque, not someone's door or
    doorway
I sit at the roadside, why should anyone remove me?

Yes, she's not a believer. Fine, she's unfaithful
If he cares so much for faith and heart, why should he
    even go to her?

The prison of life, the bondage of grief, in truth they
    are the same
Until death comes, why should man be free of grief?

There, that pride in splendour and grace, here this cloak
    of courtesies
We won't meet on the street, and she won't invite me over.

What worldly tasks have stopped without Ghalib, the
    broken, the wounded?
Why weep so bitterly, then, why moan and wail like this?

3

Ye na thi hamaari qismat ki visaal-e-yaar hota
Agar aur jeete rehte ye hi intezaar hota

Terey vaade par jiye hum tou ye jaan jhooth jaana
Ke khushi se mar na jaate agar aitbaar hota

Koi mere dilse poochhe tere teer-e-neem-kash ko
Ye khalish kahaan se hoti jo jigar ke paar hota

Kahoon kis se mai'n ki kya hai shab-e-gham buri bala hai
Mujhe kya bura tha marna agar ek baar hota

Teri naazuki se jaana ke bandha tha ahd boda
Kabhi tu na tod sakta agar ustuvaar hota

Ye kahaan ki dosti hai ke baney hain dost naaseh
Koi chaarasaaz hota koi ghamgusaar hota

Usey kaun dekh sakta ke yagaana hai vo yakta
Do dui ko boo bhi hoti toh kahin do-chaar hota

Hue mar ke hum jo ruswa hue kyon na gharq-e-dariya
Na kabhi janaaza uth'ta, na kahin mazaar hota

Ye masaail-e-tasawwuf ye tera bayaan Ghalib
Tujhe hum wali samajhte jo na baadakhvaar hota

(It was not my destiny to be united with my beloved
Had I lived any longer, it would have been the same
   long wait.

Had I lived on your promise, it would have been a sham
Wouldn't I have died of happiness if I had trusted you?

Let them ask my heart about your half-drawn arrow
There wouldn't have been such agony had it gone right
   through [my being].

To whom shall I explain what it is? The night of grief
   is such a curse
Why would I mind dying if it happened only once?

I realize your promise is fragile only because you are
   tender
You would never have broken it had it been stronger.

What friendship is this, friends become preachers
I wish someone brought solutions, someone shared my
   sorrows.

Who can see Him, for He is unique and He is matchless
Had there been even a whiff of duality, He might have
   been spotted somewhere.

Death brought me notoriety, why didn't I drown in a
   river?
There would have been no funeral, there would have
   been no tomb.

These mystical issues, and your explanations, Ghalib—
We would have considered you a saint, had you not
   been a boozer.

4

Husn ghamze ki kashaakash se chhuta mere baad
Baar-e-aaraam se hain ahl-e jafa mere baad

Shama bujhti hai toh us mein se dhuan uthta hai
Shola-e-ishq siyah-posh hua mere baad

Gham se marta hoon ke itna nahin duniya mein koi
Ke kare taaziyat-e mehr-o-wafa mere baad

Kaun hota hai hareef-e-mai-e mard-afgan-e-ishq
Hai mukarrar lab-e -aaqi mein sala mere baad

Aaye hai bekasi-e-ishq pe rona Ghalib
Kis ke ghar jaayega sailaab-e-bala mere baad

(Beauty will no longer need to tease when I'm gone
Those tyrants will finally be at ease when I'm gone.

Smoke rises from a candle when it goes out,
Passion will be smothered in black when I'm gone.

I die of grief for there's no one in the world who
Will mourn for love and loyalty when I'm gone.

'Who will accept the challenge to drink the poison-wine
of love?'
The wine-bearer keeps calling out when I'm gone.

The destitution of love makes me cry, Ghalib
Whose home will the flood of ordeals drown when I'm
gone?)

5

Rahiye ab aisi jagah chal kar jahaan koi na ho
Hum-sukhan koi na ho aur hum-zubaan koi na ho

Be-dar-o-deewaar sa ek ghar banaaya chaahiye
Koi humsaaya na ho aur paasbaan koi na ho

Padiye gar beemaar toh koi na ho teemaardaar
Aur agar marr jaaiye toh nauha-khvaan koi na ho

(Let us go and live somewhere where there's no one
No one to speak to, no one to share our language.

Let us make a house without doors and walls
No neighbour next door, and no one to guard it.

If we fall sick, no one to tend to us
And if we die, no one to mourn us.)

6

Hazaaron khwaahishein aisi ki har khwaahish pe dum
     nikley
Bohot nikley mere armaan lekin phir bhi kam nikley

Nikalna khuld se Aadam ka sunte aaye hain lekin
Bohot be-aabru ho kar tere kooche se hum nikley

Mohabbat mein nahin hai farq jeene aur marne ka
Usi ko dekh kar jeete hain jis kaafir pe dum nikley

Hui jin se tawaqqo' khastagi ki daad paane ki
Vo hum se bhi zyaada khastah-e-tegh-e-sitam nikley

Kahaan maikhaane ka darwaaza Ghalib, aur kahaan vaaiz
Par itna jaante hain kal vo jaata tha ke hum nikley

(Thousands of desires have I nurtured, and each one to
     die for
Many wishes were fulfilled; but they were few and far
     between.

We've heard all our lives of Adam's expulsion from
     Eden, but
With far greater disgrace we've made our exit from your
     street.

In love, there's no difference between life and death
I live gazing upon that unfaithful one whom I die for.

Those who I hoped would applaud my broken state
Turned out to be even more wounded by the sword of
     cruelty than me.

Whither the tavern-door, whither the preacher.
But I know this—last night, as I was leaving, he tiptoed
     in!)

7

Baazeecha-e-atfaal hai duniya mere aagey
Hota hai shab-o-roz tamaasha mere aagey

Ek khel hai aurang-e-Sulemaan mere nazdeek
Ek baat hai, aijaaz-e-Maseeha mere aagey

Juz naam nahin surat-e-aalam mujhe manzoor
Juz vehem nahin hasti-e-ashia mere aagey

Hota hai nihaan gard mein sehra mere hotey
Ghista hai jabeen khaak pe dariya mere aagey

Hum-pesha-o-hum-mashrab-o-humraaz hai mera
Ghalib ko bura kyon kaho achha merey aagey

(The world is but the playground of children before me
A spectacle unfolds night and day before me.

To me, the throne of Solomon is just a game
Before me, the miracles of Christ are mere talk.

I accept the face of the universe merely as a name
Before me, the status of reality is but a superstition.

In my presence, even the wilderness hides in dust
Before me, even the river rubs its forehead on earth.

He shares my vocation, my drinks and my secrets
Don't condemn Ghalib, he's good enough for me.)

8

Ah ko chaahiye ik umr asar hote tak*
Kaun jeeta hai teri zulf ke sar hote tak

Daam-e har mauj mein hai halqa-e sad kaam-e nihang
Dekhein kya guzre hai qatre pa guhar hote tak

Aashiqi sabr-talab aur tamanna betaab
Dil ka kya rang karoon khoon-e jigar hote tak

Hum ne maana ke taghaaful na karoge lekin
Khaak ho jaaeinge hum tum ko khabar hote tak

Partav-e-khur se hai shabnam ko fana ki taaleem
Mai'n bhi hoon ek inaayat ki nazar hote tak

---

*Many singers have used 'hone tak', but the actual words in *Diwan-e-Ghalib* are 'hote tak'. It's an archaic version of 'hone tak'.

Yak nazar besh nahin fursat-e-hasti ghaafil
Garmi-e bazm hai ik raqs-e sharar hote tak

Gham-e hasti ka Asad kis se ho juz marg ilaaj
Shama har rang mein jalti hai sahar hote tak

(A sigh needs a lifetime to yield results
Who lasts till your tresses are won over?*

In the web of every wave is a ring of a hundred dragon-
mouths
Let's see what the drop goes through before it is a pearl.

Love demands patience, and longing is restless
How do I colour my heart till it bleeds to death?

Agreed, you won't ignore me, but
I'll turn to dust by the time word [of my plight] reaches
you.

From sun-rays the dew learns what destruction means
Even I'm waiting to be destroyed by her glance of favour.

The leisure of existence is no longer than a single glance,
you unmindful one
[As] the warmth of a gathering lasts only as long as the
dance of the candle flame.

The grief of life, Asad, has no cure except death
The candle burns in every colour until dawn.)

---

*The expression 'sar hona', according to various scholars, including
Shamsur Rahman Faruqi, means 'to be victorious'.

MOMIN KHAN MOMIN
The Debonair Hakim of Delhi
(1800–1851)

Aijaaz-e-jaan-dehi hai hamaare kalaam ko
Zinda kiya hai hum ne Maseeha ke naam ko

Muddat se naam suntey thay Momin ka, baare aaj
Dekha bhi hum ne us sho'ara ke imaam ko

(My poetry performs the miracle of life
I've revived the name of the Messiah.

For years we've heard of Momin, but today
We've finally seen this Imam of Poetry.)

I

DURING THE REIGN OF THE MUHGAL EMPEROR SHAH ALAM II (1759-1806), two Kashmiri brothers, Kaamdaar Khan and Naamdaar Khan—both hakims (Unani physicians)—migrated from the Valley to Delhi and joined the Mughal Court. Both earned great respect in the city and their family practice was later expanded by Hakim Naamdaar Khan's son, Hakim Ghulam Nabi Khan, who was not only a successful hakim but also a man of letters. It came as no surprise, therefore, when he decided to send his only son to a reputed school of religious learning to gain formal education in Arabic, Persian and religious studies before training him as a hakim. The boy grew up to become extraordinarily successful—not only as a hakim, who inherited and added to a vast ancestral practice, but also as a poet, of whom even Ghalib was envious.

Born in 1800 at Kucha Chelan in Delhi, Hakim Momin Khan Momin was, arguably, the most passionate, suave and charming Urdu poet of Mughal India. In his fictionalized account of Mughal Delhi's last mushaira, *Dehli Ki Aakhri Shama*, Mirza Farhatullah Baig Dehlvi gives us a detailed description of the plush house in Kucha Chelan where Momin was born, lived and died:

> Hakim Agha Jaan ke chhatte ke saamne Khan sahib ka makaan hai. Bada darwaaza hai. Andar bohot vaseeh sehen hai, aur uske chaaron taraf imaarat hai. Do taraf do sehenchiyaan aur saamne badey-badey daalaan dar daalaan. Pehle daalaan ke upar kamra hai. Saamne ke daalaan ki chhat ko kamrey ka sehen kar diya hai. Lekin munder bohot chhoti rakkhi hai. Daalaanon mein chaandni ka farsh hai. Andar ke daalaan mein beechon-beech qaaleen bichha hua hai. Qaaleen par gaao-takiye se lagey Hakim sahib baithe hain.[96]

(Khan saheb's house is opposite the chhatta* of Hakim Agha Jaan. There is a big gate. Inside, there is a huge courtyard surrounded by a building. On either side there are smaller courtyards and at the front, one large veranda after another. Above the first veranda, there is a room. The roof of the front veranda is used as a balcony for that room. But they've kept the gable rather small. White sheets are spread on the veranda floors. Right in the centre of the middle veranda is a carpet, and on the carpet Hakim sahib is sitting with his back against a bolster-pillow.)

Kucha Chelan was the same locality where Mir had lived when he first arrived in Delhi in 1733, and where Mihrparwar Begum had built a large house for Dard's family in the 1740s.[97] Momin's father was a disciple of Shah Abdul Aziz Dehlvi, son of the legendary Islamic scholar and theologist Shah Waliullah Dehlvi, and an intellectual in his own right. It was Shah Abdul Aziz Dehlvi who had named the child Momin, which literally means 'a believer in Islam', perhaps in the hope that the boy would grow up to be a devout Muslim. In one of his later couplets, in a fine example of pun, Momin complains how his name kept him away from the women he desired:

Dushman-e-Momin hi rahey bu't sada
Mujh se mere naam ne ye kya kiya

(Idols always remained enemies of Momin
Look what my name has done to me!)**

---

*'Chhatta' was the space made by joining the terraces of two houses, usually owned by the same person, but built opposite each other on either side of the same lane.

**The word 'bu't', which means 'idol', has been traditionally used by Urdu poets to refer to the beautiful beloved. For believing Muslims like him (a 'momin'), idols and idol-worship would be forbidden.

After the completion of his formal education, Momin trained under his father to be a hakim and turned out to be a most sought-after physician. His biographer, Karimuddin, claims that Momin was such a great hakim that he surpassed even Avicenna, the father of medicine, in the art of pulse-reading.[98]

For Momin, the practice of medicine was almost a divine calling. He ran his clinic from his home and attended to a large number of patients. He prided himself on being a hakim with an exceptional healing touch, one who could revive his patients' senses in no time. To convey that he could diagnose pain by just looking at his patient's face, Momin used a remarkable romantic metaphor in one of his poems:

> Hakim vo hoon, ke jaate rahein hawaas agar
> Karey muaarza-sar daftar-e-uqool-o-nufoos
>
> Tabeeb vo hoon, ke ho soz-e-seena-e-bulbul
> Nazaara-e- rukh-e-gulfaam se mujhe mehsoos
>
> (I'm a hakim who, even if consciousness is lost
> Can revive the patient's mind and soul
>
> I'm a physician who, just by looking at the face of the rose
> Can read the fire burning in the nightingale's heart.)

In keeping with his belief in the transcendence of his occupation, Momin never charged his patients a penny. When Momin's grandfather, Hakim Naamdaar Khan, joined the Mughal Court, Emperor Shah Alam II had awarded him the estate of Narnaun, which was then situated in the Province of Jhajjar. The British Government later awarded the entire Province of Jhajjar to Nawab Faiz Talab Khan and the estate also went to the Nawab. However, a handsome annuity of one thousand rupees was reserved for

Hakim Naamdaar Khan, which was later inherited by his descendants. In addition to this annuity, four other hakims of the family received pensions from the British Crown, out of which Momin got his share through his father who, in any case, had accumulated sufficient wealth. Consequently, the poet led a fairly comfortable life on inheritance and bequests, a fact that is reflected in Farhatullah Baig's description of his residence in *Dilli Ki Aakhri Shama*.

Momin had started writing at the age of sixteen. Following the tradition of training under an ustaad, he became the pupil, for some time, of Shah Naseeruddin Naseer, alias Kaale Saheb, the poet and spiritual leader who had trained other prominent poets and was a dear friend of Ghalib's. But Momin's talents extended to other arts, too. He was also an adept astronomer, a gifted singer, an ardent connoisseur of the flute and a master chess player. It is believed that the celebrated flute maestro of his times, Mir Nasir Ahmed, shunned the flute after Momin's death, saying that after the poet, the city was left with no real qadradaan (connoisseur) of the instrument. Added to these extraordinary qualities of science and art were Momin's debonair disposition and charming persona. He dressed impeccably and sported long tresses. A section of *Dehli Ki Aakhri Shama* contains a vivid description of his sartorial sense:

> Badan par sharbati malmal ka neechi choli ka angarkha tha lekin uske neeche kurta na tha aur jism ka kuchh hissa angarkhe ke parde mein se dikhaayi de raha tha. Galey mein siyaah rang ka feeta, usmein chhota sa sunehri taaweez. Kaakrezi rang ke dupatte ko bal de kar kamar mein lapeit liya tha aur uske donon sirey saamne padey hue thay. Haath mein patla sa khaarpusht, paaon mein surkh gulbadan ka paijaama, mohriyon par se tang, upar

ja kar kis qadar dheela. Kabhi kabhi ek bar ka paijaama
bhi pehente thay magar kisi qism ka bhi ho, hamesha
reshmi aur qeemti hota tha. Chaura surkh nefa. Angarkhe
ki aasteenein aage se kati huin, kabhi latakti rehti thiin
aur kabhi palat kar charha lete thay. Sar par gulshan ki
dopalri topi, us ke kinaare se par-baareek lace. Topi itni
badi thi ki sar par achhi tarah mundh kar aa gayi thi.
Andar se maang aur maathe ka kuchh hissa aur baal
saaf jhalakte thay. Gharazeke nihaayat khush-poshaak
aur jaama-zeb aadmi thay.[99]

(He was wearing a wine-coloured muslin tunic with a low
bodice but no kurta underneath, and some of his skin
could be seen through a slit in the tunic. Round the neck
was a black cord with a small golden amulet. A violet
sash had been folded like a waistband with its two ends
left dangling in front. In his hand was a tiny khaarpusht*,
and he wore red gulbadan** pyjamas, tight at the ankles,
rather loose above. Sometimes he also wore single-girth
pyjamas; whatever be the style, it was always silk and
expensive with a wide red band. His tunic sleeves were
cut from the front. Sometimes he let them dangle full
length, sometimes he would roll them up. On his head
was a double-band gulshan cap with extremely delicate
lace on the hem. The cap was so big that it would cover
his head rather well but would clearly reveal the parting
in his hair and a portion of his forehead. In short, he was
an extremely well-dressed and fashionable man.)

---

*The word 'khaarpusht' literally means 'hedgehog'. Even though some
writers have suggested that Momin may be carrying a small hedgehog
in his hand, like people used to carry quails, the word probably refers
here to some kind of a prickly staff or maze.

**Literally, 'flower like body', but the term is also used for a variety
of cloth which is very fine.

It was no wonder, then, that Momin was a highly desirable man and was involved in a series of amorous affairs. Though no name other than that of one Saheb ji finds mention in any of Momin's works or biographies, by closely going through his works, one can reasonably conclude that in his fifty-one years the poet was romantically involved with at least five women.[100] There is considerable debate on the real identity of Saheb ji. However, it is commonly believed that Saheb ji was the sobriquet of a Lucknow courtesan, Ummul Fatima, who visited Delhi in the 1820s and stayed with her hosts in Kucha Chelan. The story goes that one day Saheb ji fell ill and her hosts requested Momin to examine her in purdah. Called to feel her pulse, Momin fell for her hennaed hands and extolled their beauty in verse:

> Saaf sandal se zyaada vo haath
> Narm makhmal se zyaada vo haath
>
> (Fairer than sandalwood, those hands
> Softer than velvet, those hands.)

When the veiled affair became public, Saheb ji was forced to return to Lucknow. After Saheb ji's return, Momin fell in love with a girl from Rampur, to meet whom he often travelled all the way to that province, an admission that he makes in this couplet:

> Dilli se Rampur mein laaya junoon ka josh
> Veerana chhor aaye hain veerana-tar mein hum
>
> (The zeal of madness has brought me from Delhi to
>   Rampur
> I've left one wilderness for another even more desolate.)

At the age of twenty-three, Momin was married to the daughter of a rural zamindar. However, the marriage did not last long. Either his wife was too traditional and provincial to satisfy his intellectual needs or she could not endure his rather liberal approach to matters of the heart. After his first marriage broke down, Momin married an educated woman from a well-known family of highly distinguished scholars. Her father was Khwaja Naseer, who was the son of Zeenat-un-Nisa Begum, daughter of the poet and Sufi Khwaja Mir Dard. Her mother was the daughter of Dard's son, Khwaja Saheb Ilm.

Momin took great pride in having married a woman with such a scholarly and spiritual legacy, and on one occasion, became deeply involved in the family's affairs. When his father-in-law, Khwaja Naseer, died, a dispute arose on the appointment of the Sajjada-nasheen (successor to the shrine) of Khwaja Mir Dard. Some members of the family appointed Khwaja Nasir Ameer, a maternal grandson of Khwaja Naseer through his first wife, as the Sajjaada-nasheen. Momin, who believed that this would dilute Dard's Sufi legacy, got his wife and sister-in-law to file a lawsuit challenging the appointment. He engaged a prominent lawyer of the time, Mir Tafazzul Husain, as their advocate. The other side was represented by an equally eminent lawyer, Mughal Jan. Though the court demarcated the shares of all parties in accordance with Islamic law, to fund the litigation, both parties had to sell their respective ancestral properties. As was expected, the litigation resulted in permanent animosity between the families.

Momin was a close friend of Ghalib's and stood by him like a rock through many a difficult and turbulent time. In 1847, when Ghalib was incarcerated for six months for the offence of gambling, Momin was one of his few friends who not only made all possible attempts to bail him out but also supported his family during those months. While this may have been out of admiration for Ghalib the poet, it is more likely it was out of friendship. For Momin, somewhat superciliously, hardly considered any other poet his equal. No one, not even Ghalib, was in his league:

> Momin ye shaairon ka mere aagey rang hai
> Joon pesh aaftaab ho be-noor har chiraagh

> (Momin this is how poets fare before me
> Like lightless lamps in the presence of the sun.)

He was of the firm belief that only someone who could not understand the real meaning of his poetry would consider any other poet superior to him:

> Momin usi ne mujh se di bartari kisi ko
> Jo past-fehem mere ashaar tak na pahuncha

> (Momin, only he accorded superiority to someone else
> Who could not even begin to understand my poetry.)

The renowned Urdu poet and Ghalib's biographer, Maulana Altaf Hussain Hali, has narrated the following incident in *Yaadgaar-e-Ghalib*:

> In one of his Persian couplets, Mirza contended that he was at least equal to (the distinguished Persian scholar) Sheikh Ali Hazin. When Momin heard that couplet, he agreed with Ghalib. This was not because he considered Ghalib a great Persian scholar, but because he considered Sheikh Ali Hazin inferior to himself.[101]

Ghalib, on the contrary, despite his incessant self-adulation, held Momin in high esteem as a poet. He is reported to have offered to trade his whole diwaan for just this single couplet by Momin:

> Tum mere paas hotey ho goya
> Jab koi doosra nahin hota

(You are with me, as if
When there is no one else.)

The couplet is incredible, and its translation exceedingly challenging. Momin could have simply said:

You are with me
When there's no one else.

However, by using the word 'goya', he has indulged in an amazing wordplay, one of the most outstanding examples of paronomasia in Urdu poetry. Goya would be best translated in English as 'as if'. The inclusion of this single short word in the first misra of this couplet has accorded it an understated touch of mystical magic and has rendered the couplet open to a wide canvas of interpretations. The couplet could mean:

Even when I am alone, it seems you are there with me
or
When you are with me, no one else is
or
When you are there with me, others do not seem to exist
or
When there is no on else, it is as if you are (or, pared down further, 'When no one is, you are').

It is simply impossible to capture the essence of what Momin is saying in this couplet and it is this impossibility that enthralled Ghalib. Some scholars have also suggested that the word 'goya' here means 'to speak' and, therefore, Momin is really saying that his beloved (or God) speaks to him when there is no one else. This interpretation, however, seems anomalous. In 1966, in a song written for the Bollywood film *Love in Tokyo*, the poet and lyricist Hasrat Jaipuri used a slightly changed version of this couplet. Joy

Mukherjee sings to Asha Parekh in the voice of Mohammad Rafi in a Tokyo setting:

O mere shah-e-khubaan, O meri jaan-e-jaanaana
Tum mere paas hote ho, koi doosra nahin hota

(O my beautiful ruler, O love of my life
Only you are always with me, no one else is.)

Like Mir, Momin was also extremely sensitive in matters of self-respect. He did not believe in taking favours or accepting endowments. Since he had no ambitions of being close to the Mughal royalty, he did not eulogize them in his poetry. We do not, therefore, find many qaseedahs in his works, even though his contemporaries, including Ghalib and Zauq, have dozens of qaseedahs to their credit. The two notable exceptions are the qaseedahs that Momin wrote for the Prince of Tonk, Nusrat Jung, and the brother of the Maharaja of Patiala, Ajeet Singh. In fact, the circumstances necessitating these two poems only establish the truth of the assertion that Momin never took the burden of favours.

Prince Nusrat Jung had invited Momin to travel with him at his expense to perform the pilgrimage of Hajj. Momin politely declined the invitation but, to express his gratitude for the offer, penned some verses for the Prince. His reasons for eulogizing Ajeet Singh are quite different but, again, stem from his profound sense of pride and dignity. Once Ajeet Singh invited Momin to his house and he and his friends spent a leisurely evening listening to Momin's poetry. When the evening came to an end, Ajeet Singh, out of his deep appreciation for Momin's poetry, gifted him an elephant. When Momin tried to escape the favour by saying that he was a poor man and would not be able to feed the elephant, his host also gifted him a hundred rupees to take care of the pet's expenses. Bound by politeness and etiquette, Momin could not refuse the gifts. However, this 'beastly burden' was troubling him. Therefore, to return the appreciation and make things even, the very next day Momin penned a qaseedah in praise of his generous host and sent it to him in lieu of the previous day's gifts.

Unlike his contemporaries, Momin was also not in the habit of making courtesy calls on noblemen and aristocrats. While most of his friends were busy writing longish odes in praise of their benefactors, when Momin visited Nawab Hamid Ali Khan, a powerful Mughal courtier, he congratulated the Nawab, rather condescendingly, for befriending a perfect man like himself:

Momin aaya hai bazm mein teri
Sohbat-e-aadmi Mubarak ho
Tahniyat khwaan-e-kaamyaabi se
Sila-e-dosti Mubarak ho

(Momin has come to your gathering
Congratulations on achieving the company of Man.
From one who felicitates your success
Accept greetings on this friendship.)

Once, the Maharaja of Kapurthala offered him the position of poet laureate in his court with an attractive salary of three hundred and fifty rupees a month. Momin turned down the offer on the ground that the salary of the court musician was also the same. Though even had the salary been twice as much, Momin might not have accepted the honour.

For, Momin adored his Delhi. He was offered a lectureship at Delhi College by his friend, the British Secretary Thompson,[102] at a salary of eighty rupees a month. Momin demanded a hundred rupees. Thompson agreed but subject to the condition that Momin would have to occasionally travel with him outside Delhi. When Momin came to know of this condition, he refused to accept the offer, saying that he would not 'sell Delhi' for hundred rupees a month. He recommended Ghalib for the position and when Ghalib also refused to accept it, the post went to Imam Bakhsh Sehbai.

—

Momin's connection with Delhi was not only by birth and ancestry; it was also spiritual. He was a follower of Syed Ahmad Rai Barelvi, author of *Sirat-e-Mustaqeem* (The Straight Path) and a major exponent of Wahhabism in India, who had based himself in Delhi. But Momin also drew inspiration from the teachings of various other scholars, the prominent among them being the highly revered theologian of Delhi, Shah Waliullah Dehlvi (1703-1762), who is best known for his annotated Persian translation of the Quran and his classic book on the Islamic way of life, *Hujjatullah-al-Baligha* (The Profound Evidence of God)[103]. Rai Barelvi had himself been inspired by Shah Waliullah in many ways. However, there was an essential difference between the opinions of the two scholars. Rai Barelvi's Wahhabism sought to rid Islam of what he thought were extraneous influences and restore it to its puritanical form where there is no mediator between man and God. Consequently, he rejected Sufi traditions. Shah Waliullah, on the other hand, believed in tolerance and reconciliation of conflicting beliefs within Islam. Momin seemed to fight this dichotomy between the beliefs of Shah Waliullah and Syed Ahmad Rai Barelvi all his life.

On the one hand, Momin tried to be a practising believer and, on the other, a passionate lover indulging in worldly pleasures. It was perhaps because of this paradox that Momin's real personality bloomed and it was in this dichotomy that his individuality was hidden. It was what made him such a fine poet who inspired many others. Some of his disciples became famous poets themselves. One of them was Shefta, who published the complete Urdu works of Momin, *Kulliyaat-e-Momin*, in 1843. A Persian diwaan was also in place by the same time.

In 1851, a hale and hearty Momin was supervising some repairs on the terrace of his house when he slipped, fell and injured himself badly. The instinct of a physician told him that the fall would prove fatal. He died within five days. He was buried next to the graves of his father's spiritual mentor, Shah Abdul Aziz Dehlvi—who had given Momin his name at birth—and Shah Saheb's father, Shah Waliullah—who had himself had a considerable influence on Momin's philosophy. Momin's great grand father-in-law, Khwaja Mir Dard, also lay buried in the vicinity.

Momin's sudden death came as a grave loss not only to his friends but also to the entire literary landscape of Delhi. Ghalib was devastated. In a letter to one Nabi Bakhsh, he wrote:

> Suna hoga tum ne ki Momin Khan mar gaye. Aaj un ko marey hue dasvaan din hai. Momin Khan mera hum-asr tha aur yaar bhi tha. Bayaalees-taintaalees baras hue, yaani chaudah-chaudah, pandrah-pandrah baras ki meri aur us marhoom ki umr thi ki mujh mein rabt paida hua. Is arsey mein kabhi kisi tarah ka ranj-o-malaal darmiyaan nahin aaya. Hazrat, chaalis chaalis baras ka dushman bhi nahin paida hota. Dost toh kahaan haath aata hai.[104]

> (You must have heard that Momin Khan is dead. Today is the tenth day of his death. Momin Khan was my contemporary and also my friend. It has been forty-two or forty-three years, both of us were about fourteen or

fifteen years old when we befriended each other. In this period never did we nurture any complaint or grievance against each other. Sir, even an enemy of forty years is difficult to find, let alone finding a friend of these many years.)

II

AS WE HAVE OBSERVED, THE SOURCE OF MOMIN'S extraordinary poetry lay perhaps in the conflict between his allegiance to a rather austere interpretation of his faith and his robustly romantic disposition. A lot of his verse deals beautifully with this clash between Momin the devout and Momin the lover. Urdu poetry has had a rich heritage of using distinctive metaphors, similes and allusions for the beloved and the beautiful. The words bu't and bu'tkhaana, which literally mean idol and idol-house (or temple), have been traditionally used by Urdu poets to refer to the beauteous and to the house of beauty, both of which are as abhorred in orthodox Islam as idols and idol-worship. Momin indulges in a beautiful use of the two metaphors in his poetry.

On the one hand, he urges himself to turn towards religion:

> Chal ke kaabe mein sajda kar ae Momin
> Chhor is bu't ke aastaane ko

> (Go and prostrate yourself in the Ka'aba, O Momin
> Come away from this habitat of the idol.)

And on the other hand, he chides himself for trying to take the sacred path:

> Allah re gumrahi, bu't-o-butkhaana chhor kar
> Momin chala hai kaabe ko ek paarsa ke saath

(Oh God, the limit of going astray! Having turned away
    from idols
Momin now walks with the pious to the Kaaba.)

However, when disappointed in love, a dejected Momin
turns towards God:

Chal diye soo-e-haram koo-e-bu'taan se Momin
Jab diya ranj bu'ton ne toh khuda yaad aaya

(From the lane of idols, I head for the mosque
Momin, when idols gift me sorrow, I remember God.)

After having spent a lifetime indulging his love of beauty
and splendour, Momin wonders if he can now be a devout
Muslim:

Umr saari toh kati ishq-e-bu'taan mein Momin
Aakhri waqt mein kya khaak musalmaan hongey

(I've spent all my life in love with idols, Momin
What kind of Muslim will I make in my final hour!)

Finally, he decides to revel in this seemingly irreconcilable
difference and makes a virtue of it. He rejoices in the fact
that he has had the best of both the worlds:

Momin ko sach hai daulat-e-duniya-o-dil naseeb
Shab butkadey mein guzri hai din khaanqaah mein

(Momin has gained the wealth of the world and of the
    heart
His nights are spent in the idol-house, his days in the
    khanqah [Sufi monastery].)

Momin is a poet of intense romantic character, who makes
remarkably effective use of the tropes and traditions of
classical Urdu poetry. In the same ghazal that contains the
couplet Ghalib envied, he complains that his beloved is

utterly insensitive. Had she accepted his proposal, all his desires would have been fulfilled. But he is condemned to silent anguish and endless waiting:

Asar usko zara nahin hota
Ranj raahat-faza nahin hota

Tum hamaare kisi tarah na hue
Varna duniya mein kya nahin hota

Us ne kya jaane kya kiya le kar
Dil kisi kaam ka nahin hota

Kyon sune arz-e-muztar ae Momin
Sanam aakhir khuda nahin hota

(Nothing affects her at all
Grief brings no comfort.

No matter what I did, you wouldn't be mine
What couldn't have been mine in this world otherwise?

God alone knows what she did with it
The heart, after all, is a useless thing.

Why should she hear the pleas of the distressed
O Momin, the idol after all is not God.)

Letting his restlessness be known to his beloved is futile, for it will make no difference to her:

Kya naame mein likkhoon dil-e-vaabasta ka ahwaal
Maaloom hai pehle hi ki vo va na kareinge

(In my letter, what should I say of the state of my heart?
I already know, she won't be moved.)

The faithless ways of the beloved, the inconstancy of love, are a recurring theme in Urdu love poetry (written, as some have noted, by men who were rarely faithful or steadfast in love themselves). Momin excels in this literary tradition. In this simple, heartrending couplet, for instance:

Kisi ka hua aaj, kal tha kisi ka
Na hai tu kisi ka, na hoga kisi ka

(With someone today, you were with another yesterday
You don't belong to anyone and you never will.)

In a fine display of literary prowess, Momin applauds his
beloved for breaking up with him, for even he has been
unhappy with his continued fidelity towards her:

Mai'n bhi kuchh khush nahin wafa kar ke
Tum ne achha kiya nibaah na ki

(Even I don't particularly prize my loyalty
You did well to break up with me.)

Before the complaint and heartbreak, sometimes, there is
humour, as in this description of the beloved's fury:

Kya jaane kya likha tha usey iztiraab mein
Qaasid ki laash aayi hai khat ke jawaab mein

(God knows what I wrote to her in my restless state
In reply, she has sent me the poor messenger's body.)

Though Momin has to his credit numerous remarkable
ghazals in the romantic tradition, if there is one ghazal
that deserves to be nominated as the poet's chef-d'oeuvre,
it is, without doubt, the sublime 'Vo jo hum mein tum mein
qaraar tha'—the remembrance of love that has ended, sung
with such restrained emotion by Begum Akhtar that it is
like a knife in the heart. The complete ghazal, which is in
the selection at the end of this chapter, begins with these
couplets:

Vo jo hum mein tum mein qaraar tha tumhein yaad ho
    ke na yaad ho
Vahi yaani vaada nibaah ka tumhein yaad ho ke na
    yaad ho

Vo naye giley, vo shikaayatein vo mazey-mazey ki
    hikaayatein
Vo har ek baat pe roothna tumhein yaad ho ke na yaad ho

(The ease that was once between us, you might remember
    or you might not
That promise we made to stay together, you might
    remember or you might not.

Those ever-new laments, a thousand complaints, those
    heady tales we told one another
How every little thing was a reason to be cross, you might
    remember or you might not.)

And it ends with this couplet:

Jisey aap gintey thay aashna, jisey aap kehte thay ba-wafa
Mai'n vahi hoon 'Momin-e-mubtala', tumhein yaad ho
    ke na yaad ho

(The one you once counted as an acquaintance, the one
    you once called faithful
I am the same Momin-in-anguish, you might remember
    or you might not.)

This one ghazal, alone, would have made Momin immortal.
For its sophistication and emotional impact, it is unsurpassed
in classical Urdu love poetry. But this master of romance
doesn't rule the popular imagination as Ghalib or Mir do. In
the mohalla that was his, however, his memory does survive.
Though Momin's birthplace and house in Kucha Chelan
no longer exist, a lane in the neighbourhood carries his
name. It had been named after him as Gali Hakim Momin
Khan Momin at one time. Later, the name was shortened
to Gali Momin Waali. To reach this gali, one has to enter
Kucha Chelan from Daryaganj, through a lane just ahead
of Golcha Cinema. Residents of the neighbourhood claim

that the many small houses in the lane once formed part of Momin's palatial bungalow. A mosque at the end of the lane is claimed to have been frequented by him. In Hakim Agha Jaan ka Chhatta, the building right opposite Momin's house, a banquet hall popularly called Inayat ka Shaadi Hall (Inayat's Wedding Hall) and a sweet shop are being run.

Momin's grave forms part of the enclosed precincts of the mosque surrounding the Dargah of Shah Waliullah at one end of the Mehndiyaan graveyard next to the campus of Maulana Azad Medical College, New Delhi. It is well-preserved, and on a tombstone erected on it some decades ago are inscribed, in fading letters, some of Momin's better-known couplets.

It is, however, a travesty of literary history that not much is found on the multifaceted life of this not so archaic genius even in fairly well-stocked Urdu libraries. Perhaps Urdu lovers should follow Momin's own 'reverse metamorphosis' advice and pray that his legacy fades away, for that might be the only way of ensuring that it does not:

Maanga kareinge ab se dua hijr-e-yaar ki
Aakhir toh dushmani hai asar ko dua ke saath

(From now on I will pray for separation from my beloved
After all, there's enmity between my prayers and their
    answer.)

III

SELECTED GHAZALS OF MOMIN

I

Vo jo hum mein tum mein qaraar tha, tumhein yaad ho
ke na yaad ho
Vahi yaani vaada nibaah ka, tumhein yaad ho ke na
yaad ho

Vo naye giley, vo shikaayatein, vo mazey-mazey ki
hikaayatein
Vo har ek baat pe roothna, tumhein yaad ho ke na yaad
ho

Koi baat aisi agar hui, ki tumhaare ji ko buri lagi
Toh bayaan se pehle hi bhoolna, tumhein yaad ho ke
na yaad ho

Kabhi hum mein tum mein bhi chaah thi, kabhi hum se
tum se bhi raah thi
Kabhi hum bhi tum bhi thay aashna, tumhein yaad ho
ke na yaad ho

Vo jo lutf mujh pe tha beshtar, vo karam ke tha mere
haal par
Mujhe sab hai yaad zara-zara, tumhein yaad ho ke na
yaad ho

Suno, zikr hai kayi saal ka, ki kiya ik aap ne vaada tha
So nibhaane ka toh zikr kya, tumhein yaad ho ke na
yaad ho

Vo bigadna vasl ki raat ka, vo na maan'na kisi baat ka
Vo nahin-nahin ki har aan ada, tumhein yaad ho ke na
yaad ho

Jisey aap gintey thay aashna, jisey aap kehte thay ba-wafa
Mai'n vahi hoon 'Momin-e-mubtala', tumhein yaad ho
ke na yaad ho

(The ease that was once between us, you might remember
or you might not

That promise we made to stay together, you might
remember or you might not.

Those ever-new laments, a thousand complaints, those
heady tales we told one another

How every little thing was a reason to be cross, you might
remember or you might not.

If words were ever spoken that displeased you—to
remember those words

And forget them before they were spoken again; you
might remember, or you might not.

That you and I shared a desire once, that you and I could
work miracles together

That you and I once knew each other; you might
remember or you might not.

Those joys that fell upon me like a benediction, that sweet
concern for my condition

I can remember all of that, bit by bit, you might remember
or you might not.

Listen, this did happen many years ago—you made me
a promise

I don't expect it to be fulfilled, but you might remember
it. Or you might not.

Getting annoyed with me on that night of union, not
listening to any of a hundred pleas

That manner of saying 'no' to everything—you might
remember or you might not.

The one you once counted as your acquaintance, the one
you once called faithful

I am the same Momin-in-anguish, you might remember
or you might not.)

2

Asar usko zara nahin hota
Ranj raahat-faza nahin hota

Tum hamaare kisi tarah na hue
Varna duniya mein kya nahin hota

Us ne kya jaane kya kiya le kar
Dil kisi kaam ka nahin hota

Haal-e-dil yaar ko likhoon kyon kar
Haath dil se juda nahin hota

Chaara-e-dil siva-e-sabr nahin
So tumhaare siva nahin hota

Tum mere paas hotey ho goya
Jab koi doosra nahin hota

Kyon sune arz-e-muztar ae Momin
Sanam aakhir khuda nahin hota

(Nothing affects her at all
Grief brings no comfort.

No matter what I did, you wouldn't be mine
What couldn't have been mine in this world otherwise?

God alone knows what she did with it
The heart, after all, is a useless thing.

How should I write her of the state of my heart?
My hand is fastened to my heart.

There's no cure for this heart but patience
And that, I cannot have without you.

You are with me, as if
When there is no one else.

Why should she hear the pleas of the distressed, Momin
The idol, after all, is not God.)

3

Ulte vo shikve karte hain aur kis ada ke saath
Be-taaqati ke taane hain uzr-e-jafa ke saath

Bahr-ayaadat aaye vo lekin qaza ke saath
Damm hi nikal gaya mera aawaaz-e-pa ke saath

Maanga kareinge ab se dua hijr-e-yaar ki
Aakhir toh dushmani hai asar ko dua ke saath

Allah re gumrahi, but'-o-butkhaana chhor kar
Momin chala hai kaabe ko ek paarsa ke saath

(She turns the tables on me, and with such flair
Her excuses for cruelty come with taunts about my
     feebleness.
She came to ask after me, but brought Death along
My breath left me when I heard her footsteps.

From now on I will pray for separation from my beloved
After all, there's enmity between my prayers and their
     answer.

Oh God, the limit of going astray! Having turned away
     from idols
Momin now walks with the pious to the Kaaba.)

4

Roya kareinge aap bhi pehron isi tarah
Atka kahin jo aap ka dil bhi meri tarah

Aata nahin hai vo tou kisi dhab se daav mein
Banti nahin hai milne ki us ke koi tarah

Nae taab hijr mein hai na aaraam vasl mein
Kambakht dil ko chaiyn nahin hai kisi tarah

Maashooq aur bhi hain bata de jahaan mein
Karta hai kaun zulm kisi par teri tarah

Mar chuk kahin ke tu gham-e-hijraan se chhoot jaaye
Kehte toh hain bhale ki va-lekin buri tarah

Hoon jaan-ba-lab butaan-e-sitamgar ke haath se
Kya sab jahaan mein jeete hain Momin isi tarah

(Even you will cry for hours like this
If your heart is hooked like mine.

There's no trick to tame her
There's no way to make her mine.

No comfort in separation, nor relief in union
This wretched heart will find no solace either way.

There are other lovers in the world, but tell me
Who oppresses someone like this?

'Go die somewhere, so you are rid of the sorrows of
       separation.'
They say it for my good, but they say it in a terrible way.

The tyranny of these idols has brought me to death's door
Does everyone live in this world, O Momin, the same
       way?)

BAHADUR SHAH ZAFAR

An Emperor's Affair with Urdu
(1775–1862)

Dil ki mere beqaraari mujh se kuchh poochho nahin
Shab ki meri aah-o-zaari mujh se kuchh
poochho nahin

Ae Zafar jo haal hai mera karoonga gar bayaan
Hogi un ko sharm-saari mujh se kuchh poochho nahin

(Don't ask me about the restlessness of my heart
Don't ask me about my night of crying and wailing.

O Zafar, if I speak of my condition
They'll be put to shame; don't ask me.)

I

WILLIAM DALRYMPLE'S BOOK *THE LAST MUGHAL: THE Fall of a Dynasty, Delhi 1857,* opens with the following description of a nondescript funeral:

> At 4 pm on a hazy, humid winter's afternoon in Rangoon in November 1862, soon after the end of the monsoon, a shrouded corpse was escorted by a small group of British soldiers to an anonymous grave at the back of a walled prison enclosure...The bier of the State Prisoner—as the deceased was referred to—was accompanied by two of his sons and an elderly, bearded mullah...The ceremony was brief. The British authorities had made sure not only that the grave was already dug, but that quantities of lime were on hand to guarantee the rapid decay of both bier and body. When the shortened funeral prayers had been recited—no lamentations or panegyrics were allowed—the earth was thrown in over the lime, and the turf carefully replaced so that within a month or so no mark would remain to indicate the place of burial.[105]

The funeral described so memorably by Dalrymple is not of a notorious criminal or common prisoner but that of the last Mughal Emperor of India, Mirza Abu Zafar Sirajuddin Muhammad Bahadur Shah—an accomplished music composer, a revered Sufi, a distinguished theologian, a great connoisseur of art and poetry and a poet himself, known to the world as Bahadur Shah 'Zafar'.

For more than two hundred years, Zafar's Timurid ancestors had ruled the larger chunk of South Asia with a splendid and ostentatious display of wealth and authority, frequently translated into matchless architectural wonders and peerless artistic marvels. However, after the death of

Aurangzeb in 1707, the empire had started fragmenting. By the time Zafar inherited the throne in 1837, he was already sixty-two and frail. Delhi had changed. The territorial limits of the Empire barely extended beyond the walls of the Qila-e-Moalla, the Red Fort, and the grandeur of the Mughal crown had almost faded away, forcing Zafar to compare it with a beggar's bowl:

Ya mujhe afsar-e-shaahaana banaaya hota
Ya mera taaj gadaayaana banaaya hota

Roz maamoora-e-duniya mein kharaabi hai Zafar
Aisi basti se toh veeraana banaaya hota

(You should have sent me to earth as a Royal Officer
Or given me a beggar's bowl for a crown.

This teeming world is wrecked anew every day, Zafar
A desolate ruin would be a better habitation than this.)

This ageing Emperor, still referred to as Zill-e-Subhaani—the Shadow of God—by people out of respect, habit, decency or only nostalgia, was in fact a helpless man burdened with an impossible history. His writ ran no further than the quarters of his family and a few retainers and advisors, and even that under conditions set by the real ruler of Hindustan, The East India Company, which paid him a stipend to supplement his small income from other sources. In *Asar-al-Sanadid*, Sir Syed Ahmad Khan discloses the Emperor's then annual income as a total of rupees sixteen lakhs and three thousand.[106] The book does not make it clear whether this was Zafar's personal income or the annual revenue of the Mughal Empire. Interestingly, in 1908, British Orientalist Stanley Lane-Poole, in his book *Aurangzib and the Decay of the Mughal Empire*, writes that the annual revenue of the Mughal Empire during Akbar's reign in 1605 was more than nineteen million pounds and, under Aurangzeb's rule, had risen to more than forty-three million pounds by 1697.[107] In just 160 years, it would all be dust and history.

—

Born on 24 October 1775 in Delhi, Zafar was the son of Emperor Akbar Shah II and his Hindu Rajput wife, Lalbai. Zafar's father had presided over a speedily crumbling empire for three decades till his death in 1837. Consumed by a false sense of royal pride, he had refused audience to the British Governor General—except if the latter agreed to appear as a Mughal subject—resulting in serious curtailment of his powers and his near incarceration in his own fort. To protest this shabby treatment, he had appointed the Bengali reformer Ram Mohan Roy as his special envoy to travel to the Court of St. James in London, conferring upon him the title of Raja, but Roy's efforts in this regard had only limited success, and Akbar Shah II died a disappointed man. Bahadur Shah Zafar ascended to the Mughal throne, such as it was, a few days later, on 28 September 1837.

Zafar was not his father's preferred choice as the Wali-ahad (heir apparent). He succeeded Akbar Shah II only because his step brother, Mirza Jahangir, who was his father's choice, had been exiled in Allahabad after he tried to attack the British Resident, Archibald Seton, at the Qila-e-Moalla. The inheritor of a powerless, immobilized throne, Zafar turned his attention to non-political matters and had soon assembled a galaxy of matchless Urdu and Persian poets in his court. Among them were Mirza Asadullah Khan Ghalib, Hakim Momin Khan Momin, Mufti Sadruddin Aazurdah, Imaam Bakhsh Sehbai, Nawab Mustafa Khan Shefta and, of course, the Emperor's ustaad and Poet Laureate, Shaikh Mohammad Ibrahim Zauq.

Mushairas at the Qila, presided over by Zafar himself, were extraordinary literary gatherings, of the kind that Delhi had not seen before, and never again would.

The only rival to Zafar's court in this matter was the haveli of Hakim Ahsanullah Khan, Zafar's Royal Physician, who was himself a great connoisseur of poetry and a man of letters. In this huge haveli in Lal Kuan, the Hakim would host glamorous mushairas, invitations to which were considered a great honour for poets of the time. The haveli was later split into various small and large structures. Its drawing room—baithak, or mardaana—was later acquired and made part of the Excelsior Cinema. (The building can still be found at the junction of Lal Kuan Bazar and Kucha Pandit in old Delhi, but the cinema, which was in business till recently, has shut down.)

However, the stars of Urdu poetry shone most brightly in Zafar's little empire. A ghazal by a Mughal prince, Mirza Qadir Bakhsh Saabir, describes how he benefitted from the company of the brilliant Urdu and Persian poets in the Court of the last Mughal:

Pehle ustaad thay Ehsaan-o-Naseer-o-Momin
Hui Ehsaan se pur-islaah tabiyat meri

Phir hua Hazrat-e-Sehbaai ki islaah ka faiz
Taba baareek hui unki badaulat meri

Aur hum-bazm rahe Momin-o-Zauq-o-Ghalib
Ustaadon se hi hardam rahi sohbat meri

Munaqqid hoti hai jab sheher mein bazm-e-Insha
Karte hain ahl-e-sukhan waqat-o-izzat meri

(At first, my tutors were Ehsaan, Naseer and Momin
It was Ehsaan who guided my ideology.

Then I benefitted from the guidance of Sehbaai
Because of him I acquired sensitivity in my temperament.

And Momin, Zauq and Ghalib have been my fellow-
poets;
I have always been in the company of masters.

Whenever a gathering is organized in the name of Insha
The literati accord me stature and respect.)

Zafar, however, was not taken seriously as a poet by his
contemporaries. In his list of the seventeen greatest Urdu
poets of nineteenth-century Delhi, Sir Syed does not name
Zafar.[108] It is believed that even Ghalib, who took over
as Zafar's ustaad rather late in life, did not consider him
a particularly good poet. But Zafar took his poetry quite
seriously. Soon after becoming Emperor, he had appointed
as his ustaad Shaikh Mohammad Ibrahim Zauq, whose
literary rivalry with Ghalib successfully kept the latter
out of the Mughal court for long years. Many critics who
regard Zafar as a run-of-the-mill poet, have alleged that
some of the best couplets ascribed to him were actually
penned, or at least partly penned, by Zauq—an accusation
that seems speculative, if not completely unfounded. In a
tribute to the legendary Faiz Ahmed Faiz in 2010, the actor
Shabana Azmi narrated an amusing anecdote in which
Zafar figures.[109] She was shooting in Moscow once, when
she discovered that Faiz was also in town. When she went
to meet him, Faiz showed her a piece of paper on which he
had written his latest poem. Shabana's inability to read the
Urdu script infuriated Faiz, who blamed her parents—Kaifi
and Shaukat Azmi, both well-known Urdu scholars and his
close friends—for not having taught her their language.
Shabana, however, assured Faiz that despite her ignorance
of the script, she was well-versed in Urdu poetry and had, in
fact, memorized many of his poems. Flustered and nervous,
unable to think straight, she hurriedly recited a couplet,
only to be told by Faiz that it was Mir's and not his. Even

more nervous by now, she quickly apologized and recited another couplet. Faiz calmly put out the cigarette he had been smoking and said: 'Mir ki hadd tak toh theek tha, lekin Bahadur Shah Zafar ko main shaayar nahin maanta.' ('It's still okay to be mistaken for Mir, but Bahadur Shah Zafar I don't even consider a poet.')

However, there are several scholars, like Aslam Parvez, who hold the opposite view. The debate about Zafar's skill and achievements as a poet will probably never be settled one way or another. But there is no denying Zafar's talent as an artist. A man of many parts, the Emperor was deeply interested in music and would himself compose thumris and khayals. The Delhi school of Hindustani music, or the Dilli gharaana, traces its lineage to Mian Ajmal Khan, popularly called 'Mian Achpal', a great musician belonging to the school of Hindustani music known as Qawwal Bachche. Zafar had appointed Mian Achpal as the Court Musician and considered him his ustaad. Mian Achpal's illustrious disciple, Mir Qutab Bakhsh, popularly called 'Tanras Khan', would travel with Zafar during his summer sojourns to Mehrauli and teach him the art of composing khayals. Zafar not only patronized poets and artists, he also had great regard for scholars and reformers. In 1842, he bestowed upon Sir Syed Ahmad Khan—the great educationist and founder of what is now the Aligarh Muslim University—the title of Jawwaad-ud Daulah (Scholar of the Land), originally conferred upon the reformer's grandfather, Syed Hadi, by Emperor Shah Alam II, in the middle of the eighteenth century. Later, Zafar conferred upon Sir Syed the further military title of Arif Jung, signifying the latter's inclusion into the nobility of Delhi.

Zafar was also a devout Sufi and a disciple of the highly revered poet-seer of his time, Shah Naseeruddin Naseer, alias Kaale Saheb. In fact, the Emperor would also himself accept disciples in the Sufi tradition of Piri and Mureedi (teacher and taught). It is said that before his rise to the Mughal throne, Zafar lived the life of a dervish in the Qila, in complete contrast to his three prodigal brothers, Mirza Jahangir, Salim and Babur. He firmly believed in the divinity of God:

> Kiski himaayat dhoondein hum aur kis se marham
>   chaahein Zafar
> Rakhte nazar hain apne khuda par vo hi hamaara haami
>   hai
>
> (Whose favour shall I seek and whom should I ask for
>   a cure, Zafar
> I keep an eye on my God, He alone is my benefactor.)

The pluralism that was intrinsic to the philosophy and lifestyle of many Sufis came naturally to Zafar. Born to a Hindu mother, he would celebrate the Hindu festivals of Holi, Dussehra and Diwali with as much fervour as he did the two Eids.

Zafar and his family were devotees of the thirteenth-century Sufi Saint Khwaja Qutubuddin Bakhtiyar Kaki and would often pay homage at his dargah at Mehrauli. In 1812, when Zafar's step-brother, Mirza Jahangir, was imprisoned by the British in Allahabad, his mother, Queen Zeenat Mahal, vowed to make offerings at the dargah if he was released. The prince was soon released and the queen organized a week-long multi-religious celebration at the dargah. The pluralist nature of this celebration appealed to the people of Delhi so much that they decided to convert it into an annual affair. Now called 'Phoolwalon ki Sair' ('Stroll of the Flower-sellers'), the celebration takes place every year with great pomp and show. During the celebration in his time, Zafar would move his court to a building adjacent to Bakhtiyar Kaki's dargah at Mehrauli. The building had been originally built by his father, but Zafar added an impressive gate and a baradari—a twelve-door pavilion—to the structure and renamed it Zafar Mahal. Inside the Mahal, he chose a spot for his own burial, next to the graves of his father and grandfather.

Zafar's idea of piety and his attitude to religion were closer to those of the ordinary people of his land than of austere theologians and the clergy. According to some of his biographers, he was predisposed to common, earthy beliefs—for instance, that pirs and saints possess supernatural powers. He had his own inner circle of astrologers, soothsayers and clairvoyants. As protection against 'the evil eye', he would himself use, and also distribute to his disciples, all kinds of charms and would regularly sacrifice animals, donate cows to the poor, bury eggs and order arrests of black magicians.[110] He was not only convinced of the existence of jinns but also believed that they were amongst his loyal subjects. When the British began the massacre of Delhi to crush the 1857 'mutiny', Zafar was initially unperturbed because his spiritual advisers had persuaded him to believe that no harm could come to an Emperor who was being protected by jinns.

Zafar was well aware that the Mughal throne he had inherited was a sham, and the Empire mere fiction. Even to travel up to the dargahs at Nizamuddin or Mehrauli from his Qila, he had to seek permission of the British Resident. As his two-decade-long symbolic rule progressed and years passed by, he became more and more distraught by a situation that he could do nothing about. Even age was not on his side. He felt worthless and helpless. A ghazal that has been ascribed to Zafar for years, but may or may not be his, depicts this deplorable condition rather lucidly. It opens with this sher:

> Na kisi ki aankh ka noor hoon na kisi ke dil ka qaraar
>   hoon
> Jo kisi ke kaam na aa sakey ma'in vo ek musht-e-ghubaar
>   hoon

> (Neither the light of anyone's eyes, nor the solace of
>   anyone's heart
> I am no use to anyone; I am just a fistful of dust.)

This ghazal was always believed to be one of Zafar's, though, interestingly, for almost a century after his death it did not appear in any of Zafar's published collections, despite the fact that oral tradition had for years attributed it to him. In 1958, for the first time, the ghazal was formally ascribed to Zafar in writing and included in a new collection of his works titled *Nawa-e-Zafar.* Twenty years before that, in 1938, the renowned Urdu poet Jan Nisar Akhtar, in an article published in *Suhail,* an Urdu periodical, had claimed that the ghazal had been authored by his father, the well-known poet Muztar Khairabadi (1862-1927) and that it was part of Muztar's handwritten diary, which had come into his possession. In 1963, in an article titled *Shah Zafar nahin, Muztar Khairabadi* ('Not Emperor Zafar but Muztar Khairabadi') which appeared in a Pakistani periodical, *Nigaar-e-Pakistan,* Yunus Hasani reiterated Jan Nisar's claim. Almost eighty years after Jan Nisar's startling revelation, in 2015, his son and Muztar's grandson, the celebrated lyricist and poet Javed Akhtar, published Muztar's collection of poems called *Khirman* and included this ghazal in it. Javed announced that he had found the original in his grandfather's handwritten diary passed on to him by his father.

Royalty has always loved being eulogized and Zafar was no different. In 1850, presumably on the recommendation of some of his advisors, including Hakim Ahsanullah Khan and Kaale Saheb, he commissioned Mirza Ghalib to write an account of the history of the Mughal Empire in Persian poetry and conferred upon him the titles of Dabir-ul-Mulk and Najm-ud-Daulah[111]. A bi-annual honorarium was fixed for him. Ghalib, who was continuously in debt, would rather have had a monthly remuneration. One day while in attendance in the royal court, Ghalib, who was aware of the Emperor's soft corner for adulatory poets, beseeched him in a longish poem to convert his bi-annual honorarium into a monthly one, holding that the practice of paying someone just twice a year was a slur on Mughal generosity:

Ae Shehenshah-e-aasmaan aurang
Ae jahaandaar-e-aaftaab aazaar

Baar-e-naukar bhi ho gaya sadd-shukr
Nisbatein ho gayin mushakhkhas chaar

Na kahoon aap se toh kis se kahoon
Mudda-e-zaroori-ul-izhaar

Kuchh khareeda nahin hai ab ke saal
Kuchh banaaya nahin hai ab ke baar

Raat ko aag aur din ko dhoop
Bhaad mein jaaein aise lail-o-nahaar

Meri tankhvaah jo muqarrar hai
Uske milne ka hai ajab hanjaar

Rasm hai murde ki chhe-maahi ek
Aur chhe-maahi ho saal mein do baar

Bas ke leta hoon har maheene qarz
Aur rehti hai sood ki takraar

Aap ka banda aur phiroon nanga
Aap ka naukar aur khaaoon udhaar

Meri tankhvaah kijiye maah-ba-maah
Ta na ho mujh ko zindagi dushwaar

Tum salaamat raho hazaar baras
Har baras ke hon din pachaas hazaar

(O Emperor! Adorner of the Throne!
O Sovereign shining like sun!

Thanks to you, now I am a servant too
And four relationships are thus identified with you

Whom shall I tell, if not you
The crucial issue that I must state?

Nothing have I bought this year
Nothing have I acquired this time

Fire in the night, sun in the day
Doomed be such days and nights

The salary that has been fixed for me
It is disbursed in a strange way

Like the dead are counted once in six months
This six-monthly practice is followed twice a year

Every month, I take a loan
And I'm reminded to pay interest

Your subject, with not a dress to wear
Your servant, sunk in debt

Grant me a monthly salary
so that my life isn't such a struggle.

May you live a thousand years
And may there be fifty thousand days to each year.)

Zafar was so impressed with this poetic appeal that, within minutes, he passed an order converting Ghalib's bi-annual honorarium into a monthly one.

However, though fond of adoration, Zafar remained God-fearing and never let his royal status touch his humility.

He believed that one who forgets God in luxury or rage fails the test of human-ness:

> Zafar aadmi usko na jaaniyega, ho vo kaisa hi sahib-o-fahm-o-zaka
> Jisey aish mein yaad-e-khuda na rahi, jisey taish mein khauf-e-khuda na raha
>
> (Don't consider him human, Zafar, howsoever intellectual or wise he may be
> Who, in luxury, doesn't remember God; who, in rage, doesn't fear Him.)

—

Zafar had been Emperor for twenty years when the Ghadar—the revolt of 1857—broke out. He was almost eighty-two, infirm and ailing, but the revolt jolted him out of his melancholic stupor. He himself hadn't proactively done anything to initiate the uprising, but the Indian sepoys of the East India Company who had risen in revolt found in the Mughal Emperor a figure under whom all of them could unite across religious, communal and territorial lines. Legal luminary A.G. Noorani explains the circumstances under which Zafar got involved in the Ghadar:

> Bahadur Shah was the one around whom both the [Hindu and Muslim] communities rallied as a symbol of revolt and unity...In him have still been centred the hopes and aspirations of millions. They have looked upon him as the source of honour and, more than this, he has proved the rallying point not only to Muhammadans, but to thousands of others with whom it was supposed that no bond of fanatical union could possibly be established.[112]

On 11 May 1857, sepoy regiments from Meerut, which had been among the first to revolt, reached Delhi and sought audience with their Emperor. It appears that Zafar, feeling guilty about his inaction and lack of resolve in the face of British atrocities, decided to meet them the next day and, sunk in emotion, promised them his full support. He immediately issued a Shaahi Farmaan (Royal Decree) calling upon all his subjects to join the revolt, clearly stating that he had decided to stand by his people. But the revolt failed, and terrible retribution followed. British forces began to slaughter captured sepoys and also the civilian population in towns and villages across Northern India. In places like Kanpur, the sepoys themselves had killed unarmed British families, and the British used this to legitimize their brutality. By the time Company forces reached Delhi, terror and tyranny had become their official policy. During the four-month siege of Delhi by the British forces, there was a wholesale massacre in Delhi in order to force Zafar and the rebel sepoys who now owed allegiance to him, to surrender.

Hakim Ahsanullah Khan, the Royal Physician and Zafar's advisor—whom many would later accuse of betraying Zafar—has recorded the developments that followed the arrival of the mutinying sepoys. A page from his fascinating account, which was published by the Journal of the Pakistan Historical Society in 1958, reads thus:

> I was in my house that evening and was unable to get out of the Fort owing to the vast crowd of sepoys in the Bazaar and at the principal Gate. On the morning of Friday [18 September] I sent a man who returned saying the door of the Diwan-i-Khas was closed. I heard nothing more. But in the afternoon of the same day one of the residents of the Fort ascertained the fact I have recorded [that the King had fled]. Being astonished I wrote a petition to the King asking the reason of his departure without informing me of it. In the evening

a reply came summoning me and saying that a verbal explanation of the King's bad case would be given me. In reply to the above I sent another petition in the morning stating that my bearers and syce had run off and that I had no means of travelling, that if His Majesty could furnish me with a conveyance I would go off at once to him. In the afternoon of Saturday two elephants came, on one of which I placed my things and on the other my brother Hakim Ghulam Najaf Khan and myself. We started for the Court towards the close of the afternoon. On the road the mutineer army abused me and called me a Christian. In short, I reached the King in the evening and at night the conversation turned on the conduct of the army to the King. The King said, 'Well, what could I do against them?'

In the morning I saw the whole army in retreat, and after them came Bakht Khan, with the Risaldars. He importuned the King go with him whithersoever he went. I said, 'You have just escaped to this place from the Fort, where will you wander with these runaways? We must now trust to our Fate. Be pleased to remain here. Wait for an answer to the mukhtarnamah sent yesterday to Captain Hodson (Hodson Sahib) by the Queen through Mirza Illahi Bakhsh. Perhaps some chance of bettering ourselves may turn up, though the time has gone for that.' The King then told Bakht Khan, that he could not go with him, saying, 'Whither will you wander in your ruined condition? If you could do anything why are you running away?' He answered, 'The Hakim who is in league with the English is leading you astray, you'll suffer for it in the end.' He then brought a palki and wished the King to start. At last I told the members of the Royal Family to talk to the King and not allow him to proceed, that if he did accompany Bakht Khan it would be a great misfortune. If he were seized his life would be in danger.

Many of the Royal Family forbade his going, and much abuse was bandied about. The officers, being unable to effect their object, went off.

A parwanah was written to Mirza Illahi Bakhsh to settle matters quickly and come over. The order was sent to the Arab Sarai (near Homayun's Tomb) forbidding any conflict with any of the Government (English) people who might come there. Several orders were sent in succession to the mutineer army not to encamp at the Tomb, but to go where they [wished].

In the afternoon Prince Muhammad Azim came with his troops and wished to encamp at the Tomb. He was ordered to go on, and not stop there, for His Majesty had lost all confidence in the rebel army.

In the morning Qadir Baksh came and he also asked the King to accompany the army. He also got his answer, and was told that the King would await his fate, that he now placed no trust in anyone but God. After 12 o'clock Mirza Illahi Bakhsh arrived and stated there was a pass for the safety of the Queen and Mirza Jawan Bakht and Samsham-ad-Daulah [the Hakim] and showed an English signature, probably Hodson Sahib's. He said that on condition that all present would lay down their arms and the King go off alone in his palki, he would be allowed to remain in the Queen's apartments, and that other particulars would be settled hereafter: that Maulvi Rajab Ali had come with 25 Sikh Sawars [of the British force] to the Tomb and that Hodson Sahib would come to meet the King.

Having reassured the King, and having started him and the Queen off, we went off too. The Maulvi [Rajab Ali] presented his nazr outside the Arab Sarai, and reassured the King, and when the cavalcade neared the city, having caused the palki to be put down, he wrote informing Captain Hodson that the party had got so far.

'Be pleased to come in person.' After a while he came, and I, having got down from the elephant, advanced to meet him and saluted him. He came near the King, took off his hat to him, and taking the party along with him came to the Delhi Gate of the city: Thence we arrived in front of the Fort. He told the Queen's party and all of us to go away and took the King with 8 or 10 men inside the Fort, by the Lahore Gate, to meet the General [Hodson].[113]

Zafar was charged and tried on four counts, two of aiding rebels, one of treason, and one of being party to the murder of forty-nine British residents of Delhi who had taken shelter in the Qila fearing massacre at the hands of the rebel sepoys. Soon, Act XIV of 1857 was enacted to provide for the trial and punishment of persons who had instigated 'mutiny and sedition' among the Forces of the East India Company and also for trial of offences against the State.[114] A court martial was conducted, presided over by a low-ranking army officer, one Lt. Col. Dawes of the Horse of Artillery. The prosecution was conducted by a Deputy Judge-Advocate General, one Major F.J. Harriott. A month-long trial commenced at the Diwaan-e-khaas where, until some weeks ago, the accused would grant audiences as Emperor of India to his few distinguished visitors. By now, Zafar was sick, feeble and almost unintelligible. He was kept imprisoned in a small room in the Qila and not given even a pen to write with. He waited for the ceaselessly painful days to end:

Subah ro-ro ke shaam hoti hai
Shab tadap kar tamaam hoti hai

(I weep the morning into evening
All night I tremble in restlessness.)

When the victory of British forces became certain, Zafar took refuge in Humayun's Tomb, near the dargah of Hazrat Nizamuddin which, at that time, was an area considered to be on the outskirts of Delhi. On 20 September 1857, English forces led by Major William Hodson surrounded the tomb and secured his surrender, on the condition that he would not be sentenced to death. Zafar was brought back to the Qila and imprisoned there. Percival Spear evocatively describes the aftermath of Zafar's surrender:

> For the citizens of Delhi the aftermath of the Mutiny was a case of the scorpions of Rehoboam following the whips of Solomon...they had been subjected to shortages and insecurity, to extortion and plunder...We may pass over the scenes which occurred during the actual fighting within the city, for no troops could be expected to be altogether restrained after the privations which the British Army had endured on the Ridge and the exertions it had made over a period of months. Hindus and Muslims were at first indiscriminately killed; women and children were however spared and respected. But it was the events after 20 September which burnt themselves into the consciousness of the Delhi people. 'In the city no man's life was safe,' reported Main-ud-din; 'all able-bodied men who were seen were taken for rebels and shot.' 'For several days after the assault,' wrote Mrs. Saunders (wife of the Commissioner of Delhi), 'every native that could be found was killed by the soldiers, women and children were spared.' 'The troops,' wrote Saunders himself, 'were completely disorganized and demoralized by the immense amount of plunder which fell into their hands and the quantity of liquor which they managed to discover in the shops of the European merchants of Delhi.' After this first collapse, the reaction of exhausted and over-wrought men, there followed a more systematic

reign of terror, which lasted for several months...There was much indiscriminate shooting besides drum-head court martials and summary hearings.[115]

The Emperor was spared, but not his sons. Hodson, while bringing back Zafar's three sons, Princes Mirza Mughal, Mirza Khazr Sultan and Mirza Abu Bakr, killed them near the Khooni Darwaza, opposite what is today the Maulana Azad Medical College. It is widely believed that their headless bodies were then hung in front of the Kotwali, the present-day Fountain Chowk opposite Gurudwara Sisganj Saheb in Chandni Chowk—the same place from where more than a hundred years ago, on 22 March 1739, Nadir Shah had begun his ruthless onslaught on the people of Delhi.

The aged and ailing emperor could hardly understand that he was facing a trial. He read out a short written defence in Urdu and denied any connection with the 'Mutiny', contending that he had been a helpless prisoner of the rebel sepoys. He did not cross-examine any witness. The prosecutor maintained that Zafar had engineered the revolt as part of a larger organized 'Islamic conspiracy'. On 9 March 1858, at 11 am, Hariott closed his final submissions. After four hours, at 3 pm the same day, all members of the court martial unanimously declared Zafar guilty 'of all and every part of the charges preferred against him' and sentenced him 'to be transported for the remainder of his days, either to one of the Andaman Islands or to such other place as may be selected by the Governor General in council'.[116]

On 7 October 1858, Zafar left Delhi for Rangoon on a bullock cart, accompanied by his wives, his two surviving sons and some servants.

In Burma, the ex-Emperor who was now a convicted life-prisoner, was met by the British Commissioner, Captain

H. Nelson Davies. The family was then incarcerated in a quarter near the Shwe Dagon Pagoda. Records say that the family was provided four rooms of sixteen square feet each and four Indian attendants—a peon, a water carrier, a washer-man and a sweeper. Zafar was denied pen, ink and paper but the poet in him was not yet dead. It is believed that the forlorn Emperor used a burnt stick to inscribe his last verses on a wall of his room. Generations of ghazal-lovers have grown up thinking that this oft-quoted and oft-sung ghazal was Zafar's last poem written by him in exile in Rangoon:

> Lagta nahin hai ji mera ujdey dayaar mein
> Kis ki bani hai aalam-e-napaayedaar mein
>
> Keh do in hasaraton se kahin aur ja basein
> Itni jagah kahaan hai dil-e-daagh-daar mein
>
> Kitna hai badnaseeb Zafar dafn ke liye
> Do gaz zameen bhi na mili koo-e-yaar[117] mein
>
> (My mind is not at rest in this ruined place
> In this unstable world, who has ever been happy?
>
> Tell these desires to find another home
> Where's the space for them in this charred heart?
>
> How unfortunate is Zafar, that for his burial
> He's denied even two yards of earth next to his beloved.)

Some scholars have, however, disputed the authorship of this ghazal and have claimed that it was actually written by Seemab Akbarabadi, a poet who was born much after Zafar's death and died in Karachi in 1951. The couplet which is believed to be the best of the best of this ghazal (haasil-e-ghazal sher) and is quoted most frequently is:

> Umr-e-daraaz maang ke laaye thay chaar din
> Do aarzoo mein kat gaye, do intezaar mein

(I had asked and I was granted a long life of four days
Two passed in desiring, and two in waiting
   [for fulfilment].)

Urdu academic Zaheer Ahmed Siddiqui has taken pains to establish that this is, indeed, Seemab's couplet and the first misra is actually this:

Umr-e-daraaz maang ke 'laayi thi' chaar din

([My] Long-life asked for, and was granted just four days.)

Those who dispute the authorship of the entire ghazal argue that since this couplet has been proved to have been authored by Seemab, the entire ghazal must have been written by him and, just because the verses seem to narrate the sad story of an exiled Emperor and the takhallus 'Zafar' occurs in the maqta, the ghazal cannot be ascribed to Zafar.[118] Despite this line of argument, the fact remains that the ghazal—without this one sher—is found in almost every compilation or selection of Zafar's poetry.

On 7 November 1862, almost six years after his conviction, Bahadur Shah Zafar died at the age of eighty-seven. Fearing a backlash, his last rites were performed in secrecy. The news of his death was made public only after a week of his burial. After twenty-four years of his death, his wife, Zeenat Mahal, also died in Rangoon and was buried next to him. In 1907, the British government agreed to erect a railing around the site of the emperor's grave with an inscription which read: 'Bahadur Shah, the ex-king of Delhi, died at Rangoon on November 7th 1862 and was buried near this spot.'

II

BAHADUR SHAH ZAFAR'S MEMORY, AND HIS IMAGE IN THE popular imagination—both as an emperor and a poet—is associated, and perhaps always will be, with 'Na kisi ki aankh ka noor hoon', the ghazal made famous by the great playback singer Mohammed Rafi, who sang it for the Bollywood film *Lal Qila* (1960), a romanticized telling of the 1857 revolt. But there are several other poems of Zafar's that are remarkable. The mood is often, but not always, melancholic. In fact, given the quiet despair and sadness that mark his best-known verses, the following couplets may surprise many readers. He is critical of the poet Sauda for the endless complaints in his poetry:

> Hum kehte Zafar hoti jo Sauda se mulaqaat
> Kyon karta basar aah-o-fughaan mein hai tu auqaat
>
> Tang aa ke jo humsaaya tere kehte hain ye baat
> Sauda teri faryaad se aankhon mein kati raat
>
> (Zafar, I would have told Sauda, had I met him
> Why do you waste your existence sighing and weeping?
>
> Fed up with you, even your neighbours complain
> 'Your endless laments, Sauda, keep us awake all night!')

But given how the Last Emperor's own poetry came to be full of lamentations, Sauda may well have replied with one of Zafar's own couplets and advised him to look within himself before pointing fingers at others:

> Na thi haal ki jab hamein apne khabar, rahe dekhte auron
> 　　ke aib-o-hunar
> Padi apni buraaiyon par jo nazar toh nigah mein koi
> 　　bura na raha

(When I wasn't aware of my self, I sat in judgement over
   everyone
When I noticed my own flaws, I could see no faults in
   anyone.)

The Last Mughal is also a conventional romantic, completely
mystified by the disorienting side-effects of falling in love.
In one of his famous ghazals, sung by a number of popular
singers in diverse styles—by Mehdi Hassan, Runa Laila and
Jagjit Singh, among others—he is at a loss to know why he
has suddenly become a stranger to himself:

> Baat karni mujhe mushkil, kabhi aisi toh na thi
> Jaisi ab hai teri mehfil kabhi aisi toh na thi
>
> Le gaya chheen ke kaun aaj tera sabr-o-qaraar
> Be-qaraari tujhe ae dil kabhi aisi toh na thi

> (I never had to struggle so much to say something
> Never was your gathering like this before.
>
> Who has snatched your patience and peace?
> O heart, you were never as restless as this before.)

Like all conventional lovers, Zafar is convinced that the
real world is full of betrayals and treachery:

> Hum ne duniya mein aa ke kya dekha
> Dekha jo kuchh so khvaab sa dekha
>
> Ab na dijiye Zafar kisi ko dil
> Ke jisey dekha be-wafa dekha

> (What have we seen upon coming to earth?
> Whatever we've seen was just a dream.
>
> Don't give your heart to anyone, Zafar
> Everyone I've met, I've found unfaithful.)

However, despite this stark realization, he is always game
for wine and romance:

Jaam hai sheesha hai saaqi bhi hai barsaat bhi hai
In dinon baada-kash din bhi hai aur raat bhi hai

Yaar hai, yaar ke saath Zafar bos-o-kinaar
Aur agar chaahiye kuchh baat toh vo baat bhi hai

(There's wine, goblet, wine-bearer, and there's rain too
Nowadays the day is intoxicated and the night too.

There's the beloved, and there's Zafar kissing and hugging
    her
And should you want something more, there's that too.)

Zafar is credited with some exceptional poetry in long metre—lambi beher—a feat not easy to achieve even for seasoned poets:

Ja kahiyo un se naseem-e-seher mera chaiyn gaya meri
    neend gayi
Tumhein meri na mujh ko tumhaari khabar mera chaiyn
    gaya meri neend gayi

Kehta hai yahi ro-ro ke Zafar meri aah-e-rasa ka hua
    na asar
Tere hijr mein maut na aai abhi mera chaiyn gaya meri
    neend gayi

(Go tell her, O morning breeze, I've lost my peace and
    my sleep
Neither do you know of my well-being, nor I of yours;
    I've lost my peace and my sleep.

This is what Zafar says, crying and wailing, 'My sighs
    have gone in vain'
Separated from you I haven't died yet, I've lost my peace
    and my sleep.)

K.C. Kanda, who has compiled some of Zafar's poetry and made an admirable effort to translate it into English, though sometimes inaccurately, maintains that the 'loss of

Zafar—the King—was the gain of Zafar—the poet'.[119] His position having been reduced to a mere titular one, he had no State functions to perform. He, therefore, immersed himself in art and poetry and soon created a court, and wrote poetry, of unique character.

Perhaps that art gave him solace as he lay dying, even when he composed lines soaked in sadness: 'Do gaz zameen bhi na mili koo-e-yaar mein.' ('...denied even two yards of earth next to his beloved.')

The spot Zafar had once chosen for his burial—the 'do gaz zameen'—in Zafar Mahal, near the grave of the Sufi saint Bakhtiyar Kaki in Mehrauli, would never receive his bones. Today, though a monument officially protected by the Archaeological Survey of India, Zafar Mahal is in a hopelessly dilapidated condition. Commercial and residential buildings have risen haphazardly around it, and illegal construction on its boundary walls continues right under the nose of the authorities. During the day, the precincts of the Mahal are used as gambling and drinking grounds by unemployed men in the vicinity. For fear of being assaulted, the lone guard posted at the imposing entrance turns a blind eye to what goes on inside, and the local police can't be bothered.

A road and some avenues have been named after the Emperor. But in history books there is barely a trace of his poetry, or of his struggle to find some dignity in circumstances imposed upon him by history; he is only portrayed as the most timid and pitiable sovereign India has ever had. In films and television serials he has appeared repeatedly as a tragic caricature. In Yangon—Rangoon— the story is a little different. The Burmese Muslims regard him as a Sufi saint and have converted his burial spot into a shrine. In 1991, some labourers digging a drain at the back of the shrine uncovered the brick-lined grave of the emperor three feet under the ground and twenty-five feet away from the shrine. The shrine is now managed by a trust called the Bahadur Shah Zafar Mausoleum Committee and has become a favourite tourist spot, especially for visiting statesmen, most of whom have heard of him only as a frail and feeble emperor, and not as an accomplished Urdu poet. Visitors to the shrine hardly value his literary stature.

Even among those who know Zafar as a poet and value his literary work, few would be aware that a lot of what he wrote was lost or destroyed in the aftermath of the Revolt of 1857. What survived and was later compiled as the *Kulliyyat-i-Zafar* (Complete Works of Zafar) is, perhaps, only half of his oeuvre. Zafar had already foretold this fate:

Pas-e-marg merey mazaar par jo chiraagh kisi ne jala diya
Usey aah daaman-e-baad ne sarey shaam hi se bujha diya

(After my death, if someone were to light a lamp on my grave
Alas, it would be blown out by the first evening breeze.)

III

SELECTED POEMS OF ZAFAR

I

Baat karni mujhe mushkil kabhi aisi toh na thi
Jaisi ab hai teri mehfil kabhi aisi toh na thi

Le gaya chheen ke kaun aaj tera sabr-o-qaraar
Be-qaraari tujhe ae dil kabhi aisi toh na thi

Chashm-e-qaatil meri dushman thi hamesha lekin
Jaise ab ho gayi qaatil kabhi aisi toh na thi

Unki aankhon ne khuda jaane kiya kya jaadu
Ke tabiyat meri maail kabhi aisi toh na thi

Kya sabab tu jo bigadta hai Zafar se har baar
Khu teri, hoor-shamaail, kabhi aisi toh na thi

(I never had to struggle so much to say something
Never was your gathering like this before.

Who has snatched your patience and peace?
O heart, you were never as restless as this before.

The assassin's gaze was always my enemy
But never was it as lethal as this before.

God knows what magic her eyes have played on me
Never was I drawn to anyone like this before.

Why do you get so angry with Zafar all the time?
Your nature, O angel-face, was never like this before.)

2

Ya mujhe afsar-e-shaahaana banaaya hota
Ya mera taaj gadaayaana banaaya hota

Apna deewaana banaaya mujhe hota tu ne
Kyon khirad-mand banaaya, na banaaya hota

Khaaksaari* ke liye garche banaaya tha mujhe
Kaash khaak-e-dar-e-janaana banaaya hota

Nashsha-e-ishq ka gar zarf diya tha mujh ko
Umr ka tang na paimaana banaaya hota

Sufiyon ke jo na tha laayaq-e-sohbat toh mujhe
Qaabil-e-jalsa-e-rindaana banaaya hota

Roz maamoora-e-duniya mein kharaabi hai Zafar
Aisi basti se toh veeraana banaaya hota

(You should have sent me to earth as a Royal Officer
Or given me a beggar's bowl for a crown.

---

*The word 'khaaksaar' literally means 'someone who touches dust'
but is used in Urdu to refer to a person who is 'humble' and, hence,
'khaaksaari' would refer to 'humility' or 'humbleness'. In this couplet,
however, Zafar uses the word in both in its literal as well as allegorical
meanings.

You should have made me your [senseless] deewaana*
You made me wise, you shouldn't have.

If you've made me a creature of humility**
You should have made me the dust of the beloved's house.

If you've bestowed on me the ability to get drunk on love
You shouldn't have made the goblet of life so small.

If I wasn't worthy of the company of Sufis, I should have
Been made fit for the assembly of the drunk.

This teeming world is wrecked anew every day, Zafar
A desolate ruin would be a better habitation than this.)

3

Ja kahiyo un se naseem-e-seher, mera chaiyn gaya meri
    neend gayi
Tumhein meri na mujh ko tumhaari khabar, mera chaiyn
    gaya meri neend gayi

Na haram mein tumhaara yaar pata, na suraagh daiyr
    mein hai milta
Kahaan ja ke dekhoon ma'in jaaoon kidhar, mera chaiyn
    gaya meri neend gayi

Kehta hai yahi ro-ro ke Zafar, meri aah-e-rasa ka hua
    na asar
Tere hijr mein maut na aai abhi, mera chaiyn gaya, meri
    neend gayi

(Go tell her, O morning breeze, I've lost my peace and
    my sleep
Neither do you know of my well-being, nor I of yours;
I've lost my peace and my sleep.

Neither are you found in the mosque, my friend, nor is
    there a trace of you in the temple

---

*The word 'deewaana' literally means 'mad' or 'crazy' but is used in
Urdu poetry for a person who is madly in love with someone.

**See footnote above, about 'khaaksaari'.

Where do I look for you? Where do I go? I've lost my
peace and my sleep.

This is what Zafar says, crying and wailing, 'My sighs
have gone in vain.'
Separated from you I haven't died yet, I've lost my peace
and my sleep.)

4

Lagta nahin hai ji mera ujdey dayaar mein
Kis ki bani hai aalam-e-napaayedaar mein

Keh do in hasaraton se kahin aur ja basein
Itni jagah kahaan hai dil-e-daagh-daar mein

Kaanton ko mat nikaal chaman se, O baaghbaan
Ye bhi gulon ke saath pale hain bahaar mein

Bulbul ko baaghbaan se na saiyyaad se gila
Qismat mein qaid likkhi thi fasl-e-bahaar mein

Kitna hai badnaseeb Zafar dafn ke liye
Do gaz zameen bhi na mili koo-e-yaar mein

(My mind is not at rest in this ruined place
In this unstable world, who has ever been happy?

Tell these desires to find another home
Where's the space for them in this charred heart?

Don't turn out the thorns from the garden, O gardener
Even they have grown up with flowers in spring

Neither with the gardener nor with the hunter does the
nightingale have any complaints
She was simply destined to be imprisoned in springtime

How unfortunate is Zafar, that for his burial
He's denied even two yards of earth next to his beloved.)

(As explained earlier, some scholars have disputed the authorship of
this ghazal and have claimed that the ghazal, or at least part of it,
was actually written by Seemab Akbarabadi.)

5

Na kisi ki aankh ka noor hoon, na kisi ke dil ka qaraar
   hoon
Jo kisi ke kaam na aa sakey, main vo ek musht-e-ghubaar
   hoon

Na toh ma'in kisi ka habeeb hoon, na toh main kisi ka
   raqeeb hoon
Jo bigad gaya vo naseeb hoon, jo ujad gaya vo dayaar
   hoon

Mera rang-roop bigad gaya, mera yaar mujh se bichhar
   gaya
Jo chaman fizaan mein ujad gaya, ma'in usi ki fasl-e-
   bahaar hoon

Paye faateha koi aaye kyon koi chaar phool charhaaye
   kyon
Koi aa ke shama jalaaye kyon ma'in vo bekasi ka mazaar
   hoon

Ma'in nahin hoon naghma-e-jaan fishaan mujhe sun ke
   koi karega kya
Ma'in badey birog ki hoon sada kisi dil-jaley ki pukaar
   hoon

(Neither the light of anyone's eyes, nor the solace of
   anyone's heart
I am no use to anyone; I am just a fistful of dust.

Neither anyone's friend, nor anyone's rival
The one that is ruined, I am that fate, the one that is
   wrecked, that land.

My beauty is ravaged, my beloved is separated from me
The garden that was ruined by autumn, I am the harvest
   of its spring.

Why should anyone say a requiem, why should anyone
   offer flowers

Why should anyone come to light a candle? I am the tomb of destitution.

I am not a soul-inspiring song, why would one listen to me?

I am the voice of a sick man, I am the cry of the broken-hearted.

(As explained earlier, some scholars have disputed the authorship of this ghazal, too, and have claimed that it was actually written by Muztar Khairabadi.)

SHAIKH MOHAMMAD IBRAHIM ZAUQ
The Poet Laureate
(1788–1854)

In dinon garche Dakan mein hai bohot qadr-e-sukhan
Kaun jaaye Zauq par Dilli ki galiyaan chhor kar

(Although poetry is greatly valued in the
Deccan these days
Zauq, who would trade that for the lanes of Delhi?)

Ab toh ghabra ke ye kehte hain ke mar jaaeinge
Mar ke bhi chaiyn na paaya toh kidhar jaaeinge

(Now we're fed up, we say we'll die
What if there is no peace even in death?
Where will we go then?)

I

IN AN UNKNOWN GRAVE IN A DIRTY CORNER OF A CROWDED
furniture market in Delhi's Paharganj area, lies buried
Shaikh Mohammad Ibrahim Zauq, Poet Laureate of the
last Mughal Court. It is not a fate Zauq would have
imagined for himself. Though not as extraordinary a poet
as the others profiled in this volume, he was the ustaad
of Emperor Bahadur Shah Zafar and, owing to his royal
position, literally ruled the world of Urdu poetry in the
mid nineteenth century. Through stories of his legendary
rivalry with Ghalib, his coterie of rich nobles and peers, his
caucus of ardent admirers and disciples, his near veneration
within and outside of the Qila-e-Moalla, Zauq emerges as
an imposing figure, presiding over a parallel empire—an
empire of verse and rhyme.

Books on the life and works of Zauq are small in number
and it is somewhat strange that all of them borrow almost
all their content from Maulana Muhammad Hussain Azad's
Aab-e-Hayaat—arguably the most widely-read commentary
on classical Urdu poetry. Zauq's father, Shaikh Mohammad
Ramzan, belonged to Shahpur, a village near the Budhana
town of what is now District Muzaffarnagar in Uttar
Pradesh, and had travelled to Delhi in search of employment.
Though a poor soldier once, he had the distinction of being a
remarkable storyteller and raconteur of historical facts. His
reputation as a dependable, trustworthy and fine gentleman
had persuaded a local noble, Nawab Lutf Ali Khan,[120] to
appoint him as the caretaker of his haramsara (seraglio).
Zauq was the only son of Ramzan. In a beautiful example
of literary pun, Azad uses the name of Zauq's father to
eulogize Zauq as the greatest poet of his time:

Us waqt kisey khabar hogi ki is 'Ramzan' se vo chaand
niklega, jo aasmaan-e-sukhan par Eid ka chaand ho kar
chamkega.[121]

Who would have known then that that the moon which
rose from this 'Ramzan' would shine in the sky of poetry
like the [elusive] crescent moon of Eid.

In Delhi, Zauq lived in a posh neighbourhood in Kabuli
Darwaaza[122], then inhabited by the elite of the city. The area
had earlier been home to Sauda. Though Kabuli Darwaaza
boasted of huge mansions, Zauq's house was perhaps one
of the smallest and most modest houses there. Today, no
remnants of this neighbourood can be found. According
to Zauq's biographer, Tanvir Ahmad Alvi, all the houses
were demolished after 1857 and the area was subsequently
acquired to build the Old Delhi Railway Station which
became operational in 1864, with its vast net of warehouses,
platforms and railway lines.[123]

At a young age, Zauq was admitted to a school run
by Hafiz Ghulam Rasool, a well-known educationist of
the time. Though a teacher by profession, Hafiz sahib
had a penchant for Urdu poetry and himself wrote under
the takhallus 'Shauq'. In this literary ambience, Zauq got
interested in poetry, and it gave him some kind of spiritual
happiness. He had learnt various couplets of the then
renowned poets by heart and would recite them at the
drop of a hat. In *Hayaat-e-Zauq* (Life of Zauq), Ahmad
Husain Lahori writes that even as a child Zauq would visit
shrines and pray: 'Ilaahi mujhe sher kehna aa jaaye.'[124]
('Lord, grant me the art of writing poetry.') Then, one fine
morning, when he was still a child, he suddenly uttered two
couplets—almost miraculously—and thus began the journey
of Zauq, the poet. The takhallus 'Zauq', which literally

means 'taste' (and is used in the sense of having a taste for the finer things of life), was obviously inspired by the takhallus of his first ustaad, Hafiz Ghulam Rasool Shauq.

After graduating from Hafiz saheb's school, Zauq was admitted for further education to the madrasa of Maulvi Abdul Razzaq. It was here that Zauq actually began showing his poetic mettle and met some of his closest friends, including Nawab Lutf Ali Khan's nephew, Mir Kazim Husain Beqaraar, who would later play an important role in his life. The story of Zauq's education will not be complete without describing, in some detail, his relationship with Shah Naseeruddin Naseer. If Zauq's Delhi boasted of many a young poet, it also prided itself on being home to many an experienced ustaad, the most towering among them being the poet-seer Shah Naseer—popular as Kaale Saheb—who tutored many numbers of the Mughal royalty. He was also close to both Ghalib and Zafar and was the ustaad of Momin. It is believed that one day Beqaraar recited a beautiful ghazal that he had recently penned. Zauq, who knew Beqaraar to be an average poet, asked him how his poetry had suddenly improved so greatly. On being told by Beqaraar that this was because he had recently been accepted as a disciple by Shah Naseer, Zauq requested Beqaraar to take him along to his new ustaad. It is said that Shah Naseer was so impressed with Zauq's poetic prowess, that not only did he agree to be Zauq's ustaad, but was soon also taking him along to mushairas as his favourite shaagird, or disciple. Unsurprisingly, this didn't make Zauq's original ustaad, Hafiz Ghulam Rasool Shauq, very happy. However, despite Hafiz sahib's displeasure, Zauq continued attending mushairas with Shah Naseer.

But Zauq's relationship with Shah Naseer was not to last. As Zauq's poetic skills improved, he did not find it necessary to consult his new ustaad for every poem he would write and, on the other hand, the accolades he began to earn did not exactly please his legendary ustaad. The rift between the two grew almost by the day. Azad writes in *Aab-e-Hayaat* that once Zauq wrote a ghazal in the style of Sauda and read it out to Shah Naseer. Though it was customary for poets to seek inspiration from the works of great poets of yesteryears, Naseer considered Zauq far too junior to attempt this and publicly reprimanded him for trying to compete with Sauda: 'Ustaad ki ghazal par ghazal kehta hai? Ab tu Mirza Rafi (Sauda) se bhi ooncha udne laga?'[125] ('How dare you write in the style of the ustaad? You'll fly higher than Mirza Rafi (Sauda), will you?')

This incident made Zauq defiant, and emboldened him even further. He began writing with greater confidence, testing new waters, and began reciting in mushairas without an ustaad. Azad also adds another angle to this souring of the relationship between Zauq and Naseer, which is best described in his own words:

> Zyaada qabaahat ye hui ki Shah sahib ke sahebzaade, Shah Wajihuddin Nayyar, jo tabiyat ki burraaqi mein apne waalid ke khalf-ul-rasheed thay, unki ghazlon mein tawaarud, ya khuda jaane kis ittefaaq se, vahi mazmoon paaye gaye (jo Zauq ki ghazlon mein thay).[126]

> (What made things worse was that Shah sahib's son, Shah Wajihuddin Nayyar, who, in terms of having an acerbic temper, was the true inheritor of his father, began writing, whether by accident or God knows what coincidence, about the same subjects in his ghazals [as were found in Zauq's].)

Around 1806, when Zauq was about eighteen, Shah Naseer travelled to Deccan for a fairly long stint and, during his absence from Delhi, Zauq's fame spread rather quickly, making his relationship with an envious Nayyar and, consequently, with Nayyar's protective father even more hostile.

The Qila-e-Moalla, despite the collapse of the Mughal Empire and the straitened circumstances of the Emperor, frequently played host to a large number of poets, writers and artists. These included Hakim Sanaullah Khan Firaq (not to be confused with the famous Firaq Gorakhpuri, who was born decades later), Mir Ghalib Ali Syed (not to be confused with Mirza Ghalib), Hafiz Abdul Rehman Khan Ahsaan, Burhanuddin Khan Zaar, Hakim Qudratullah Qasim, his son Mir Izattulah Ishq, Mian Shakeba (a disciple of Mir Taqi Mir), Mirza Azeem Beg (a disciple of Sauda) and Mir Qamaruddin Minnat and his son, Mir Nizamuddin Mamnoon. For an Urdu poet the greatest honour would be an invitation to recite at the royal mushaira in the Qila. Like most poets, Zauq too had an ardent desire to be associated with the Qila. His friend Beqaraar worked for the royal family and was engaged in the personal staff of Bahadur Shah Zafar who the then Wali-ahad, the heir apparent or crown-prince. On the advice of a few well-wishers, Zauq persuaded Beqaraar to introduce him to the Wali-ahad, which Beqaraar did. In or around 1807, when he was less than twenty years old, Zauq became a regular visitor to the Qila, and the Wali-ahad soon became extremely fond of his poetry.

The Wali-ahad was himself a poet and, like many other princes, also had an ustaad—in his case, the much-in-demand Shah Naseer. When Shah Naseer migrated to Deccan for some years, Zafar asked Beqaraar to help him improve his ghazals, but Beqaraar soon found a high-ranking position in the secretariat of a British Officer, John

Elphinstone (later Lord Elphinstone), and he too left for the South. It was then that Zauq was called upon to advise Zafar on his poetry, which the young poet began to do, but irregularly. The story goes that once, Zauq visited the Qila after a short absence and found Zafar practising archery. On seeing Zauq, Zafar said to him:

> Miyaan Ibrahim, Ustaad toh Dakhan gaye. Kazim Husain udhar chaley gaye. Tum ne bhi hamein chhor diya.

> (Miyaan Ibrahim, the ustaad has migrated to Deccan. Kazim Husain [Beqaraar] has gone to that corner. You have also left me.)

Zauq replied, with the usual courtesies, that he could never forget the Wali-ahad. Zafar handed him a newly-composed ghazal and asked him to 'mend' it. Zauq thought for a while and then recited the ghazal with some improvements. Zafar was so fascinated with the improved version that he requested Zauq to visit him more frequently and suggest improvements in his future poems too, which Zauq began to do. After some time, he was formally appointed as the Wali-ahad's ustaad and a monthly remuneration of four rupees was fixed for him. The Emperor, Akbar Shah II, it seems, was as impressed with Zauq's poetry as was his son and, following a qaseedah written by Zauq in his praise, conferred upon him the title of Khaqaani-e-Hind (Khaqaani of India) after the great twelfth-century Persian poet.

Akbar Shah II died in September 1837 and Zafar succeeded him as Emperor. Immediately upon Zafar's coronation, Zauq wrote an impressive and longish qaseedah' which began with the following couplets, comparing him to a shining sun that brightens up everything in the world:

> Hain aaj jo yoon khushnuma noor-e-seher rang-e-shafaq
> Partau hai kis khursheed ka noor-e-seher rang-e-shafaq

Ye josh-e-nasreen-o-saman ye lala-o-gul ka chaman
Gulshan mein goya chha gaya noor-e-seher rang-e-shafaq

(If they are so pleasing today, the morning light, the
    colour of twilight
The splendour of which sun are they, this morning light,
    this colour of twilight?
This blossom of wild rose and jasmine, this garden of
    tulips and flowers
As if the flower garden bathes in the morning light, the
    colour of twilight.)

Overwhelmed by the poetic adulation, the Emperor
appointed him Malik-ul-Shoara (literally, 'King of Poets',
but used to refer to the Poet Laureate). Though the position
of Malik-ul-Shoara was reasonably high-ranking in the
hierarchy of the Qila-e-Moalla, Zauq continued to be paid
the meagre monthly stipend of four rupees that was fixed for
him when he had joined as the ustaad of the Wali-ahad. He
also continued to live in his small house in Kabuli Darwaaza
rather than move to a state accommodation in the Qila.
The Treasurer of the Mughal Court, Mirza Mughal Baig, it
seems, did not consider the position of Poet Laureate grand
enough to be equated with other similar positions in the
Court. As long as Baig remained the Treasurer, there were
only minor enhancements in Zauq's monthly remuneration,
and the highest it rose to was thirty rupees—an amount far
too low for the status that Zauq enjoyed. It was only when
Nawab Hamid Ali Khan succeeded Mirza Mughal Baig as
Treasurer after many years that Zauq's remuneration was
raised to a respectable figure of hundred rupees a month.
However, Zauq never complained. Zafar, though a feeble
ruler, who couldn't even command his own Treasurer to
enhance Zauq's remuneration, had the greatest reverence for

Zauq. This royal veneration made Zauq a highly respected figure in and outside the Qila. Zauq was more than happy with the admiration he received from the Emperor and was far too devoted to him to grumble about his remuneration.

Zauq remained the Emperor's ustaad and the Poet Laureate of the Mughal Court for seventeen years, till he died in 1854. During this period, he wrote more than 350 ghazals and about 60 qaseedahs. He firmly believed that his poetry would make him immortal:

> Rehta sukhan se naam qayaamat talak hai Zauq
> Aulaad se rahe yahi do pusht chaar pusht

> (Poetry makes your name known till eternity, O Zauq
> Children make it known only for a generation or two.)

Zauq had a vibrant literary life even outside the Qila. He had close associations with many of the city's elite and aristocrats who would invite him to chair literary gatherings and preside over mushairas. His life narratives, however, are so inextricably intertwined with episodes relating to the Qila that it is difficult to divorce the two and think of an incident involving the poet outside his royal position.

With Nawab Mirza Ilahi Bakhsh Khan Maaroof, he shared a special friendship. Ilahi Bakhsh was the father of Hatim Zamani Begum, the second wife of Bahadur Shah Zafar's son, Mirza Fathul Mulk Bahadur, alias Mirza Fakhru, who would later be designated as the last Wali-ahad. It is believed that Ilahi Bakhsh later served as a spy for the British and would provide to them sensitive information relating to the Qila. When Zauq was about twenty, Ilahi Bakhsh, having heard about his talent as a young poet, had invited him for a cup of tea. During the course of the tea, Ilahi Bakhsh requested Zauq to recite his verse. Zauq had just penned a fresh ghazal and when he recited the highly romantic matla (opening couplet), the Nawab fell head over heels for his poetry and thus began a long journey of friendship, camaraderie and admiration:

> Nigaah ka vaar tha dil par dharakne jaan lagi
> Chali thi barchhi kisi par kisi par aan lagi

> (Her lethal gaze sought my heart, but my soul began to tremble
> Her spear was directed at one, but hit the other.)

But there was one prominent Dilliwaala who never became part of Zauq's inner circle. This was Mirza Ghalib, nine years Zauq's junior, who had acquired quite a reputation as a poet even in his youth but had gained only limited access to the Qila-e-Moalla. Zauq, being a stickler for traditional values and etiquette, did not like the bohemian and nonconformist Ghalib at all, and Ghalib believed that his entry into the Mughal Court was being impeded by Zauq. He did not consider Zauq a great poet, either. There was no love lost between the two and each would frequently try to show the other up as a second-rate poet. The resulting literary skirmishes provided regular entertainment to the people of Delhi.

Even though Zauq continued to live in a small house in Kabuli Darwaaza, he would move around the city in style, in a palanquin, observing royal decorum and protocol, and would usually be accompanied by a few of his admirers and hangers-on. Once, when he was going somewhere with some followers in tow, Ghalib publicly sneered at him, commenting that his only claim to fame was his royal connection: 'Hua hai sheh ka musaahib phirey hai itraata.' ('Having become the King's companion, he struts around, puffed up.')

Zauq's admirers made a strong complaint to the Emperor. In the next mushaira at the Qila, Zafar asked Ghalib if he had actually made this comment. Ghalib admitted its authorship but added that it was not a comment on Zauq; it was the first line of the maqta of his latest ghazal, which he had composed upon receiving the invitation for the royal mushaira. The Emperor asked him to recite the whole maqta, and Ghalib immediately obliged:

Hua hai sheh ka musaahib phirey hai itraata
Wagar na sheher mein Ghalib ki aabroo kya hai

(Having become the King's companion, he struts around, puffed up
Otherwise, what reputation does Ghalib command in the city?)

Ghalib's poetic genius won the day for him and the matter was closed. However, on another occasion, Ghalib had to apologize to Zauq, clarifying that he had not intended to make the royal ustaad the object of his sarcasm. Zafar's son Prince Mirza Jawan Bakht was getting married and lavish wedding ceremonies had been planned. It was customary for well-known poets to be asked to compose wedding poems, called sehra, for the bridegroom. On the request of Jawan Bakht's mother Zeenat Mahal Begum, the most influential of Zafar's queens, Ghalib composed a remarkable sehra for the Prince which ended with this maqta:

Hum sukhan-fehem hain,Ghalib ke tarafdaar nahin
Dekhein is sehre se keh de koi behtar sehra

(We appreciate good poetry, we're not partial to Ghalib
Let's see if someone can compose a better sehra than this.)

Zafar thought, and perhaps rightly so, that this was a comment on Zauq who, despite not being as good a poet as Ghalib, had been appointed Poet Laureate. He asked Zauq to compose a sehra in reply to Ghalib's. Zauq wrote an equally remarkable sehra in which he responded to Ghalib's maqta with this sarcastic couplet:

> Jisko daawa ho sukhan ka ye suna do usko
> Dekh is tarah se kehte hain sukhanwar sehra

> (He, who stakes claim over good poetry, go tell him
> This is how good poets write a sehra.)

Ghalib realized that his maqta had not gone down well with either the Emperor or his ustaad. It was all right to needle and make snide remarks that could later be denied, but this time he had been too direct. He did not want to get on the wrong side of these powerful men by publicly humiliating the royal ustaad and, consequently, showing disrespect to the Emperor himself. To redeem himself and pre-empt any future damage, he immediately penned an apology in the form of a qita, a quadruplet, which included the following verses:

> Kya kam hai ye sharaf ke Zafar ka ghulaam hoon
> Maana ke jaah-o-mansab-o-sarwat nahin mujhe

> Ustaad-e-Sheh se ho mujhe purkhaash ka khayaal
> Ye taab ye majaal ye taaqat nahin mujhe

> Maqte mein aa padi hai sukhan-gustaraana baat
> Maqsood us se qata-e-mohabbat nahin mujhe

> (Is it not a singular honour that I am a slave of Zafar?
> Agreed, I don't have position, rank or power.

> To think of quarrelling with the royal ustaad
> Such nerve, such audacity, such strength I don't possess.

> An impudent thought has crept into the maqta
> But disrespect was not my intention in any way.)

It seems that even this apology did not yield the desired result and the Emperor remained displeased with Ghalib for quite some time. This incident and the verses associated with it have become legendary. Ghalib's misras 'hum sukhan-fehem hain Ghalib ke tarafdaar nahi*n*' and 'ye taab ye majaal ye taaqat nahi*n* mujhe' are today used idiomatically. More than a hundred years after this incident, Kaif Bhopali, most popular for having composed some songs for the film *Pakeezah* (1972), wrote:

> Janab-e-Kaif ye Dilli hai Mir-o-Ghalib ki
> Yahaan kisi ki taraf-daariyaan nahin chaltin

> (Dear Kaif, this is the Delhi of Mir and Ghalib
> Taking sides doesn't work here at all.)

But it was also the Delhi of Zauq. Like Mir and Ghalib, he was in love with Delhi. Despite the modest salary that he received from an impoverished royalty, and despite more lucrative opportunities in the Deccan that even his ustaad Shah Naseer could not turn down, he refused to leave the city: 'Kaun jaaye Zauq par Dilli ki galiyaa*n* chhor kar'. Even today, lovers of Delhi express their attachment to the city with this line.

Zauq lived to the age of sixty-six. He died in 1854, three years before the Ghadar of 1857, and was thus spared the horror and agony of the bloodbath in its aftermath. In early October 1854, he had come down with high fever and a severe gastrointestinal condition. The fever subsided in three days but the abdominal disease could not be controlled and became the cause of his untimely death on 18 October. Though the Emperor wanted Zauq to be buried in the royal graveyard inside the Qila-e-Moalla, in his lifetime Zauq had himself expressed a desire to be buried near Dargah Qadam

Sharif (Shrine of the Holy Foot), not far from where he lived. Zauq's wishes were honoured. As news of his death spread, a cloud of gloom engulfed the literati of Delhi. Even Ghalib went into a state of shock and depression, perhaps in realization of the uncertainty of life and the futility of one-upmanship. Scores of dirges and elegies were written in Persian and Urdu and the mourning continued for weeks.

II

ZAUQ'S POETRY IS DISTINCTIVE FOR HIS VERY 'CORRECT' AND precise style. He is both a perfectionist and a conformist. He is very particular about the established conventions and forms of ghazal-writing and never deviates from them. Zauq does not believe in experimenting. His works are a testament to the classical style of romantic Urdu poetry which, after him, finds place in the works of his shaagird, Daagh Dehlvi.

He is a master of what is called the 'pure ghazal' (khaalis taghazzul ki shaayri), a highly romantic form of poetry:

> Waqt-e-peeri mein shabaab ki baatein
> Aisi hain jaise khvaab ki baatein
>
> Phir mujhe le chala udhar dekho
> Dil-e-khaana-kharaab ki baatein
>
> (In old age, talking of beauty
> Is like talking of dreams.
>
> Look how it takes me to her door yet again
> Ah, the ways of this ruined heart.)

In Urdu ghazal, the word 'kaafir' (literally, 'infidel') as a metaphor has different connotations. 'Kaafir nigaah', for instance, would mean a gaze that leads you astray. In a brilliant play of words, Zauq refers to his beloved's tresses as 'kaafir zulfein' and then calling his heart the Kaaba, rather deftly, uses the literal meaning of the word kaafir to tell her why she does not care for it:

> Zulfein teri kaafir unhein dil se mere kya kaam
> Dil Kaaba hai aur Kaaba Musalmaan ke liye hai

> (Your infidel tresses, what do they have to do with my heart?
> The heart is the Kaaba, and the Kaaba is only for the Muslim [the believer].)

Characteristic of Zauq's poetry is its colloquialism, the use of the idioms of spoken Urdu. *Kulliyaat-e-Zauq* (The Complete Works of Zauq) is full of couplets with Hindustani idioms, phrases and figures of speech used by the common people of Delhi—like 'tooti bolna' ('being famous all around'), 'lahu laga ke shaheedon mein milna' ('pretending to become a martyr'), 'ghar ka kaatne ko daudna' ('being haunted by loneliness') and 'kuein ka pyaase ke paas jaana' ('The mountain coming to Muhammad'). Sample a few:

> Hai qafas se shor ek gulshan talak faryaad ka
> Khoob tooti bolta hai in dinon sayyaad ka

> (From the prison to the garden, the noise of his pleas
> These days the prisoner is famous all around.)

> Gul us nigah ke zakhm-raseedon mein mil gaya
> Ye bhi lahu laga ke shaheedon mein mil gaya

> (Now the flower's been wounded by her gaze
> So here's another one pretending to be a martyr.)

> Din kata jaaiye ab raat kidhar kaatne ko
> Jab se vo paas nahin, daude hai ghar kaatne ko

(The day's been spent, now where should we spend the
　　night?
Ever since she's not close by, loneliness haunts me.)

Kehne laga ki jaata hai pyaasa kuein ke paas
Ya jaata hai kuan kahin tishna-dehen ke paas

(Does the thirsty man go to the well, he asked
Or does the well come to the parched mouth?)

Like a deprived lover, Zauq is unhappy that his beloved,
instead of meeting him, has sent him a bouquet of flowers
through someone else. He treats this as her insensitivity
towards his just desires, shown in passive defiance of the
etiquettes of love. Zauq uses a classic Hindustani idiom to
express his feelings:

Hamein nargis ka dasta ghair ke haathon se kyon bheja
Jo aankhein hi dikhaani theen dikhaate apni nazron se

The first line is easily translated:

Why did you send me a nargis bouquet through a
　　stranger?

The second line if translated somewhat literally would mean:

If you had to show me [what is in] your eyes, you should
　　have done it with your own eyes.

However, 'aankhein dikhaana' is a phrase commonly used
to mean 'showing defiance/anger'. What Zauq, therefore,
means is that if the beloved had to show her defiance or
anger, she should have done it in person rather than sending
the message by using a stranger as a courier.

One of the most celebrated Urdu poets of the twentieth
century, Firaq Gorakhpuri, in his magnum opus on classical
Urdu poets, *Andaaze*, has, in his imitable style, made a

fascinating comment on Zauq's expertise in using idioms and phrases as also on his pellucid, scintillating and free-flowing language:

> Zauq ko 'Ustaad Zauq' kaha jaata hai. Is khitaab ki mauzooniyat sirf is liye nahin musallam hai ke Zauq Badshaah ke Ustaad thay, balki is liye bhi hai ki mukhtalif-ul-unwaan ash'aar kehne mein rozmarrah muhaavron, kahaavaton, aise alfaaz aur fiqron ko jo ba-zaahir sheyr mein khapaaye nahin ja sakte thay, belaag bandh jaane mein, aur us sab ko le kar ta'aqeedon ka kaawa kaat'te hue kuchh shehsawaaron ki tarah yoon aage barh jaane mein, ki haath ka paani tak na hiley, Zauq apna saani nahin rakhte thay.[127]

(Zauq is called *Ustaad Zauq*. This title is appropriate not only because Zauq was the tutor of the Emperor but also because he had the unsurpassable knack of using—and so effortlessly—such commonplace idioms, sayings, words and phrases in his poetry that usually cannot be employed in a couplet. In weaving them together and moving forward like an elegant rider who makes sure that his ride is so smooth that even the glass of water in his hand does not spill, Zauq had no match.)

The distinguished Urdu academic Sadiq-ur-Rahman Kidwai maintains that the worth of Zauq lies not in any depth in his poetry but in his contribution to the linguistic heritage of Urdu:

> You will not find any depth or philosophical dimension in Zauq's poetry, like you find in Ghalib's or Mir's. But what you will find in it is the extensive use of the colloquial language of the Delhi of his time in a such a way that it makes his poetry a great medium of communication; and therein lies its appeal. The greatness of Zauq and

other poets like him lies in the fact that they took the
linguistic heritage of Urdu places.[128]

Zauq himself admits that, despite trying hard, he and others
like him failed to emulate the great Mir in ghazal-writing:

> Na hua par na hua Mir ka andaaz naseeb
> Zauq yaaron ne bohot zor ghazal mein maara

> (They couldn't, they just couldn't emulate Mir's style
> Zauq, the fellows worked hard on their ghazals.)

Zauq's own circumstances, the conventions he lived by,
are the subject of many of his verses. Here, for instance,
he revels in the company of old friends and chooses them
even over a messiah and a prophet:

> Ae Zauq, kisi hamdam-e-dereena ka milna
> Behtar hai mulaaqaat-e-Maseeha-o-Khizr se

> (O Zauq, to meet an old friend
> Is better than meeting the Messiah or Khidr.)

Messiah here refers to Jesus Christ, who is believed to
have had the power to infuse life in the dead and Khidr
was a prophet who had defied death by drinking an elixir
and would show the right path to people who went astray.
Zauq gives old friends a stature even higher than the one
accorded in scriptures to Christ and Khidr.

Having led a life full of decorum, protocol and
officialdom, Zauq is also aware that formality and
observance of customary etiquette is not easy to follow:

> Ae Zauq, takalluf mein hai takleef saraasar
> Aaraam mein hai vo jo takalluf nahin karta

> (O Zauq, in formality there is constant pain
> Those who don't get into formalities live in peace.)

In what is, perhaps, his most well-known, widely-read and widely-sung ghazal, Zauq acknowledges the inevitability of life and its many inescapable elements. The ghazal begins with these couplets:

> Laayi hayaat aaye, qaza le chali, chaley
> Apni khushi na aaye, na apni khushi chaley
>
> Behtar to hai yahi ki na duniya se dil lagey
> Par kya karein jo kaam na be-dillagi chaley
>
> (Life brought me in, death takes me away
> Neither did I come on my own, nor am I leaving at my will.
>
> It's best not to get attached to this world
> But what does one do, some things just don't get done without getting attached.[129])

Zauq has his own views on love and romance, which keep varying from ghazal to ghazal. He frequently allows his heart to rule over his mind:

> Ae Zauq, jaana hosh-o-khirad ki salaah par
> De ishq jo salaah vahi hai baja salaah
>
> (O Zauq, compared to the advice of reason and wisdom
> The advice given by love is the correct one.)

But he is also conscious of the ebb and flow of love:

> Jab kiya ishq ke dariya ne talaatum ae Zauq
> Toh kahin mauj bani aur kahin gardaab bana
>
> (When the river of love turned turbulent, O Zauq
> A wave appeared somewhere, and somewhere a whirlpool.)

In a monograph on Zauq, Kausar Mazhari maintains that the essence of Zauq lies in his resolve not to use any complex or complicated themes or to create unnecessary moods of sensuality or eroticism while dealing with love. The fact that Zauq looks at this subject from the standpoint of a common man, engrossed in his daily ordeals, as against incessantly fantasizing about it, is what distinguishes him from his contemporaries.[130]

In love, as in life, Zauq also often comes across as a practical, realistic man, one who prefers pragmatism over fantasy and despair:

Ab toh ghabra ke ye kehte hain ke mar jaaeinge
Mar ke bhi chaiyn na paaya toh kidhar jaaeinge

(Now we're fed up, we say we'll die
What if there is no peace even in death? Where will we
    go then?)

Elsewhere, he says we make our own choices. Life is short, it is best to be pragmatic:

Ae shama teri umr-e-tabiyyi hai ek raat
Hans kar guzaar ya isey ro kar guzaar de

(O Candle, your natural age is just one night
Spend it laughing or spend it crying.)

—

Zauq was a believer. He also had a deep sense of devotion towards the Prophet Muhammad. In what is present-day Paharganj, just north-west of the New Delhi Railway Station, in a nook called Qila in the Multani Dhanda market is situated a dilapidated mausoleum known as Dargah Qadam Sharif (Shrine of the Holy Foot). The mausoleum boasts of a stone on which, it is believed, is etched the footprint of the Prophet. The stone is said to have been brought for Sultan Firoz Shah Tughlak from Mecca in the fourteenth century. The shrine derives its name from this holy footprint. It is believed that Zauq used to visit the shrine to pay his respects to the Qadam Sharif, the holy footprint, every Thursday.

However, despite his religious beliefs, Zauq does not spare the mullah. Known to be a teetotaller, Zauq extols the virtues of intoxication almost like an alcoholic. He closes a purely romantic ghazal by advising that the only cure for the righteous mullah is that he be brought to the tavern:

> Zauq jo madrase ke bigdey hue hain mullah
> Un ko maikhaane mein le aao sanwar jaaeinge
>
> (Zauq, these mullahs spoilt by their madrasas
> Bring them to the tavern, they'll be set right.)

Of course, the common reference to alcohol in Urdu poetry is often a reference to being consumed by love and passion.

In another couplet, in an interesting use of the idiom 'munh kaala karna' ('to blacken one's face', that is, to shame oneself publicly, or to be publicly shamed), he mocks the two-faced preachers of morality who, while making public discourses on piety, crave to lead a life of desire and debauchery:

> Baaqi hai dil mein Shaikh ke hasrat gunaah ki
> Kaala karega munh bhi jo daarhi siyaah ki
>
> (The Shaikh still nurtures a desire for sin
> He has blackened his beard, he'll blacken his face too.)

In yet another incredible use of a Hindustani idiom, Zauq tells the devout that his faith is not so shaky as to be corrupted by having a drink or two:

> Zaahid sharaab peene se kaafir hua mai'n kyon
> Kya derh chullu paani mein imaan beh gaya

(O devout, why do you call me an infidel just because
I drink?
Is faith so puny it will drown in a palm-full of water?)

The second line draws from the Hindustani idiom 'chullu
bhar paani mein doob marna'. Literally translated as 'kill
oneself by drowning in a palm-full of water', the idiom is
used in the sense of being ashamed of oneself, or rather,
being asked to acknowledge the shame one has brought
upon oneself and kill or hide oneself away.

In a rather audacious couplet which, if written today,
would have earned the poet a fatwa, Zauq beseeches those
who drink to remember the distinct sound of liquor being
poured, comparing it with prayer calls from the mosque:

Ho ye labbaik-e-haram ya ye azaan-e-masjid
Mai-kasho, qulqul-e-meena ki sada yaad rahe

(Whether it is the pilgrimage call or the call to prayer
from the mosque
O drinkers, always remember the glug and gurgle of the
wine bottle.)

At the same time, he also advises that it is best to stay
away from the compulsive addiction of drinking. Again, he
uses an idiom—'munh lagaana'—which would translate as
'touching with (or bringing to) the mouth', but means to
pay heed to something or someone:

Ae Zauq, dekh dukhtar-e-raz ko na munh laga
Chhut'ti nahin hai munh se ye kaafir lagi hui

(O Zauq, don't touch that daughter of the grape with
your mouth
The infidel won't quit your lips once you bring it there.)

To both Zauq and Ghalib, kindness and basic humanity are
the true attributes of faith, not empty or heartless rituals.

Both these poets are disgusted by the appalling lack of compassion in their fellow-beings. While Ghalib laments:

> Bas ke dushwaar hai har kaam ka aasaan hona
> Aadmi ko bhi mayassar nahin insaan hona
>
> (It is difficult for all things to be easy
> As for man it isn't easy to be human.)

Zauq goes a step further, reserving particular scorn for preachers and other 'learned' men:

> Aadmiyyat aur shai hai, ilm hai kuchh aur shai
> Kitna tote ko parhaaya par vo haivaan hi raha
>
> (Humanity is one thing, knowledge quite another
> The parrot was taught so well, but he remained an
>   animal.)

Zauq believes in the oneness of mankind and declares that religious disputes are created by the wicked:

> Kya momin, kya kaafir, kaun hai sufi, kaisa rind
> Saare bashar hain bande haq ke, saare shar ke jhagdey
>   hain
>
> (What believer, what infidel? Who's the Sufi, who's the
>   drunk?
> All are but fellows of God, these are quarrels of the evil.)

—

Zauq was a master of qaseedahgoi—the art of writing a qaseedah, or panegyric in verse. About a sixth of his work consists of qaseedahs written in praise of either Akbar Shah II or Bahadur Shah Zafar. The qaseedah that Zauq wrote in praise of Emperor Akbar Shah II, and for which he was conferred the title of Khaqani-e-Hind, contains eighteen couplets in eighteen different languages or dialects. In his qaseedahs, Zauq shows the same facility in playing with the language which is typical to his ghazals. In two outstanding couplets found in one of his later qaseedahs, he describes his failing health and old age with grace and refinement:

Haddiyaan hain is tan-e-laaghar mein khas ki teeliyaan
Teeliyaan bhi vo jo hovein sau baras ki teeliyaan

Josh-e-giriya mein hua ye ustakhvaan-e-tan ka haal
Jis tarah gal jaati hain paani mein khas ki teeliyaan

(The bones in this frail body are like twigs of the khus
And twigs that are a hundred years old.

In my zeal for crying, the bones of my body
Have decayed like twigs decay in water.)

His bones were buried in his beloved Delhi, whose lanes he could not bear to be parted from. It is a pity that in the same Delhi, there is no trace of the house he lived in. On his grave in a filthy bylane called 'Koodakhatta' ('dump yard') near Gali No. 13 of the Multani Dhanda area in Paharganj, the Municipal Corporation built public conveniences in 1961. These lavatories continued to be there till about twenty years ago. In the late 1990s the Archaeological Survey of India, upon judicial intervention, acquired the property, demolished the lavatories and built a small memorial called 'Yaadgaar-e-Zauq' (Zauq's Memorial). The tiny enclosure which houses Zauq's grave has a couple of marble blocks with his couplets inscribed on them. It is usually locked. The Archaeological Survey of India, which has not cared to put up any description of the memorial, has erected a board outside announcing that the grave is a 'protected monument' of 'National Importance' and has posted a guard there who arrives and leaves at his own will. In search of Zauq, Anant Raina and I reached the crowded furniture market of Multani Dhanda one morning. It took us more than an hour to find the memorial. No one in the vicinity had either heard of Zauq or his memorial. We could locate it only with the help of a photograph that was published in *The Hindu*. When we showed it around, almost like the photograph of a missing person, some school-going boys said they had seen a similar structure near Koodakhatta but did not know what it was. We followed their directions and reached the 'monument'.

It is heartbreaking that Zauq lies buried in an abandoned corner, near a refuse dump, just a few minutes away from the Fort from where he once ruled the literary capital of Mughal India. On our return from Paharganj, consumed with the bitter realization that history will forget you unless it suits someone's political will, all we could do was to utter 'Amen' in response to what Zauq had written just three hours before his death:

Kehte hain aaj Zauq jahaan se guzar gaya
Kya khoob aadmi tha, khuda maghfirat karey

(They say, Zauq has left this world today
What a fine man he was, may he rest him in peace.)

III

SELECTED POETRY OF ZAUQ

I

Laayi hayaat aaye, qaza le chali, chaley
Apni khushi na aaye, na apni khushi chaley

Behtar to hai yahi ki na duniya se dil lagey
Par kya karein jo kaam na be-dillagi chaley

Hum se bhi is bisaat pe, kam honge bad-qimaar
Jo chaal hum chaley, so nihaayat buri chaley

Ho umr-e-Khizr bhi, toh kaheinge ba-waqt-e-marg
Hum kya rahe yahaan, abhi aaye, abhi chaley

Naazaan na ho khirad pe, jo hona hai ho vahi
Daanish teri, na kuchh meri daanishwari chaley

Duniya ne kis ka raah-e-fana mein diya hai saath
Tum bhi chaley chalo yoon hi jab tak chali chaley

Jaate hawa-e-shauq mein hain is chaman se Zauq
Apni bala se baad-e-saba ab kabhi chaley

(Life brought me in, death takes me away
Neither did I come on my own, nor am I leaving at my
    will.

It's best not to get attached to this world
But what does one do if nothing is achieved without
    attachment?

In this game of chess, bad players like me would be far
    and few
Every move that I made was a really bad one.

Even if I were granted immortality, at the time of death
    I'll say
'I've hardly lived here. I've only just arrived, and now
    it's time to leave.'

Don't take pride in your wisdom, whatever will be will be
Neither your intellect nor mine will be of any use.

In the journey of death, when has the world walked all
    the way with anyone?
You too should carry on, as long as you are able.

I leave this garden, Zauq, riding the wave of desire
Fair winds may now blow whenever, what do I care?)

2

Ab toh ghabra ke ye kehte hain ke mar jaaeinge
Mar ke bhi chaiyn na paaya toh kidhar jaaeinge

Hum nahin vo jo karein khoon ka daawa tujh par
Balki poochhega khuda bhi toh mukar jaaeinge

Aag dozakh ki bhi ho jaayegi paani paani
Jab ye aasi araq-e-sharm se tar jaaeinge

Shola-e-aah ko bijli ki tarah chamkaaoon
Par mujhe dar hai ke vo dekh ke dar jaaeinge

Zauq jo madrase ke bigdey hue hain mullah
Un ko maikhaane mein le aao sanwar jaaeinge

(Now we're fed up, we say we'll die
What if there is no peace even in death? Where will we
   go then?

I'm not the man to blame you for my murder
Even if God asks, I'll deny the charge.

Even hell-fire will turn into water
Drenched in shame, when we sinners pass by.

I'd flash the flame of pain like lightning
But I fear that it will scare her.

Zauq, these mullahs spoilt by their madrasas
Bring them to the tavern, they'll be set right.

3

Aankh us pur-jafa se ladti hai
Jaan kushti qaza se ladti hai

Shola bhadke na kyon ke mehfil mein
Shama tujh bin hawa se ladti hai

Qismat us bu't se ja ladi apni
Dekho ahmaq khuda se ladti hai

Shor-e-qulqul ye kyon hai dukhtar-e-raaz
Kya kisi paarsa se ladti hai

Dekh us chashm-e-mast ki shokhi
Jab kisi paarsa se ladti hai

(My sight fights her cruelty;
My soul wrestles with death.

Why won't a spark flare up? In the gathering
Without you, the candle battles the air.

My destiny has challenged the idol
The fool, she fights with God!

Why does the wine glug and gurgle so much?
Is it at war with a pious man?

Behold the mischief in those intoxicated eyes
When they fight with a pious man!)

4

Waqt-e-peeri mein shabaab ki baatein
Aisi hain jaise khvaab ki baatein

Phir mujhe le chala udhar dekho
Dil-e-khaana-kharaab ki baatein

Mahjabeen yaad hain ke bhool gaye
Vo shab-e-mahtaab ki baatein

Qissa-e-zulf-e-yaar dil ke liye
Hain ajab pech-o-taab ki baatein

(In old age, talking of beauty
Is like talking of dreams.

Look how it takes me to her door yet again
Ah, the ways of this ruined heart.

O beautiful one, do you remember or have you forgotten
The things we said on that full-moon night?

The story of her tresses! For this heart
They are tales of strange twists and turns.)

NAWAB MIRZA KHAN DAAGH DEHLVI
The Last Casanova of Delhi
(1831–1905)

Nahin khel ae Daagh yaaron se keh do
Ke aati hai Urdu zabaan aate-aate

(It is no child's play, O Daagh, go tell them
It takes some doing to master the Urdu language.)

⁓

Tere vaade par sitamgar, abhi aur sabr karte
Agar apni zindagi ka hamein aitbaar hota

(I would have believed your promise a little longer,
my oppressor
Had I known how long I would live.)

I

ON A SUNNY WINTER AFTERNOON IN DECEMBER 2017, sitting outside his house in a Delhi suburb, wrapped in copious layers of wool and sipping tea, the nonagenarian bard of Delhi, Pandit Anand Mohan Zutshi 'Gulzar Dehlvi', pronounces: 'Ghalib ko Ghalib banaane waala Daagh tha.' ('It was Daagh who made Ghalib what he was.')

At my surprise, the ninety-two-year-old romancer of Shahjahanabad goes on to explain that initially Ghalib used to write very difficult verse in Persianized Urdu, which was the primary reason for his lack of popularity. However, when he saw how Daagh Dehlvi, a lad young enough to be his son, was rising to fame because of his simple and direct poetry, Ghalib decided to change his language and style so that he would be easily understood by the common man. Had it not been for Daagh, therefore, Ghalib would never have acquired the fame that he ultimately did. I am amused by this claim, but do not dare to contest it out of the immense respect that the claim-maker commands.

Some weeks later, I repeat Gulzar Dehlvi's statement to Shamim Hanfi and Sadiq-ur-Rahman Kidwai, both highly distinguished Urdu professors. They laugh it off, saying that it flies in the face of historical facts. Gulzar Dehlvi, of course, has his own reasons for making the claim. His father, Pandit Tribhuvan Nath Zutshi 'Zaar Dehlvi', was Daagh's pupil. For this reason, the aged poet refers to Daagh as 'Ustaad Dada' (Grand Ustaad). But the factual accuracy or otherwise of his claim notwithstanding, it is undeniable that the last of the classical Urdu poets of nineteenth-century Delhi, Daagh was also, arguably, the one who earned the greatest and widest popularity in his lifetime. And to this day he is the most widely-sung classical Urdu poet after Ghalib.

Daagh's life-story is richly complicated—he was born in Delhi, sent to Rampur as a child, made to return to Delhi when he was not yet fourteen, forced to go back to Rampur at twenty-eight, compelled to leave Rampur and travel to Hyderabad at fifty-seven, constrained to return to Delhi at fifty-eight, finally settling, at fifty-nine, in Hyderabad, where he managed to live in some peace, till his death at the age of seventy-four.

Daagh was born in Chandni Chowk to Wazir Khanum, a woman who had the reputation of being one of the strongest and most fiercely liberal and independent women of imperial Delhi. In his spellbinding book *Kayi Chaand Thay Sar-e-Aasmaan* (translated into English and published as *The Mirror of Beauty* in 2006)[133], Shamsur Rahman Faruqi tells the riveting story of Wazir Khanum, alias Chhoti Begum. Though he calls it 'historical fiction', Faruqi maintains that his novel is based entirely on facts and does not contain any fiction, except in one incident which he has tweaked a bit for lack of sufficient credible historical material. In a well-researched piece on Daagh published in 2016 by the Daagh Academy, Khalid Ashraf describes the role of Daagh's mother in the poet's early life in some detail.[134] Faruqi's and Ashraf's accounts and other biographical material available on Daagh reveal a fascinating family history, making Daagh's life-story read like the script of a film, with his mother playing the lead role.

Wazir Khanum was born sometime around 1811 to Mohammad Yusuf, a Delhi-based goldsmith of Kashmiri origin. She grew into a stunning woman of rare intelligence and chutzpah who did not believe in submitting to societal norms. She had an eye for men but would not settle for someone she did not like. She is believed to have told her elder sister: 'Mujhe jo mard chaahega, usey chakkhoongi.

Pasand aayega toh rakkhoongi, varna nikaal baahar
karoongi.'[135] ('I will first taste the man who desires me. If
I like him, I'll keep him. Otherwise, I'll throw him out.')

When she wasn't yet sixteen, Wazir Khanum met
Marston Blake, an English officer. It happened on a mid-
summer evening. Wazir and her father were returning home
from the Dargah of Khwaja Qutubuddin Bakhtiyar Kaki in
Mehrauli, when their bullock-cart met with an accident in a
wilderness. Her father thought that they would not survive
the night; there was no help around, it was oppressively
hot and the area was very unsafe. Just then, the convoy of
an English officer happened to pass by. Faruqi narrates the
story in his epic novel:

> Yet none can touch those whom God desires to save.
> A nimbus of dirty yellow light, like a patch of cloud
> shot through with the light of a dim sun, was descried
> moving along the road from the direction of Delhi. Then
> came the musical tinkle of the bells worn by dromedaries
> around their ankles. Then a horse-rider, before and
> behind whom were two lance-bearers, their faces covered
> against the dust and the wind, but putting each steady
> and firm foot with deliberate slowness. The horse too
> was highly trained so that the slaps of the gusting wind,
> or its roaring rush through the trees were quite unable
> to disrupt its concentration. To the right and left of the
> rider were two foot soldiers, one of them with a flambeau
> in hand...The dromedary rider and the lance-bearers
> continued up the road, but the rider stopped at some
> distance, flanked by his light bearers...On his part, the
> cart driver quickly determined that he and his travellers
> weren't confronted by dacoits or robbers, and succour
> could be sought from them.
>
> The cart driver took a few tentative steps forward.
> The dromedary rider commanded his mount quickly to

block the driver's progress. 'Who are you? And what are you doing here at this hour? Aren't you aware that it is prohibited to saunter around after sundown unescorted by a caravan or a posse of soldiers?...Where is your master? Let him present himself before the Company sahib!'...Wazir Khanum's father came forward a bit, having extricated himself from the broken cart. The horse rider set his mount in motion and in a moment he and the travellers were face to face. In the meantime, the lance-bearer had lit a lantern too; the wind was freshening further and the flame of the lantern was smoking and spluttering. Suddenly, a strong gust, and the chador that Wazir Khanum had wrapped around her body fluttered free and her full face was revealed. Her face, full of fear and shame, felt dark and hot below her large brown-black eyes, like a deer's whose forehead had been burnt brown and black by a harsh sun. And the lantern's thrilling, trembling flame highlighted her body just a bit more. The Englishman stared, quite still. The importunate waves of youth, realizing the absorption of an attractive male in herself, became a little more impudent. Their eyes met for a split second. The cart driver, pulling out another chador quickly, veiled her body again.

The Englishman was Marston Blake, going to Arab Sarai to spend the night with his mistress.[136]

Marson Blake escorted Wazir Khanum and her father back to the city, and soon became a regular visitor to their house. Wazir and Marston fell in love but Wazir's father would not marry her to a Christian Englishman. So they eloped and got married. The couple later had two children. In early 1830, Blake was killed in Jaipur in a riot. Upon his death, the British administration refused to recognize their marriage and accord Wazir the benefits of an English officer's widow. She had to return to Delhi, where her long list of admirers included the Nawab of Loharu and Firozepur Jhirka, Mirza Shamsuddin Ahmed Khan, and the British Resident Agent to the Governor General of India, William Fraser. Though the British Resident was a powerful man, he appears not to have been to Wazir's taste; she did not reciprocate his attention fully, dismissed his advances and got married to the Nawab. Fraser took this as brazen humiliation and vowed to avenge himself. (Interestingly, Nawab Shamsuddin was a cousin of Mirza Ghalib's wife, Umrao Begum, and had duped Ghalib of a substantial amount of money on the pretext of trying to settle his pension dispute with the British.[137])

From Wazir's marriage to Shamsuddin, on 25 May 1831 was born Nawab Mirza Khan, later to be known as Daagh Dehlvi. Shamsuddin had two more wives but Daagh was his first child. The haveli where the Nawab lived was in a lane in Chandni Chowk, almost opposite the present-day Fountain Chowk. The haveli has since been split into small houses and shops selling fake leather accessories. The area has been named after Daagh as Kucha Ustaad Dagh. It is a ten-minute walk from the Mahavir Jain Temple on the main Chandni Chowk Road.

On 22 March 1835, Fraser was assassinated by one Kareem Khan, who claimed to have been hired by Shamsuddin. It was alleged that Shamsuddin wanted to eliminate Fraser because, even after Shamsuddin's marriage to Wazir, Fraser had not stopped eying her. Following a brief police investigation, Shamsuddin was summarily tried for conspiracy to murder Fraser, sentenced to death and hanged on 3 October 1835. Most of his estate was impounded. Daagh was four years old then. Wazir had no option but to send Daagh to her elder sister, Umda Khanum, who was living with Nawabzada Yusuf Ali Khan of Rampur. In 1840, when Yusuf's father, Nawab Saeed Khan, succeeded his cousin Ahmed Ali Khan as the Nawab of Rampur, Daagh was admitted as a member of the Nawab household. Thus began Daagh's education along with other children of the Rampur aristocracy, not only in language and literature but also in horse-riding and calligraphy. He was tutored in Urdu and Persian by a renowned academic of those days, Mulla Ghayasuddin Rampuri. Soon Wazir joined her son in Rampur. On the one hand, men—eligible and ineligible—obsessed over her and, on the other, the princely state began bristling with stories of her two earlier marriages. Turab Ali, an affluent gentleman besotted with her, proposed marriage. To avoid further tittle-tattle, Wazir accepted his proposal and in 1842 the two got married. The very next year, in 1843, Turab Ali was killed by dacoits and Wazir was widowed for the third time. From her marriage to Turab Ali, a child was born posthumously, who would become a reputed Urdu scholar, known to the world as Agha Mirza Shaaghil.

It seems that the family stayed in Rampur for another year. Daagh, around fourteen by now, had already begun his innings as a poet and his ghazals were being commended even by seasoned poets. Rampur was then inhabited by scores of aristocrats and nobles who patronized literature and art. The literary environs of Rampur afforded Daagh the opportunity to show his poetic mettle. Many years earlier, Nawab Mohammad Yar Khan Amir of the nearby town of Tanda, himself a poet, had established a small court which boasted of eminent poets, including Shaikh Ghulam Hamdani Mushafi, Qayam Chandpuri and Qudratullah Shauq. Tanda kept alive its love for art and culture even after the Nawab's death. Daagh was a regular participant in the mushairas held there. Khalid Ashraf narrates an interesting incident where a highly-respected poet of the day, Hakim Maula Qalaq Meeruthi, a disciple of Hakim Momin Khan Momin, objected to the use by Daagh of the expression 'aashiyaan-e-Shahbaz' ('home of Shahbaz') in a couplet. Shahbaz is a fabled bird which, it is believed, does not make a nest or a home and Qalaq reminded Daagh of this salient quality of the bird. Daagh respectfully replied that the expression was not coined by him but by the celebrated poet Kaleem Hamdani in one of his Persian couplets and proceeded to recite Hamdani's couplet. The senior poet was so impressed that he embraced Daagh warmly and showered blessings on him.[138]

In late 1844, Wazir, Daagh and the young Agha Mirza returned to Delhi and again occupied Shamsuddin's haveli in Chandni Chowk. Though fairly young even then, Daagh started visiting poets and scholars and reciting his poems in mushairas and private gatherings. His poetry was gaining fame. It is believed that Mohammad Ali Tishna—an eccentric poet close to the Mughals—advised Daagh to seek pupillage with Ustad Zauq, Poet Laureate in Emperor Bahadur Shah Zafar's court, but Daagh was more concerned about the well-being of his thrice-widowed mother and younger half-brother than his own poetic training. For him, it was far more important to earn a living to help run the family, and pupilage with Zauq would not have left him with either the time or the energy to work.

Around this time, as luck would have it, the Mughal Prince Mirza Fath-ul-Mulk Bahadur, popularly known as Mirza Fakhru, son of Zafar, upon seeing a picture of Wazir, fell in love with her and decided to propose marriage. Though the Mughal Empire had long been robbed of its splendour and glory, the proposal was one that Wazir did not want to refuse in the interest of her children's future and her own social security. In January 1845, Wazir got married to Mirza Fakhru and was bestowed the title of Shaukat Mahal. As part of a pre-nuptial understanding, Daagh was granted a scholarship of five rupees a month by the Emperor and was also admitted as a pupil of Ustad Zauq, besides being entitled to pursue his further studies and training with the other Mughal princes.

Being the Emperor's step-grandson now, Daagh got opportunities to regularly meet with the great poets of the time. He began reciting at prestigious gatherings in the Qila-e-Moalla and also outside—most notably, at the legendary mushairas held at the haveli of Hakim Ahsanullah Khan, one of Delhi's richest men, at Lal Kuan.[139]

In Delhi, Daagh also forged some formidable friendships, including with two young poets, Khwaja Qamaruddin Raqim and Sayyid Zahiruddin Husain (whose father, Sayyid Jalaluddin Haider, was a great calligraphist and had taught the Emperor himself). Both Raqim and Zahir were pupils of Mirza Ghalib, which fact alone gave them bragging rights.

In Urdu poetry there is a tradition of holding 'tarahi' mushairas. A tarahi mushaira is somewhat competitive in nature, where a misra (line of a couplet)—usually the first misra of the opening couplet—is set as a model and all the poets are expected to compose a ghazal each on the same pattern and rhythmic metre. In those days, a new ghazal of Khwaja Haider Ali Aatish—one of Lucknow's most illustrious poets—was becoming popular, the opening verse of which was:

Magar usko fareb-e-nargis-e-mastaana aata hai
Ulat'ti hain safein gardish mein jab paimaana aata hai

(But she does know how to deceive with the intoxicated
    eye
There's a stampede when the goblet is on the move.)

At a tarahi mushaira in Delhi, Daagh composed a beautiful ghazal on the same pattern:

> Mujhe ae ahl-e-Kaaba yaad kya butkhaana aata hai
> Udhar deewaana jaata hai idhar mastaana aata hai

> Rukh-e-raushan ke aage shama rakh kar vo ye kehte hain
> Idhar jaata hai ya dekhein udhar parwaana jaata hai

> Dagha shokhi sharaarat be-hayaayi fitnapardaazi
> Tujhe kuchh aur bhi ae nargis-e-mastaana aata hai

> (Do I, O People of Kaaba, miss the idol-house?
> The crazy one goes there, the inebriated comes here.

> Before that glamourous face they place the candle, and say
> 'Now let us see where the moth goes, here or there.'

> Deceit, coquetry, mischief, shamelessness, guile
> Do you, O intoxicated eye, know anything else?)

Daagh's ghazal gained immense popularity. Soon it reached Ghalib who, though not entirely happy with Daagh's growing fame, owing to the young poet's association with his long-time rival Zauq, was mightily impressed. He especially liked the second couplet of the ghazal. One evening Daagh was wandering around the lanes of Shahjahanabad with Raqim and Zahir, reciting his new ghazal. When the three passed by Ghalib's haveli in Gali Qasimjaan, the senior poet called out to them. In *The Mirror of Beauty* Shamsur Rahman Faruqi recreates Daagh's first meeting with Ghalib:

> Mirza sahib happened to espy them from the upper balcony of his house. Flower garlands around their wrists; fashionable, curled toe slippers on their feet; loose, flapping trousers on their legs; caps worked in gold; a very slight but discernible line of kohl below the eyes; seemingly without a care in the world, three young men sauntering in the bazaar like casual tourists in the city.

Mirza sahib called out impulsively from the height of the balcony, 'Hey young fellows, gentlemen at large, where are you going? Come here, come to me!'

The three looked up, startled, and saw Mirza Ghalib sahib's face, radiant with goodwill and high intelligence, handsome beyond measure, looking at them avidly. If they were a little shy and confused at having been addressed so precipitately by such a grand personality, they recovered quickly, and calling out 'Yes sir, very well, sir', managed to trundle up the stairs to the balcony.[140]

Daagh was sceptical about how Ghalib would treat him. After all, he was a pupil of Ghalib's arch rival. There was also the bitter family history—his father, Shamsuddin, had tricked and swindled Ghalib. But Daagh's apprehensions were immediately laid to rest when Ghalib hugged him, referring to his father as a 'brother'. Ghalib made the three young men feel at home and, after offering them some sumptuous kebabs, asked Daagh to recite his new ghazal. Daagh obliged and received such applause from the veteran as most young poets of the time could only dream of.

While Daagh remained somewhat in awe of Ghalib, most of his poetry was, in a fundamental way, different from the master's. Daagh concerns were not metaphysical; his poetry was about the here and now, and in that, too, as much about the pleasures of physical love as about the heartache of romantic desire. Influenced by his ustaad, Zauq, he aimed for simplicity, and kept his images simple and direct, too, which made him popular with the common man. At the same time, his mastery of rhyme and metre earned him the respect of critics as well.

Clearly aware of this near universal acknowledgement by poetry-lovers, Daagh wrote:

Raqeeb bhi toh usey kaan rakh ke sunte hain
Ajeeb tarah ka maza hai mere fasaane mein

(Even enemies listen to it carefully
There's a strange pleasure in my story.)

———

Daagh fell in love with his cousin, Fatima, who was the daughter of Wazir Khanum's eldest sister, Anwari Khanum. In 1847, not yet seventeen, Daagh, with the blessings of Mirza Fakhru, married Fatima and soon the couple shifted to the Chandni Chowk haveli. The marriage lasted half a century, until Fatima's death in 1897, but during this time Daagh had several affairs, few of them clandestine. He was incapable of fidelity, his romantic and sexual needs being a little more urgent than those of the average male poet of the time. Of course, no records will be found of what Fatima thought of all this. Fatima and Daagh had a daughter who was later married to Daagh's disciple and one of Delhi's better-known poets, Nawab Sirajuddin Ahmad Khan 'Saail Dehlvi'. Much later, after Daagh's death, Saail would get involved in a bitter battle with Daagh's favourite disciple, Bekhud Dehlvi, to inherit Daagh's literary legacy.

In 1849, upon the death of Emperor Zafar's eldest son and Wali-ahad (crown prince), Mirza Dara Bakht, a succession dispute arose between the Mughal princes and finally the British recognized Mirza Fakhru as the Wali-ahad on the condition that Zafar would be the last Mughal Emperor and, after him, Fakhru would be treated as the head of the Timurid Dynasty and would live in Zafar Mahal, Emperor's Summer Palace in Mehrauli, far from the Qila-e-Moalla, the royal fort. By now, Daagh's poetry was finding numerous admirers among the public at large. His verses were being recited by young men and women and sung by courtesans. The plummeting fortunes of the Mughal royalty, therefore, did not affect him much. He was living a comfortable and carefree life, participating in literary gatherings, sharing stage with great poets. Left to him, he would not give up this life for anything:

> Hazrat-e-Daagh ko Dilli ki hawa khoob lagi[141]
> Raat din aish hai jalson mein basar karte hain
>
> (The very air of Delhi, how well it suits Sir Dagh
> He makes merry night and day, he revels in gatherings.)

But these were the illusions of heady, self-absorbed youth.

The five-year period between 1851 and 1856 proved to be one of sorrow and grief for Delhi and, particularly, for Urdu poetry. In 1851, the celebrated poet Hakim Momin Khan Momin suddenly died of an injury at just fifty-one. Two years later, in 1853, the all-powerful British Agent at the Mughal Court, Sir Thomas Metcalfe, died of a gastrointestinal disease. It was rumoured that he was being slow-poisoned by Queen Zeenat Mahal for intruding into the affairs of the Qila. Some years ago, it was Sir Thomas who had decided the heirship dispute in favour of Mirza Fakhru, thereby rejecting the claim of Zeenat Mahal's son, Mirza Jawan Bakht. The very next year, Ustaad Zauq passed away after a brief illness at the age of sixty-six. With the ustaad's death, Daagh suffered a personal setback. In July 1856, Mirza Fakhru died of cholera. Soon after his death, Zeenat Mahal ordered Wazir Khanum to leave the Qila and Wazir, widowed for the fourth time now, moved in with her son at the Chandni Chowk haveli.

The following year proved to be decisive in the history of India. On 10 May 1857 began the Ghadar—the Great Indian Revolt—which started in the form of a sepoy mutiny in Meerut, less than 100 kilometres from Delhi. The revolt was crushed by the British but not without a bloodbath, most horrifically in the streets of Delhi. While Ghalib wrote an account of the massacre in Persian in his diary, *Dastanbu,* Daagh briefly captured its scenes in his shehr-ashob (a poem lamenting the loss of a city's soul), which was later included in his collection *Gulzar-e-Daagh.* Daagh's shehr-aashob, bemoaning the fall of his beloved city, is in the form of a musaddas—a poem in which each unit consists of six misras. He draws a graphic sketch of the carnage:

> Lahu ke chashme hain chashm par aab ki soorat
> Shikasta kaasa sar hain hubaab ki soorat
>
> Lutey hain ghar dil-e-khaana-kharaab ki soorat
> Kahaan pe hashr mein tauba azaab ki soorat
>
> (Streams of blood flow like rivers of tears
> Broken skulls rise like bubbles.
>
> Homes plundered, like ruined hearts
> As if the doomsday curse is upon us.)

Bahadur Shah Zafar was exiled to Rangoon in 1858 and the Mughal Empire was finally history. With this, Daagh lost his royal remuneration and was left with no income.

Delhi had been completely brutalized by the British. However, Rampur State (also called Mustafabad) had not been affected since its ruler Nawab Saeed Khan had declared allegiance to the British and refused to participate in the revolt. In his childhood, Daagh had already spent some years in Rampur with his aunt, Umda Khanum, and he now approached his aunt again. She arranged for his relocation to the court of the Nawab of Rampur, and thus Daagh was back in Rampur after about fourteen years. Already a popular poet by now, he was received well in

Rampur and soon became a close friend of the Nawabzada Kalb-e-Ali Khan, next in line to become the Nawab. Upon succeeding his father in 1865, Kalb-e-Ali Khan appointed Daagh as Darogha-e-Astabal (Superintendent of Stables) with a handsome remuneration—about which a local poet, employing a pun on the word 'daagh' (the expression 'daagh dena' means to shoot), famously quipped:

Shehr-e-Dehli se aaya ek mushki
Aate hi astabal mein 'daagh' hua

(From the city of Delhi came a black horse
And was immediately shot into the stable.)

It was in Rampur that Daagh met and became a close compatriot of the renowned poet of the day, Ameer Minai, now best-known for his ghazal 'Sarakti jaaye hai rukh se naqaab aahista-aahista'. Daagh's closeness to the Nawab, too, was growing by the day. The Nawab was so fond of Daagh that he was invited to join the Nawab for the Haj pilgrimage to Mecca in 1872. Daagh performed Haj in great comfort and luxury and, upon his return to Rampur, wrote of the Nawab's hospitality in verse:

Saath nawwaab ke Haj kar ke phirey hum ae Daagh
Hind mein dhoom hai mehmaan-e-Hijaz aaye hain

(With the Nawab I performed Hajj and roamed around,
　O Daagh
There's talk all over Hind [India] that the guests of the
　Holy city are back.)

It was a time of personal and professional success for Daagh. Rampur suited him well. Then, in 1879, his mother, the remarkable Wazir Khanum, died, and he was devastated. Daagh was highly attached to his mother. His father had died when he was only four years old and it was Wazir who had raised him. It was because of her connections and influence that Daagh could reach places. His early education at the Qila-e-Moalla with the Mughal princes and later at the Rampur Nawab's household had been possible only because of Wazir. She had been central to his life in so many ways, that her passing left him at a loose end and emotionally overwrought. It was shortly after this that one of the more notorious and long-lasting of Daagh's many adulterous affairs began.

Nawab Kalb-e-Ali Khan used to hold an annual week-long fair called Benazir ka Mela in his estate, Benazir Baagh, just outside Rampur. Courtesans, musicians and artists from far off places would be invited to the fair. In March 1881, a Calcutta-based courtesan, Munni Bai Hijaab, was invited to perform at Benazir ka Mela. Daagh fell for her at first sight. Completely smitten, he made his feelings known to Hijaab and invited her to stay with him on her next visit to Rampur. Hijaab visited Rampur shortly thereafter but rejected his offer. Khalid Ashraf cites extensive correspondence exchanged between the two showing Daagh's desperation for Hijaab and her reluctance. In one of his letters to Hijaab Daagh writes:

> Main tumhaare liye bilbila raha hoon. Ye khaufnaak kaali kaali raatein aur tanhaai! Kya kahoon, kyon kar tadap-tadap kar subah ki soorat dekhta hoon. Yaqeen jaano, aise tadapta hoon jaise bulbul qafas mein.[142]

> (I weep like a baby in my desire for you. The terror of these pitch-dark nights, this loneliness! You'll never know how I writhe in agony waiting for the morning. Believe me, I suffer like a caged nightingale.)

Finally, Hijaab agreed to meet Daagh in Calcutta (now Kolkata). It is believed that before proceeding for Calcutta, Daagh also wrote to Malika Jan, the influential courtesan of Calcutta and mother of the legendary Gauhar Jan, expressing his desire for Hijaab, perhaps in the hope that she would facilitate their union. It is not known if Malika played a role in changing Hijaab's mind.

In April 1882, Daagh left Rampur on a voyage to Calcutta. On his way there, he stayed in Patna (known as Azimabad back then) for a month with his pupil Mir Baqar. It was in Patna that he recited these famous couplets:

> Bhanvein tanti hain khanjar haath mein hai tan ke baithe
>   hain
> Kisi se aaj bigdi hai ki vo yoon ban ke baithe hain
>
> Bohot roya hoon main jab se ye maine khwaab dekha hai
> Ke aap aansu bahaate saamne dushman ke baithe hain
>
> Koi chheenta padey toh Daagh kalkatte chaley jaaein
> Azimabad mein hum muntazir saawan ke baithe hain
>
> (Eyebrows tense, with a dagger in hand, she sits upright
>   and stiff
> Has she had a fight with someone, or is this her make-
>   up for the day?
>
> I haven't stopped crying since I dreamt of you
> Sitting before the enemy and shedding tears.
>
> Should even a drop fall, Daagh will go to Calcutta
> He's been waiting for the monsoon in Azimabad.)

Daagh reached Calcutta in June 1882 and stayed there for about a month, during which time he would meet Hijaab almost every day. Soon, on account of his lack of discretion in conducting the affair—which did not behove a noble—he was summoned back to Rampur by the Nawab.

In the meanwhile, Ghalib had died in Delhi in 1869 and the golden age of classical Urdu poetry was all but over. Mughal rule had ended and the court at Lucknow had been ruined. Rampur was still a comfortable refuge for a poet like Daagh, but in 1887, Nawab Kalb-e-Ali Khan died and his successor, Nawab Mushtaq Ali Khan, terminated Daagh's services. Once again, Daagh was left to fend for himself. The only other princely state which was still patronizing poets and artists was Hyderabad, where Asaf Jah VI Mir Mahboob Ali Khan was the presiding Nizam. He was well-read, known to have a literary bent of mind and was well versed in at least four languages, Urdu, Persian, Arabic and English. For some months, Daagh travelled in North India, meeting his admirers and disciples, reciting at mushairas and finally, in April 1888, reached Hyderabad. Despite his continuous efforts and influence, Daagh failed to secure an audience with the Nizam. Dejected, he returned to Delhi. In 1890, he again travelled to Hyderabad. This time he met the Nizam per chance and recited a couplet to him:

Daagh har ek zabaan par ho fasaana tera
Vo din aate hain vo aata hai zamaana tera

(Daagh, may every tongue speak your story
Here come your good days, here comes your time.)

The couplet did not appear to have impressed the Nizam, who was a poet himself. Some months passed by and there seemed no hope of royal patronage. Suddenly, one fine morning in early 1891, Daagh received a request from the Nizam to make improvements in one of his ghazals and thus began Daagh's journey in the court of the Nizam of Hyderabad. With time, Daagh, the charmer, became one of the Nizam's closest confidants and was honoured with a minor storm of titles: Dabir-ud-Daula, Faseeh-ul-

Mulk, Bulbul-e-Hindustan and Jahan Ustad.[143] He was also bestowed the title of Nazim Yar Jung, symbolic of his inclusion in Hyderabad's aristocracy.

In 1897, Daagh lost his wife, Fatima. In 1899, he travelled to Calcutta with the Nizam and was devastated to find that Hijaab had got married. He could not meet her. However, her marriage was short-lived and she soon got divorced. In 1901, Hijaab travelled to Hyderabad to be with Daagh who, by then, was seventy. Hijaab not only insisted that Daagh marry her but also began making financial demands on him for herself and her family in Calcutta. This became a nuisance and Daagh wrote a couplet about it:

Daagh se kehte hain sab de do mujhe
Jo mila hai tum ko Asif Jah se

(She tells Dagh, give me everything
That you have received from Asif Jah.)

Unable to cope, Daagh parted ways with Hijaab. The end of this affair resulted in a long poem on Hijaab—a masnavi (epic) titled *Faryaad-e-Daagh* (Daagh's Plea) containing more than 1700 verses.

―

In 1903, to celebrate the succession of Edward VII and Alexandra of Denmark as Emperor and Empress of India, Viceroy Lord Curzon organized a grand celebration at Delhi called the Delhi Durbar. The Durbar was held at what is now called Coronation Park or Coronation Memorial, near Nirankari Sarovar on Burari Road in North Delhi. It was attended by more than 100,000 people, including a number of princes and aristocrats from all over India. Daagh attended the Durbar with the Nizam and during his stay in Delhi in the Nizam's camp, was visited by a number of his disciples and admirers. This was his last visit to Delhi. Though his disciple Bekhud Dehlvi has written that even at the age of seventy-two Daagh longed for carnal pleasures, others say that he seemed to have sobered down and become inclined towards religion. Daagh himself admits this change:

> Vo din gaye ki Daagh thi hardam bu'ton ki yaad
> Parhte hain paanch waqt ki ab toh namaaz hum

> (Those days are gone, Daagh, when idols were always
>   on my mind
> Now I say the namaz five times a day.)

And he admits that people change and time waits for no one:

> Aao mil jaao ki ye waqt na paaoge kabhi
> Ma'in bhi hamraah zamaane ke badal jaaoonga

> (Come, meet me once, for this time will not return
> The world is changing, and I will change with it.)

Back in Hyderabad, at the age of seventy-four, Daagh had a minor paralytic attack which affected his left side. He did not survive for long. On 17 March 1905, Daagh passed away and was buried at the graveyard of Dargah Yousufain in Nampally.

II

DAAGH WAS A ROMANTIC POET IN THE LITERAL SENSE OF the term. Unlike Ghalib, he did not deal with existential questions, nor, like Mir, did he seek to invest love with the intensity of mysticism. It wouldn't be an exaggeration to say that his shrines were the human heart and body. Being a pupil of Zauq, he also followed his ustaad in composing easily comprehensible and melodious poetry using expressions from spoken Urdu. He wrote for the common man and, because of the simplicity of his verse, he was popular in his lifetime and remains popular to this day.

Daagh's ghazals may not be profound but they are melodious, and almost always memorable. Which lover of poetry and music can claim not to have been swayed by Begum Akhtar singing Daagh in her soulful voice:

Uzr aane mein bhi hai aur bulaate bhi nahin
Baais-e-tark-e-mulaqaat bataate bhi nahin

Khoob parda hai ki chilman se lage baithe hain
Saaf chhupte bhi nahin saamne aate bhi nahin

(She hesitates to come to me, she doesn't call me either
And she doesn't tell me the reason why we cannot meet.

What purdah is this, you sit pressed up against the curtain
You won't hide yourself, you won't show yourself either.)

This a lovely example of how simple, melodious and exquisitely playful Daagh can be. He had learned the craft well from him his ustaad, Zauq.

Unlike Zauq, however, Daagh has no inhibitions in using sensual, delicately erotic imagery. In matters of romance and beauty, he is direct and straightforward and does not believe in symbolism or metaphor, so much so that his critics have often accused him of 'debauchery':

Di shab-e-vasl muazzin ne azaan pichhli raat
Haaye kambakht ko kis waqt khuda yaad aaya

(Last night the muezzin gave the call to prayer just at
     the moment of union
Damn it! What a time to remember God.)

Some critics have gone to the extent of holding his mother's past responsible for Daagh's allegedly 'dissolute' and,

therefore, frivolous poetry. The renowned Urdu poet Brij
Narain Chakbast (d. 1926), known best for his depiction
of scenes from the *Ramayana* in Urdu poetry, has referred
to Daagh's poetry as 'ayyaashi ki shaayri' ('poetry of
debauchery')[144]. Recently, Shamim Hanfi remarked that he
considers most of Daagh's poetry 'sasti shaayri' ('cheap
poetry').[145] The suave and gracious poet of Delhi, Mumtaz
Mirza (d. 1997) has, however, vehemently refuted such
critiques, arguing that if there was no substance in Daagh's
poetry, people wouldn't have been reciting and singing it—
also trashing it—even over a century after his death.[146] She
maintains that the real test of substance is not whether his
poetry is 'dissolute' or 'lofty', but whether it is predicated
on reality and truth. Daagh did not make claims of being
a poet of spirituality or mysticism. He stayed away from
the disputes of worldly versus divine love and did not shy
away from praising the feminine form. His poetry mirrored
his life and ways. Mirza says that as long as his poetry
represents a true image of his actual life, there is no need
to weigh it on any other scale.

That Daagh's poetry did actually represent a true image
of his own life has been admitted even by his worst critics.
In fact, in the same piece where Chakbast has referred
to Daagh's works as 'ayyashi ki shaayari', he has also
acknowledged that Daagh's poetry reflects his persona and
temperament, which makes it distinctive:

> Daagh ka kalaam shuru se aakhir tak uski tabiyat ke
> qudrati rang mein dooba hua hai. Uska sher zabaan-
> e-haal se pukaar kar kehta hai ki main Daagh ka sher
> hoon.[147]

> (Daagh's poetry, from the beginning to the end, is
> immersed in the natural colour of his temperament. His

verse, from its very character, calls out and says, 'I am Daagh's verse.')

Like the language he uses, Daagh's concerns in love, his complaints to and about the object of his passion, are also simple and direct:

Aap ka aitbaar kaun karey
Roz ka intezaar kaun karey

Zikr-e-mehr-o-wafa toh hum karte
Par tumhein sharmsaar kaun karey

Hijr mein zeher kha ke mar jaoon
Maut ka intezaar kaun karey

(Why should anyone trust you?
Why should anyone wait every day?

I might have talked of kindness and loyalty
But why should one embarrass you?

In separation, I'd rather drink poison
Why should one lie waiting for death?)

In a lot of his poetry—as in the work of most Urdu poets of the classical era—Daagh's grievance against his beloved remains the same—her false promises and indifference:

Ghazab kiya tere vaade pe aitbaar kiya
Tamaam raat qayaamat ka intizaar kiya

Kisi tarah jo na us bu't ne aitbaar kiya
Meri wafa ne mujhe khooob sharmsaar kiya

(A fool, I believed your promise
I waited all night for the hour of Judgement.

The idol will have no faith, no matter what I do
My constant fidelity now shames me no end.)

In another couplet, Daagh is so restless with passion that he can barely wait for the heartless beloved to respond to his letter and ends up writing to himself on her behalf:

Kya-kya fareb dil ko diye iztiraab mein
Unki taraf se aap likhe khat jawaab mein

(How I've deceived the heart in my restlessness!
I've replied to my own letters on her behalf.)

A letter figures in another ghazal, included in the third section of this chapter. Here are two couplets from it:

Hamaare khat mein naya ik salaam kis ka tha
Na tha raqeeb toh aakhir vo naam kis ka tha

Har ek se kehte hain kya Daagh bewafa nikla
Ye poochhe un se koi vo ghulaam kis ka tha

(In your letter to me, who was that new greeting from?
If I haven't lost you to another, whose name was it then?[148]

She asks everyone, 'Has Daagh turned out to be
    unfaithful?'
Someone should ask her, 'Whose slave was he?')

Note how beautifully Daagh assimilates the Hindi expressions 'poochh-gachh' and 'aao-bhagat' in a sher found in the same ghazal, bearing clear testimony to the inclusiveness and universality of the Urdu language:

Na poochh-gachh thi kisi ki na aao-bhagat
Tumhaari bazm mein kal ethimaam kis ka tha

(No one was being given attention, no one was being
    welcomed
Who had arranged this celebration for you last night?)

The beloved is always a sadist and a tease. Daagh will have his revenge on the day of judgment:

Bada maza ho jo mahshar mein hum karein shikwa
Vo minnaton se kahein, chup raho, khuda ke liye.

(What fun it would be on Judgment Day, that I complain
and
She pleads, 'Please, for the love of God, keep quiet.')

But Daagh's complaints are usually not of the kind we would associate with the tragic, constant lover who pines away for the beloved. He is, after all, Casanova, not Majnu. As she delays their love-making, playing games with him while his passion demands consummation, he gives up on her:

Is nahin ka koi ilaaj nahin
Roz kehte hain aap aaj nahin

Kal jo tha aaj vo mizaaj nahin
Is talavvun ka kuchh ilaaj nahin

(Your 'no' is an incurable affliction
Every day you say, 'Not today.'

A different mood yesterday, yet another today
Your fickleness is an incurable affliction.)

While Ghalib bemoans his misfortune in being denied his beloved's company: 'Ye na thi hamaari qismat ki visaal-e-yaar hota, Agar aur jeete rehte, yahi intezaar hota' ('It was not in my destiny to be united with my beloved/ Had I lived any longer, it would have been the same long wait'), Daagh, using the same refrain and rhythmic metre tells us that he is fortunate, for it is this deprivation that has spared him a permanent nuisance:

Ajab apna haal hota, jo visaal-e-yaar hota
Kabhi jaan sadqe hoti, kabhi dil nisaar hota

Tere vaade par sitamgar abhi aur sabr karte
Agar apni zindagi ka hamein aitbaar hota

(What a wreck I would have been, had I been united
with my beloved
At times I would have sacrificed my life, at times offered
up my heart.
I would have believed your promise a little longer, my
oppressor
Had I known how long I would live.)

Notoriously promiscuous, Daagh is yet a diehard romantic:

Aashiqi se milega ae zaahid
Bandagi se khuda nahin milta

(Only lovers find Him, o devout
You won't find God by being pious.)

He applauds those who are in love, for according to him,
it is a very engaging occupation:

Hazaaron kaam mohabbat mein hain ma'ze ke Daagh
Jo log kuchh nahin karte kamaal karte hain

(There are a thousand pleasures to achieve in love, Daagh
Those who do nothing achieve miracles.)

In a simple ghazal, later evocatively sung by Malika Pukhraj,
Daagh implores his lady love to not force him to speak,
lest he ends up tarnishing her fair image and be blamed
for her notoriety:

Be-zabaani zabaan na ho jaaye
Raaz-e-ulfat ayaan na ho jaaye

Is qadar pyaar se na dekh mujhe
Phir tamanna jawaan na ho jaaye

(I pray my silence is not broken
Lest this secret love is revealed.

Don't look at me so lovingly
Lest desire erupt again.)

A master of long ghazals containing numerous couplets, Daagh was also brilliant at ascribing different meanings in different contexts to the same word or phrase. In a ghazal which opens with this sher, he plays gently yet masterfully with the expression 'toh gaya' (the complete ghazal is found in the selection at the end of this chapter):

> Khaatir se ya lihaaz se ma'in maan toh gaya
> Jhoothi qasam se aap ka imaan toh gaya

> (For your hospitality or out of deference, I did agree
> But you lost your faith by swearing falsely.)

Though known as a master of the pure ghazal form of Urdu poetry, Daagh also has to his credit some outstanding qaseedahs and rubaayis. His work was published in four collections, between 1878 and 1905. During his lifetime, Daagh was perhaps the most sought-after ustaad, having tutored, by one estimate, more than two thousand pupils, among whom were the well-known poets Seemab Akbarabadi, Jigar Moradabadi, Bekhud Dehlvi, Saail Dehlvi (who became his son-in-law) and the great Allama Iqbal. Of Iqbal it is said that he initially showed his work to Daagh but was later told by Daagh that his poems required no improvement. Daagh, it seems, had understood that there was a sharp difference not only between their styles but also the subjects that they wrote on. Iqbal, however, continued to regard Daagh as his ustaad and, upon his death, paid him a glowing tribute:

> Chal basa Daagh aah mayyat iski zeb-e-dosh hai
> Aakhiri shaayar Jahanabad ka khamosh hai

> Ae Jahanabad, ae sarmaaya-e-bazm-e-sukhan
> Ho gaya phir aaj paamaal-e-khizaan tera chaman

> (Alas, Daagh is dead, his body adorns our shoulders
> The last poet of Jahanabad is now silent.

O Jahanabad, O prized possession of the world of poetry,
Once again, your garden has been ruined by autumn.)

Daagh's ghazals remain popular and have been sung by most of the prominent singers of the twentieth century, including Begum Akhtar, Malika Pukhraj, Noor Jahan, Farida Khanum, Mehdi Hasan, Ghulam Ali, Jagjit Singh and Abida Parveen. Research pieces have been written and institutions, including New Delhi's Daagh Academy, have been established in his name.

Despite some critics deriding his poetry as inferior because of its populist overtones, neither can Daagh's poetry nor his contribution to the development of Urdu poetry be dismissed. Gulzar Dehlvi says, 'Taqseem ke baad agar Urdu Hindustan mein zinda hai toh ye Daagh ka hi ehsaan hai.' ('After partition, if Urdu is alive in India, it is because of Daagh.')

Whether or not we agree with Gulzar Dehlvi, we cannot entirely disagree with Daagh himself:

Urdu hai jiska naam humin jaante hain Daagh
Hindostaan mein dhoom hamaari zabaan ki hai

(That which is called Urdu, only I know what it is
Daagh, Hindustan resounds with my language.)

There may no longer be the old 'dhoom' today, but if Urdu still lives in India, some of the credit must certainly go to Daagh.

III

SELECTED POETRY OF DAAGH

I

Uzr aane mein bhi hai aur bulaate bhi nahin
Baais-e-tark-e-mulaqaat bataate bhi nahin

Kya kaha phir toh kaho, 'hum nahin sunte teri'
Nahin sunte toh hum aison ko sunaate bhi nahin

Khoob parda hai ki chilman se lage baithe hain
Saaf chhupte bhi nahin saamne aate bhi nahin

Dekhte hi mujhe mehfil mein ye irshaad hua
'Kaun baitha hai, usey log uthaate bhi nahin

Ho chuka qata ta'alluq to jafaaein kyon hon
Jin ko matlab nahin rehta vo sataate bhi nahin

Zeest se tang ho ae Daagh toh kyon jeete ho
Jaan pyaari bhi nahin jaan se jaate bhi nahin

(She hesitates to come to me, she doesn't call me either
And she doesn't tell me the reason why we cannot meet.

What did you say? Say that again—'I don't want to
   listen to you.'
Well, even I don't speak to people who won't listen to me.

What purdah is this, you sit pressed up against the curtain
You won't hide yourself, you won't show yourself either.

As soon as she saw me in the gathering, she said
'Who's this sitting here, people don't even throw him out!'

If our relationship is over, why continue to hurt me?
Those who have nothing to do with you, don't torment
   you either.

If you are sick of life, O Daagh, why do you live?
Life isn't dear to you, but you won't give it up, either.)

2

Ghazab kiya tere vaade pe aitbaar kiya
Tamaam raat qayaamat ka intizaar kiya

Kisi tarah jo na us bu't ne aitbaar kiya
Meri wafa ne mujhe khooob sharmsaar kiya

Hansa-hansa ke shab-e-vasl ashkbaar kiya
Tasalliyaan mujhe de-de ke beqaraar kiya

Suna hai tegh ko qaatil ne aabdaar kiya
Agar ye sach hai to be-shubah hum pe vaar kiya

Tujhe toh vaada-e-deedar hum se karna tha
Ye kya kiya ki jahaan ko ummeedvaar kiya

Bhula-bhula ke jataaya hai un ko raaz-e-nihaan
Chhupa-chhupa ke mohabbat ko aashkaar kiya

Teri nigaah ke tasavvur mein hum ne ae qaatil
Laga-laga ke galey se chhuri ko pyaar kiya

Fasaana-e-shab-e-gham un ko ik kahaani thi
Kuchh aitbaar kiya kuchh na aitbaar kiya

(A fool, I believed your promise
I waited all night for the hour of Judgement.

The idol will have no faith, no matter what I do
My constant fidelity now shames me no end.

On the night of union, she made me laugh so much, I cried
With her repeated reassurances, she made me restless.

The sword, we hear, was polished by the assassin
If this is true, then there's no doubt she struck me.

The promise to show yourself was only made to me
What did you do, now all the world expects the favour?

By forgetting her time and again, I've shown her the
    hidden secrets
By hiding it time and again, I've revealed my love for her.

Lost in thoughts of your eyes, O killer
Time and again I hugged and kissed the knife.

The tale of the night of grief was but a story for her
Some of it she believed, some she did not.

3

Be-zabaani zabaan na ho jaaye
Raaz-e-ulfat ayaan na ho jaaye

Is qadar pyaar se na dekh mujhe
Phir tamanna jawaan na ho jaaye

Lutf aane laga jafaaon mein
Vo kahin meharabaan na ho jaaye

Zikr unkaa zabaan par aayaa
Ye kahin daastaan na ho jaaye

(I pray my silence is not broken
Lest our secret love is revealed.

Don't look at me so lovingly
Lest desire erupt again.

I've begun to enjoy her oppression
I hope she doesn't turn merciful again.

Her mention escaped my lips
I hope it doesn't grow into a story.)

4

Ajab apna haal hota jo visaal-e-yaar hota
Kabhi jaan sadqe hoti kabhi dil nisaar hota

Gham-e-ishq mein maza tha jo usey samajh ke khaate
Ye vo zehr hai ki aakhir mai-e-khush-gawaar hota

Ye maza tha dil-lagi ka ki baraabar aag lagti
Na tujhe qaraar hota na mujhe qaraar hota

Ye vo dard-e-dil nahin hai ki ho chaarasaaz koi
Agar ek baar mit'ta toh hazaar baar hota

Tere vaade par sitamgar, abhi aur sabr karte
Agar apni zindagi ka hamein aitbaar hota

(What a wreck I would have been, had I been united
  with my beloved
At times I would have sacrificed my life, at times offered
  up my heart.

Love's sorrow would have been blissful only had I known
It's a poison, but it tastes like sweet wine.

Love would have been fun had we burned in equal fires
Neither would you have found relief, nor I.

This is not a heartache that has a healer
Every time it is cured, it returns a thousand times.

I would have believed your promise a little longer,
  my Oppressor
Had I known how long I would live.)

5

Hamaare khat mein naya ik salaam kis ka tha
Na tha raqeeb toh aakhir vo naam kis ka tha

Vo qatl kar ke mujhe har kisi se poochhte hain
Ye kaam kis ne kiya, ye kaam kis ka tha

Wafa kareinge nibhaaeinge baat maaneinge
Tumhein bhi yaad hai kuchh ye kalaam kis ka tha

Raha na dil mein vo bedard aur dard raha
Muqeem kaun hua maqaam kis ka tha

Na poochh-gachh thi kisi ki na aao-bhagat
Tumhaari bazm mein kal ethimaam kis ka tha

Har ek se kehte hain kya Daagh bewafa nikla
Ye poochhe un se koi vo ghulaam kis ka tha

(In your letter to me, who was that new greeting from?
If I haven't lost you to another, whose name was it then?

Having killed me, she goes about asking everyone
Who has done this? Who did this?

'I'll be loyal, I'll be steadfast, I'll listen to you.'
Whose words were these, do you even remember?

In my heart, there's only pain, the heartless pain-giver
    has gone
Look who's made a home there, and whom it was meant
    for.

No one was being given attention, no one was being
    welcomed
Who had arranged this celebration for you last night?

She asks everyone, 'Has Daagh turned out to be
    unfaithful?'
Someone should ask her, 'Whose slave was he?')

Afterword

In his preface to *Dehli Ki Aakhri Shama* (The Last Lamp of Delhi), his fictional account of the last mushaira of Mughal Delhi, Mirza Farhatullah Baig Dehlvi wrote:

> It is customary for a sick man to recover, momentarily, before the final stroke of death overtakes him. In the case of Urdu poets, the age of the Mughal Emperor Bahadur Shah II was such a momentary recovery before the final extinction. In his ruined and desolate city were collected not only poets, but such a host of other talented men that it would be difficult to find their counterparts in the whole of India, nay in the whole world![149]

As mentioned in the preceding chapters, the 1857 Revolt had battered and changed Zafar's Delhi beyond recognition. Amaresh Mishra, in his book on 1857, calls it India's 'untold holocaust' and claims that it killed almost ten million people over ten years, a number that has been kept a secret by the British to this day.[150] While the accuracy of this figure could, perhaps, be debated, there is no doubt that the Revolt completely transformed Delhi—culturally, socially and economically. Other transformations have happened in the years since—the biggest of these after Partition, just ninety years after the Revolt—but those are stories for another book, another time.

Zafar, the last Mughal, died in confinement in Rangoon in 1862, and the same year, ironically, the shattered or desecrated architectural landmarks of Mughal Delhi began to be repaired. In his biographical work on Mirza Ghalib, Pavan Varma gives an account of the post-1857 events.[151]

He writes that the Jama Masjid, which had been captured by British troops, and the Fatehpuri Mosque, which, too, had been confiscated and later sold to a rich trader, Lala Chunna Mal (and which remained his personal property till 1877), were restored for prayers only in 1862. Zeenat-ul-Masjid (also known as Ghata Masjid), considered the second most important mosque in Delhi, part of which had been converted into a bakery for British troops, was restored and opened to the local residents for prayers only in 1875.

In 1864, Delhi College reopened for classes, but it was not till 1867, the same year that the city saw its first passenger train, that the Delhi Canal flowed again.

Ghalib died in 1869. When he died, the only other prominent poet of Zafar's Delhi still alive was Daagh who had, by then, already migrated to Rampur, from where he would later relocate to Hyderabad. Of course, there was Hali, but he was too junior and not considered a 'Delhi poet'. The 1890s saw the beginning of industrialization in Delhi, with mills and factories coming up. Parts of the city were electrified in 1902. In 1905, Daagh died in Hyderabad and, with him, came to an end the era of Delhi's classical Urdu poets.

In the years that followed, Delhi became home to many more Urdu poets—some who were born here, others who came to the city in search of greener pastures. All of them loved the city and drew beautiful portraits of its rich cultural past in their poetry. But each one was also deeply aware of the perils and dangers that were and remain entrenched in Delhi's aggressive soul. Among those who identified themselves with the city in the beginning and the middle of the twentieth century were Bekhud Dehlvi, Pandit Tribhuvan Nath Zutshi Zaar Dehlvi, Pandit Hari Chand Akhtar, Anand Narain Mulla, Saghar Nizami, Naresh

Kumar Shad, Makhmoor Dehelvi and Kunwar Mohinder Singh Bedi Sahar, to name a few. In the mid 1930s, Majaz (1909-1955), called the 'Keats of Urdu Poetry', came to Delhi and worked first at All India Radio and then at the Hardinge Library (now called Hardayal Municipal Heritage Public Library) in Chandni Chowk. He did not stay in the city for long, however. Having lost his job and suffered a heartbreak, he returned to Lucknow. While leaving, he bid a tearful farewell to Delhi:

> Rukhsat aye Dilli teri mehfil se ab jaata hoon ma'in
> Nauhagar jaata hoon ma'in naala-ba-lab jaata hoon ma'in
>
> Tera dil dhadkaa chuke hain mere ehsasaat bhi
> Tere aiwaanon mein goonje hain mere naghmaat bhi
>
> Jannatein aabaad hain tere dar-o-deewaar mein
> Aur tu aabaad hai shaayar ke qalb-e-zaar mein
>
> (Goodbye, O Delhi, I leave your company now
> Wailing I go, with cries on my lips I go,
>
> My feelings have roused your heart too
> In your hallways my lyrics too have found echo,
>
> Heavens live in your doorways and walls
> And you live in the poet's feeble heart.)

Among the later poets, Dilliwaalas were mesmerized, among others, by Gulzar Dehlvi, Ghulam Rabbani Taban, Rifat Sarosh, Bekal Utsahi, Mumtaz Mirza, Amir Agha Qazalbash, Shuja Khawar and Saghar Khayyami—all of whom lived in Delhi or, at least, spent long years in the city. Most of them came from other parts of the country and made Delhi their home.

The spoken language of the people of Delhi was always the language that is today called Hindustani—a mix of Urdu and Hindi. In general conversations, no one ever used either Sanskritized Hindi words or Persianized or Arabicized Urdu words. The language was written in both Nastalikh or Urdu script and Devanagri or Hindi script. When 200 years of British rule of India came to an end in 1947, Independence came at a cost. The cost was the country's partition on religious lines into India and Pakistan. Apart from the obvious, Partition resulted in strange things. By a surreptitious, yet deliberate, stratagem devised to annihilate the Urdu script, the language, by some absurd logic, started being identified with Muslims and, consequently, being gradually excluded from primary level courses. Despite the fact that the language continued to be widely spoken all over North India, the Urdu script almost entirely disappeared from schools and became confined only to madrasas and Urdu Departments in universities and colleges. In this context, a poem by Sahir Ludhianvi, partly recounted earlier in this book, bears repetition. In 1969, when the Government of India decided to celebrate Ghalib's hundredth death anniversary, an agitated Ludhianvi wrote:

Jis ahd-e-siyaasat ne ye zinda zubaan kuchli
Us ahd-e-siyaasat ko marhoom ka gham kyon hai?

Ghalib jise kehte hain Urdu ka hi shaayar tha
Urdu pe sitam dha kar Ghalib pe karam kyun hai

(A political system which crushed this living language,
Why does that system now grieve for the departed soul?

The one whom we call Ghalib was a poet of Urdu
Having crushed Urdu, why be kind to Ghalib?)

And yet, although the script was hardly being taught, Urdu poetry kept enthralling audiences in mushairas. In 1954, Sir Shri Ram, founder of Delhi Cloth Mills (DCM) conglomerate, began organizing an annual mushaira in Delhi in the memory of his brother, Sir Shankar Lall 'Shankar', and son, Lala Murli Dhar 'Shad'—both of whom were Urdu poets. Known as the Shankar-Shad Mushaira, it is still held every year in Modern School, Barakhamba Road and boasts of having hosted some of the greatest poets of the language from all over the world, including Jigar Moradabadi, Faiz Ahmed Faiz, Josh Malihabadi, Ali Sardar Jafri, Shahryar, Kaifi Azmi, Zehra Nigah, Jaun Elia, Khumar Barabankvi and Ahmad Faraz.[152] Also, the Red Fort, once known as the Qila-e-Moalla, continued to remain the icon of the capital's grandeur. The Prime Minster addresses the nation from its ramparts every year on Independence Day.

In the mid-1900s, some of the best poets of the Urdu ghazal began to head for Bombay (now Mumbai) to try their hand at writing film lyrics. Among them were Sahir Ludhianvi, Jan Nisar Akhtar, Majrooh Sultanpuri and Shakil Badayuni. Soon, Bombay became home to full-time lyricists who would write exclusively for films. Bollywood also used works of Urdu poets living outside Bombay, like Shahryar and Qateel Shifai. All this led to the flourishing of what can be called Urdu 'film poetry'.

Back in Delhi, while the State was Sanskritizing the Hindustani language, now written exclusively in Devanagri, the spoken language of the masses remained what it always was—Hindustani. Meanwhile, in Pakistan, the language was being 'Islamized' by incorporating more and more Arabic words. Despite language politics on both sides of the border, Urdu kept charming the common man. The reason was simple—the quintessence and soul of Urdu has always been its secular and pluralistic heritage which transcends communal divides. It was this legacy that had prompted none other than the author of Pakistan's National Anthem, Hafeez Jallandhari, many years ago, to shun stereotypical distinctions and declare:

Hafeez apni boli mohabbat ki boli
Na Urdu na Hindi na Hindustani

(Hafeez, my language is the language of love
Neither Urdu, nor Hindi, nor Hindustani.)

Delhi was always the seat of political power, and by the
1980s it was brimming with the neo-rich and the wealthy,
most of whom had little time for cultural values, consumed
as they were by their tireless efforts to climb the greasy poles
of power. Bewildered by the discourtesies that had become
characteristic of Delhi's political and social elite, the poet
Bashir Badr lamented:

Koi haath bhi na milaayega jo gale miloge tapaak se
Ye naye mizaaj ka sheher hai zara faasle se mila karo

(No one here will shake your hand, though you may put
     your arms around them
This is a city of new temperaments, keep a little distance
     when you greet people.)

As Delhi's population surged, the economy began to face
challenges and it became increasingly difficult for poets and
writers to make ends meet in the capital. Fed up with soaring
inflation in the nineties, Asrar Jaameyi, a gifted satirist living
in penury in the lanes of one of the many unauthorized
colonies of Delhi, advised Emperor Zafar to remain in his
grave in Rangoon, far from the 'do gaz zameen' (two yards
of land) in Delhi that he had yearned for:

Keh do Zafar se Dilli ke us koo-e-yaar mein
Do gaz zameen milti hai ab sattar hazaar mein

(Tell Zafar that in his beloved's street of Delhi
Two yards of land now cost seventy thousand.)

With more pressing issues facing them, successive governments failed to protect the grand literary heritage that Delhi boasted of. Havelis and graves of the great poets of Mughal Delhi lay waste until some of them were restored pursuant to judicial orders passed on public interest petitions. Grieving this cultural death of Ghalib's Delhi, Anwar Jalalpuri penned an obituary of sorts:

Kuchh yaqeen kuchh gumaan ki Dilli
Anginat imtehaan ki Dilli

Maqbarey tak nahin salaamat ab
Thi kabhi aan-baan ki Dilli

Khwaab, qissa, khayaal, afsaana
Haaye Urdu zabaan ki Dilli

Be-zabaani ka ho gayi hai shikaar
Asadullah Khan ki Dilli

(The Delhi of some certainties, some fantasies
The Delhi of countless trials

Even tombs are no longer secure now
This was once the Delhi of splendour and elegance

Dreams, tales, thoughts, stories
Alas, the Delhi that belonged to Urdu

It has lost its voice
The Delhi of Asadullah Khan [Ghalib].)

And Malizada Manzoor Ahmed lamented:

Chehre pe saare shehr ke gard-e-malaal hai
Jo dil ka haal hai vohi Dilli ka haal hai

(The city's face is covered with the dust of regret
The state of my heart is the state of Delhi.)

In the year 2000, the Delhi Official Languages Act was passed, declaring Urdu, along with Punjabi, as Delhi's 'second official language', the first being Hindi. The next decade saw what some commentators refer to as the 'resurgence' or 'revival' of Urdu in Delhi, especially of Urdu poetry—a phenomenon that continues till date. Young men and women, most whose first language is not Urdu, have shown incredible interest in its literature. Delhi has also witnessed a blossoming of literary events focussing on Urdu, with the magnificent Jashn-e-Rekhta festival—attended in 2017 by more than two hundred thousand people—taking the lead. Other institutions like Hindustani Aawaz and Jashn-e-Bahar have made enormous contribution to this renaissance of sorts, especially by making the language accessible to those who cannot read the script.

With the social media revolution, Urdu poetry has found new fans. Like every other revolution, though, social media also comes with its own pitfalls—every second verse is ascribed to Ghalib and every third person who can (or sometimes cannot) rhyme has declared himself a poet, or worse, a scholar. This is not to say that there are no good poets in the city. In fact, quite to the contrary, post-modern Urdu poetry in Delhi is, perhaps, witnessing its best time. Young poets in their twenties and thirties are writing exceedingly well. For both inspiration and approval, most of them look up to established contemporary poets, prominent among them being Farhat Ehsas—known best for his poetry on the dialectics of the body and the soul. With these young practitioners of the art, Urdu vocabulary and syntax are changing. The concerns and sensibilities of these young poets are different from those of the traditional Urdu poets of the past. They are writing on subjects which their predecessors never handled—LGBTQ rights, sustainable development, and even climate change. Their poetry seems to reflect the truth underlying Firaq Gorakhpuri's words:

Zameen badli falak badla mazaaq-e-zindagi badla
Tamaddun ke qadeem aqdaar badley, aadmi badla

Firaq hum nava-e-Mir-o-Ghalib ab naye naghme
Vo bazm-e-zindagi badli vo rang-e-shaayri badla

(The earth has changed, the sky has changed, life's flavour
     has changed
Those old values of civilization have changed, man has
     changed.

Firaq, we are the voice of Mir and Ghalib, but now there
     are new songs
That assembly of life has changed, that style of poetry
     has changed.)

Tracing the literary and cultural arc over two hundred years
of a city that boasts such a rich history was not an easy
job, even for someone like me who was born and raised
in this city. The Delhi of my childhood has changed. Its
innocence has withered away, giving way to anger and
even hatred. Communal politics, which Urdu poetry has
always abhorred, is at its peak and, shamefully, its effects
are trickling down to ordinary residents of the city. I wake
up one morning to find that a prominent road named after
a Mughal Emperor has been renamed. Another morning,
the newspaper tells me that Shahjahan's Qila-e-Moalla, the
Fort from which the Prime Minister of the world's largest
democracy addresses the nation, will henceforth be managed
by a corporate group that openly supports a political
ideology whose stance on Urdu and Mughal heritage is one
of hostility, even hate. But I remain hopeful. I refuse to let
go of my optimism. I am convinced that Urdu cannot be
killed—symbols of love are immortal and Urdu is India's
truest love-symbol.

     Consumed by the romance of Urdu, I decide to drown

my newspaper sorrows in the pleasant but demanding task of rearranging my bookshelf. I chance upon Julian Barnes' *The Sense of an Ending*. A page towards the end of the book is flagged. Its opening paragraph is underlined in pencil—an old habit I cannot give up. The first sentence reads: 'This was another of our fears: that life wouldn't turn out to be like literature.' I read and re-read that line. Will life ever turn out to be like literature? As I repeat this question to myself, I stumble upon a collection of Noon Meem Rashid's poetry containing his masterpiece *Hasan Koozagar*. Again, a page is flagged and a sentence is underlined:

> Tamanna ki vus'at ki kis ko khabar hai

> (Who knows the expanse of desire?)

I recite it to myself, aloud. It gives me reason to continue to live in hope.

Acknowledgements

Shukriya

'Anyone who gave you confidence, you owe them a lot.'

—Truman Capole, *Breakfast at Tiffany's*

THERE IS A WORD IN URDU—*TAFREEHAN*. DEPENDING ON THE context, it comes close to the English expressions 'for fun' or 'as a pastime'. I had started this work tafreehan, with no intention of ending up with a book but, as Majrooh Sultanpuri puts it, 'Log saath aate gaye aur kaarvaan banta gaya'—people joined me as I went along and a caravan was formed. As the project that began tafreehan culminates into a book, I must thank those who helped me navigate the poetic alleyways of Shahjahanabad.

First things first. I must thank my parents, Naz and Tahir Mahmood, for instilling in me the love for Urdu poetry by simply using it so beautifully in our daily conversations and, indeed, for forcing me to learn the script for fear of the stick. In a marvellous piece about his father, Asif Farrukhi, the noted Urdu writer from Pakistan, wrote that he never used an Urdu dictionary as long as his father, Dr Aslam Farrukhi, was alive; he would simply call him and ask him the meaning of the word he wanted to know. The same is true for me too. Though I possess numerous Urdu dictionaries, more often than not, I simply replace them with a short call to my father. So, thank you 'beloved parents'—without you there would have been no 'Beloved Delhi'. And, thank you, Asif Saheb, for that wonderful image.

Some years ago, the literary magician we know as Rakhshanda Jalil called me and told me that, under the banner of Hindustani Aawaz, she was curating a series of monthly talks titled 'Why it Speaks to Me'. The idea was that every month an eminent speaker would talk about a particular poet. The maiden talk in the series, she told me, was being delivered by Professor Gopi Chand Narang on 'Why Ghalib Speaks to Me'. She wondered if I could persuade my father to deliver the next talk on a poet of his choice. I promised to speak to him. The same evening, I posted my impromptu translation of a short nazm of Parveen Shakir's on Facebook. She read it and called me. She asked me if I had spoken to my father. I told her that I hadn't yet. She asked me not to, and insisted that I deliver the next talk. I had spoken extensively in public, but always on law—the subject of my education, research, training and profession. I told her I was not an Urdu scholar or orator and would do a miserable job. She did not relent and told me that she was not looking for scholarship but for passion, and if the passion was accompanied by scholarship, she would treat it as a 'bonus'. A few weeks later I addressed a packed house in Delhi on 'Why Faiz Speaks to Me'. This was my first public talk on Urdu literature. I must, therefore, thank Rakhshanda Apa for releasing the proverbial genie from the bottle (my readers may well curse her for unleashing the genie on them!).

Besides these, there is a formidable list of people who have contributed in different ways to this book—both by commission and omission. Permit me, therefore, to thank—

Anant Raina, my versatile film-maker friend, who took the fabulous photographs published in this book: for being my co-conspirator and partner in this crime, and for being as excited as me to commit it;

Zehra Nigah, that unsurpassable embodiment of elegance and erudition, and one of the greatest poets of our times: for being a minefield of information on Sauda and Mir, for having spared for me hour after hour both in Karachi and Delhi, and for her continued love and blessings;

Sohail Hashmi, the incredible storyteller of Delhi: for being an encyclopaedia on the remnants of the Mughal Empire and for writing a marvellous Preface to this book;

Shamsur Rahman Faruqi, Shamim Hanfi and Sadiq ur Rahman Kidwai, who lead the shrinking list of Urdu literary giants of modern India: for their scholarly insights and for welcoming me ever so warmly into their respective houses;

Pandit Anand Mohan Zutshi Gulzar Dehlvi, the nonagenarian bard of Delhi: for his fascinating stories, his picturesque description of the nooks and crannies of Purani Dilli, and for a perspective only he could have given;

Jerry Pinto, our very own Charles Dickens: for the many projects that we had thought up together and for not giving up on me (at least not yet);

Hasan Suroor, noted journalist and my uncle: for being my English dictionary and thesaurus;

Nomaan Majid, whose arrival in Delhi in 2016 turned out to be like that of Mir in Lucknow in 1782: for thinking of and facilitating the interesting pictures of poets published in this book, for his mesmerising discourses on the philosophy of literature, for those numerous evening conversations (some of which remain incomplete) and for his constant rejection of most poetry as substandard—with a request to not take this book seriously, for it will surely fall far below his literary standards, if not his expectations from me;

Achala Sharma and Pervaiz Alam, the wonderful broadcaster couple responsible for keeping Hindustan and Hindustani 'alive and kicking' in England: for a marvellous preview of the book in London, for their continued friendship, and for much more;

Marion Molteno, the amazing *Urduwaali* in *Inglistaan*: for her valuable inputs in putting together a house style for transcription from Urdu to Roman;

Amjad Islam Amjad, whose riveting poems have taken the Urdu world by storm; Bari Mian, the charismatic 'literary Maulana' who has kept Awadhi culture alive in Karachi; Asif Noorani, Karachi's delightful young man of seventy-five whom we, across the border, claim as our own; Ali Akbar Natiq, Pakistan's maverick and craziest poet (Lord, forgive him for he knows not what he's doing!); Kami Kidwai, the passionate Urdu aficionado in London; Shanney Naqvi, who remembers a few thousand couplets of Sauda, Mir and Ghalib and whose baritone is still heard in the hills of JNU reciting Majaz and Majrooh; and Sanjiv Saraf, whose Rekhta Foundation is doing a stellar job of spearheading the resurgence of Urdu in India: for sharing their precious literary treasures with me;

Sana Rashid Siddiqui, my priceless friend and occasional (delicious) food-provider: for reading my initial drafts and continuously disagreeing with me (and not just with respect to this book);

Madhu Prasad, the distinguished academic and fierce rights activist: for that wonderful conversation on the history of Delhi College; and Ali Javed, the scholar who raised Mir Jafar Zatalli from his grave: for providing valuable references to Kalaam-e-Zatalli;

Kanishka Prasad, my distinguished friend who never agrees with anyone: for being part of the journey when we began, for taking some great photographs at the time and for not disagreeing with me (at least not as yet);

Ijaz Ahmed Zahid, my illustrious lawyer friend in Karachi: for using his Masters' in Urdu Literature to help with my translations, and for not letting his Punjabi lineage interfere with them;

Sarover Zaidi, the bohemian madcap whose work I remain in

awe of: for coming up with a beautiful title for the book; and Afia Aslam, my desi writer friend in Karachi, and Jonaki Ray, my not so desi poet friend back home: for not coming up with a title (or coming up with unmentionable ones);

Uzma Azhar, the whiz of Turkman Gate, who has defected to Greater Noida: for her ideas for the book cover (which I could not use); and Shaaz Ahmed, my distinguished sufi friend: for his help in approving the cover design;

Subinoy Das: for permitting me to use his photograph of Jama Masjid; Nicky Chandam: for offering me her photographs of Jama Masjid (which I could not use); Ahmad Ali Shaikh and Mir Zulfequar Ali: for facilitating my visit to the grave of Daagh Dehlvi in Hyderabad; Arshad Ali Fehmi: for helping me navigate the koochas and katras of Purani Dilli; Soonita Wadia: for being a reliable courier between Zehra Apa and me;

Aneela Zeb Babar, whose consummate love for Delhi is inspirational: for giving me the answer with which I have opened my Introduction to this book;

Sunny Narang, once a friend: for first coming up with the idea of a column on Urdu poets of Delhi and for introducing me to Bharat Kapur of First City; and Bharat Kapur: for enthusiastically welcoming his idea and publishing my columns;

Kamal Chaudhary, my childhood friend: for his singular role in my resurrection;

Sania Saeed, my ultra-distinguished and uber-charming celebrity sister across the border: for a list of things, which I will Whatsapp her separately;

Minoti Bahri, my friend from elsewhere: amongst other things, for persuading her brother to let out to me a beautiful house that continues to bristle with music and poetry; and Anjali and M.K. Raina, Nuzhat and Zaheer Alam Kidvai, Atiya Zaidi and

S. Irfan Habib, Salman Akhtar, Askari Zaidi, Ajmal Kamal, Meeta Mastani, Preeti Agarwal Mehta, Rangeeta Murada, Akila Jayaraman, Shupriyo Maitra, Padmalakshmi Iyengar, Shephali Frost, Saif Kidwai, Akshay Manwani, Anand Vivek Taneja, Askari Naqvi, Anish Dayal, Sanjay Rajoura, Rishi Suri, Nazia Izuddin, Radhika Mukherjee, Shwetasree Majumder, Valentina Trivedi, Kartikeya Shukla, Shaiq Ali Khan, Piyush and Priyanka Sinha Jha and Mansi and Rahul Thappa: for ensuring that the music and poetry never stop, and for the many conversations that remain incomplete (Meeta, who still doesn't know what happened to her cat, deserves an extra hug for all those 'Lit Fest kurtas'!);

Sumanta De, my law school classmate and now partner in law firm: for always being a friend in need, a friend indeed; and, more importantly, for not rendering the outrageous advice that he is capable of rendering to clients in my absence; and Vivek Agarwal and Mayank Mikhail Mukherjee, my Kanpuriya and Kalkattiya colleagues, respectively: for restraining him from doing so;

Nida, to whom I was once married: for heroically putting up with my passion for Urdu poetry for thirteen years despite not understanding a word of it, and for occasionally helping me translate it into English;

Shibal Bhartiya, who had promised to co-author this book with me: for joining me in not keeping that promise;

Ravi Singh, my wonderful publisher and outstanding editor: for believing in me and in our Beloved Delhi; and Kanishka Gupta, my literary agent, and now friend: for persuading Ravi to do so, and for his tireless persistence;

And finally, Nishtha Satyam, who got after my life to ensure I finish this book in time: for a diverse array of things, none of which either of us can put a finger on, but most importantly, for not letting her exceptionally unwieldy hair further complicate our utterly insane conversations.

Thank you all, very much.

Sitaaron se aage jahaan aur bhi hain
Abhi ishq ke imtehaan aur bhi hain

There are still more worlds beyond the stars
There are tests of love yet to be taken.

—Iqbal

Bibliography

Alvi, Tanveer Ahmed. *Khutoot-e-Ghalib ki Raushni Mein Ghalib ki Savaaneh Umri* [Urdu], Ghalib Academy, Delhi, 2004

Alvi, Tanvir Ahmad. *Zauq Dehlavi* [Urdu], Sahitya Akademi, Delhi, 1992

Ashraf, Khalid. *Daagh aur Waalida-e-Daagh* [Urdu], anthology on Daagh, Delhi, 2016

Axworthy, Michael. *The Sword of Persia: Nader Shah, from Tribal Warrior to Conquering Tyrant*, IB Tauris, New York, 2009

Azad, Muhammad Husain. *Aab-e-Hayat* [Urdu], Naval Kishore, Lahore, 1907

Azmi, Shabana. *Interview*, https://www.youtube.com/watch?v=3hI0jl2HEb4

Bijnori, Abdur Rehman. *Mahaasin-e-Kalaam-e-Ghalib* [Urdu], Delhi, 1921

Blake, Stephen P. *Shahjahanabad: The Sovereign City in Mughal India 1639-1739*, Cambridge University Press, Delhi, 1991

Blumhardt, TF. *Catalogue of Hindustani Manuscripts in the Library of the India Office, No. 146* London, 1926

Chakbast, Brij Narain. *Mazameen-e-Chakbast* [Urdu], Allahabad, 1937

Chenoy, Shama Mitra. *Delhi in Transition, 1821 and Beyond: Mirza Sangeen Beg's Sair-ul-Manaazil*, OUP, Delhi, 2018

Dalrymple, William. *The Last Mughal: The Fall of a Dynasty, Delhi 1857*, Bloomsbury, London, 2006

Dard, Khwaja Mir. *Deewaan-e-Dard* [Urdu], Maktaba Jamia, Delhi, 1989

Dehlvi, Mirza Farhatullah Baig. *Dehli ki Aakhri Shama* [Urdu], Delhi, 1910; reproduced by Anjuman Taraqqi-e-Urdu (Hind), 2009, New Delhi

Dehlvi, Mirza Khan Daagh. *Deewaan-e-Daagh* [Urdu], Delhi, 2014

Dehlvi, Mirza Khan Daagh. *Intikhaab-e-Kalaam-e-Daagh* [Urdu], Urdu Academy, Delhi, 1988

Dehlvi, Nasir Nazir Firaq. *Maikhana-e-Dard* [Urdu], Delhi, 1925; reproduced by Rekhta Books, https://www.rekhta.org/ebooks/mai-khana-e-dard-nasir-nazir-firaq-dehlvi-ebooks

Dudney, Arthur. *Delhi: Pages from a Forgotten History*, Hay House, Delhi, 2015

Farrukhi, Aslam. *Lal Sabz Kabootron ki Chhatri* [Urdu], Scheherzade, Karachi, 2005

Faruqi, Khwaja Ahmad. *Mir Taqi Mir: Hayaat aur Shaayri* [Urdu], Anjuman Taraqqi-e-Urdu, Delhi, 1954

Faruqi, Shamsur Rahman. *Kayi Chaand Thay Sar e Aasmaan* [Urdu], Delhi, Penguin Books, 2006

Faruqi, Shamsur Rahman. *Mir Taqi Mir* [Urdu], Ghalib Institute, Delhi, 1991

Faruqi, Shamsur Rahman. *The Mirror of Beauty*, Delhi, Penguin Books, 2006

Faruqi, Shamsur Rahman. *The Sun that Rose from the Earth*, Penguin India, Delhi, 2014

Faruqi, Shamsur Rahman. *Unprivileged Power: The Strange Case of Persian (and Urdu) in Nineteenth-Century India*, Annual of Urdu Studies, Vol. 13 (1998)

Figar, Dilawar. *Aadaab Arz* [Urdu], Star Publications, Delhi, 1966

Garrett, HLO. *The Trial of Bahadur Shah Zafar*, Indian Edition, Roli Books, Delhi, 2007

Ghalib, Mirza Asadullah Khan. *Dastanbu* [Persian], Urdu Traslation by Khwaja Ahmad Faruqi, NCPUL, Delhi, 1994

Ghalib, Mirza Asadullah Khan. *Deewaan-e-Ghalib* [Urdu], Ghalib Academy, Delhi, 2001

Gorakhpuri, Firaq. *Andaaze* [Urdu], Idaara Farogh-e-Urdu, Lahore, 1956

Gupta, Narayani (ed). *The Delhi Omnibus*, OUP, Delhi, 2002

Gupta, Narayani. *Delhi Between the Two Empires 1803-1931: Society, Government and Urban Growth*, OUP, Delhi, 1981

Hali, Altaf Husain. *Yaadgaar-e-Ghalib* [Urdu], Delhi, 1897

Hanfi, Shamim. *Adab, Adeeb aur Ma'ashrati Tashaddud* [Urdu], Maktaba Jamia, Delhi, 2008

Haque, Ishrat. *Glimpses of Mughal Society and Culture*, Concept Publishing, Delhi, 1992

Hashmi, Qazi Obaidur Rahman. *Khwaja Mir Dard* [Urdu Monograph], Delhi Urdu Academy, Delhi, 2008

Hussain, Intizar. *Dilli Tha Jiska Naam* [Urdu], Sang-e-Meel, Lahore, 2005

Islam, Khurshidul and Russell, Ralph. *Three Mughal Poets*, First Indian Impression, OUP Delhi, 1991

Jalil, Rakhshanda. *Invisible City: The Hidden Monuments of Delhi*, Nyogi Books, Delhi, 2013

Jalil, Rakhshanda. *Why Mirza Ghalib is Delhi's Truest Metaphor*, DailyO, 23.12.2005, http://www.dailyo.in/arts/mirza-ghalib-asadullah-khan-urdu-poetry-delhi-revolt-of-1857-ghazal/story/1/8087.html

Kanda, KC. *Bahadurshah Zafar and his Contemporaries*, Sterling, Delhi, 2007

Khairabadi, Muztar. *Khirman* [Urdu] (five volumes), edited and published by Javed Akhtar, 2015

Khan, Hakim Ahsanullah. *Accounts of the 1857 Revolt*, Pakistan Historical Society, 1958

Khan, Syed Ahmad. *Asar-ul-Sanadid* [Urdu], Complete Edition, Central Book Depot, Delhi, 1965

Kidwai, Saleem. *Dargah Quli Khan: Portrait of a City (Persian)* in Vanita R., Kidwai S. (eds) Same-Sex Love in India, Palgrave Macmillan, New York

Kuczkiewicz-Fras, Agnieszka. *The beloved and the Lover—Love in Classical Urdu Ghazal*, Cracow Indological Studies, Vol. XII (2010)

Kumar, Sunil. *The Present in Delhi's Past*, Three Essays, Delhi, 2010

Lahori, Ahmad Husain. *Hayat-e-Zauq* [Urdu], Lahore, 1895

Lane-Pool, Stanley. *Aurangzib and the Decay of the Mughal Empire*, Dublin, 1908

Lewisohn, Leonard. *The Sacred Music of Islam: Sam'a in the Persian Sufi Tradition*, British Journal of Ethnomusicology, Vol. 6 (1997)

Liddle, Swapna. *Chandni Chowk: The Mughal City of Old Delhi*, Speaking Tiger, Delhi, 2017

Ludhianvi, Sahir. *Kulliyaat-e-Sahir* [Urdu], Mushtaq Book Corner, 1990

Mahmood, Saif. *Ghalib: The Litigious Commoner*, Talk at International Seminar on Ghalib Rediscovered, Nehru Centre, London 21.10.2015

Mahmood, Tahir. *Legal Metaphor in Ghalib's Urdu Poetry*, Islamic and Comparative Law Quaterly (VIII:3), Delhi, 1988

Mahmood, Tahir. *Urdu Shaayri Mein Qanooni Istearey* [Urdu],

Ghalib Memorial Lecture, Department of Urdu, University of Delhi, 29.10.2010

Mazhari, Kausar. *Monograph: Shaikh Muhammad Ibrahim Zauq* [Urdu], NCPPUL, Delhi, 2016

Mir, Mir Taqi. *Kulliyaat-e-Mir* [Urdu], NCPUL, Delhi, 2007

Mir, Mir Taqi. *Zikr-e-Mir,* [Persian], 1783

Mir, Raza. (ed.) *The Taste of Words,* Penguin India, 2014

Momin, Hakim Momin Khan. *Deewaan-e-Momin* [Urdu], edited by Ziya Ahmed Ziya, Shanti Press, Allahabad, 1947

Moosvi, Shireen. *People, Taxation and Trade in Mughal India,* OUP, Delhi, 2008

Naim, CM. *Zikr-e-Mir,* English Translation, OUP, 2000

Naim, CM. *Mir in "Fact" and "Fiction",* paper presented at University of Virginia in 2008, http://www.columbia.edu/itc/mealac/pritchett/00garden/texts/txt_naim_2009.pdf

Naim, CM. *Syed Ahmad and His Two Books Called 'Asar-al-Sanadid',* Modern Asian Studies Vol. 45, 2010

Narang, Gopi Chand. *Ghalib: Innovative Meanings and the Ingenious Mind,* Translated from Urdu by Surinder Deol, OUP, Delhi, 2017

Narang, Gopi Chand. *Ghalib: Ma'ni-Afrini, Jadliyaati Waza', Shunyata aur Sheriyaat* [Urdu], Sahitya Academy, Delhi, 2013

Nigah, Zehra *Urdu Talk on Mir in the Hindustani Awaaz series titled "Why it Speaks to Me?",* Delhi, April 2014 https://www.youtube.com/watch?v=b_q3MM7PoWU (recorded by Aseem Asha Foundation)

Noorani, AG. *Indian Political Trials,* OUP Delhi, 2006

Parekh, Rauf. *Those who Think Mir's Poetry is Simple are Simpletons,* Dawn, 21.10.2013, https://www.dawn.com/news/1050655

Parvez, Aslam. *The Life and Poetry of Bahadur Shah Zafar,* English Translation by Ather Farouqui, Hay House, Delhi, 2017

Pritchett, Frances W. (ed). *Muhammad Husain Azad, Aab-e-Hayat: Shaping the Canon of Urdu Poetry,* Translated by Shamsur Rahman Faruqi, OUP, 2001

Pritchett, Frances W. *Convention in the Classical Urdu Ghazal: The Case of Mir, Journal of South Asian and Middle Eastern Studies;* Vol III, No.1, Fall 1979

Pritchett, Frances W. *Nets of Awareness: Urdu Poetry and its Critics,* University of California Press, 1994

Rahbar, Daud. *Urdu Letters of Mirza Asadu'llah Khan Ghalib,* SUNY Press, New York, 1987

Raza, Azra and Goodyear, Sara Suleri. *Ghalib: Epistemologies of Elegance,* Penguin Viking, Delhi, 2009

Roberts, Emma. *Scenes and Characteristics of Hindostan, with Sketches of Anglo-Indian Society,* WH Alle & Co., London, 1835

Russell, Ralph. (ed.) *Ghalib 1797—1869: Life and* Letters, OUP, Delhi, 1994

Russell, Ralph. *The Famous Ghalib: The Sound of My Moving Pen,* Revised Edition, Marion Molteno (ed), Roli Books, Delhi, 2000

Sadiq, Muhammad. *History of Urdu Literature,* OUP, London, 1964

Saxena, Ram Babu. *History of Urdu Literature,* Ra, Narain Lal, Allahabad, 1927

Sauda, Mirza Mohammad Rafi. *Kulliyaat-e-Sauda* [Urdu], Allahabad, 1971

Schimmel, Annemarie. *Pain and Grace: A Study of Two Mystical Writers of Eighteenth-Century Muslim India,* Brill, Leiden, 1976

Sharma, SR. *Ahwaal-e-Mir: Life, Times and Poetry of Mir,* Partridge India, Delhi, 2014

Shefta, Nawab Mustafa Khan. *Gulshan e Be-khaar* [Urdu], Delhi, 1832 (Reproduced by Uttar Pradesh Urdu Academy, Lucknow)

Siddiqui, Saquib and Ahmed, Anis (ed). *Khwaja Mir Dard* [Urdu], Ghalib Institute, Delhi, 1989

Siddiqui, Zaheer Ahmed. *Momin: Shakhsiyat aur Fann* [Urdu], Delhi, 1995

Singh, Khushwant (ed). *City Improbable: Writings on Delhi,* Penguin India, Delhi, 2001

Smith, RV. *A Connection So Cool,* The Hindu, New Delhi, March 2, 2014

Spear, Percival and Margaret. *India Remembered,* Orient Longman, Delhi, 1981

Spear, Percival. *Delhi: A Historical Sketch,* in Narayani Gupta(ed), *The Delhi Omnibus,* OUP, Delhi, 2002

Spear, Percival. *Twilight of the Mughals,* OUP Karachi,1982

Trivedi, Madhu. *The Making of the Awadh Culture,* Primus Books, Delhi, 2010

Vanita R. and Kidwai S. (eds). *Same-Sex Love in India,* Palgrave Macmillan, New York

Varma, Pavan K. *Ghalib: The Man, The Times*, Penguin Books, Delhi, 2008

Wig, Narendra Nath. *Ghalib: Ek Nafsiyaati Mata'ala* [Urdu], Ilmi Majlis, Delhi, 1969

Zafar, Bahadur Shah. *Deewaan-e-Zafar* [Urdu], Farid Book Depot, Delhi, 2002

Zauq, Shaikh Ibrahim. *Kulliyaat-e-Zauq* [Urdu], edited by Tanveer Ahmad Alvi, Taraqqi-e-Urdu Bureau, Delhi, 1980

Notes

1. Percival Spear, *Delhi: A Historical Sketch*, in Narayani Gupta (ed), *The Delhi Omnibus*, OUP, Delhi, 2002, p. 1
2. Khushwant Singh (ed), *City Improbable: Writings on Delhi*, Penguin India, Delhi, 2001, pp. 266-286
3. Some authors claim that, for some time, the Fort was also called the 'Qila-e-Mubarak' (Auspicious Fort)
4. For details see Swapna Liddle, *Chandni Chowk: The Mughal City of Old Delhi*, Speaking Tiger, Delhi, 2017
5. For details see Shireen Moosvi, *People, Taxation and Trade in Mughal India*, OUP, Delhi, 2008
6. Aurangzeb had famously ordered the execution of Sarmad, a naked fakir highly revered by many in Delhi, including Aurangzeb's brother, Dara Shikoh. Sarmad is believed to have been an Iranian Jew who had converted to Islam and decided to shed his clothes. Called 'Shaheed Sarmad' (Sarmad, the Martyr), he lies buried in a shrine next to Gate No. 2 of the Jama Masjid.
7. Shamsur Rahman Faruqi, *Unprivileged Power: The Strange Case of Persian (and Urdu) in Nineteenth-Century India*, Annual of Urdu Studies, Vol. 13 (1998)
8. Ibid
9. Ibid
10. This couplet can be found in at least three different versions in different collections. However, this is the most widely accepted version.
11. Agnieszka Kuczkiewicz-Fras, *The beloved and the Lover—Love in Classical Urdu Ghazal*, Cracow Indological Studies, Vol. XII (2010)
12. Literally 'Water of Life'. It is believed that Khidr, a Prophet, had drunk an elixir which made him immortal by defying death. That elixir is called *Aab-e-Hayaat*
13. Taffazul Rizvi, well-known advocate of the Supreme Court of Pakistan, is Azad's great-grandson through his daughter.
14. Though the book is in Persian, it has an Arabic title—*Sair-ul-Manazil*—which literally translates to 'Stroll of Buildings'.

However, the spelling of the word *sair* in Arabic is the same as the spelling of the word *siar*—a derivative from *seerat* which means 'character' or 'nature'. Some scholars are, thus, of the opinion that, since the book describes the character and nature of the buildings of Delhi, the title is actually *Siar-ul-Manazil*.

15. Percival and Margaret Spear, *India Remembered,* Orient Longman, Delhi, 1981, p. 98
16. Agha Shayar Qazalbaash (1871-1940)
17. TF Blumhardt, *Catalogue of Hindustani Manuscripts in the Library of the India Office,* No. 146 London, 1926, pp. 76-78
18. Ishrat Haque, *Glimpses of Mughal Society and Culture,* Concept Publishing, Delhi, 1992, p. 37
19. Frances W. Pritchett (ed), Muhammad Husain Azad, *Aab-e-Hayat: Shaping the Canon of Urdu Poetry,* Translated by Shamsur Rahman Faruqui, OUP, 2001
20. For details see Saleem Kidwai, *Dargah Quli Khan: Portrait of a City (Persian).* In Vanita R., Kidwai S. (eds) Same-Sex Love in India, Palgrave Macmillan, New York, 2000
21. Michael Axworthy, *The Sword of Persia: Nader Shah, from Tribal Warrior to Conquering Tyrant,* IB Tauris, New York, 2009, p. 6
22. Arthur Dudney, *Delhi: Pages from a Forgotten History,* Hay House, Delhi, 2015, p. 147
23. Supra n. 19
24. Narrated by different commentators in their own style including Frances W. Pritchett, *Nets of Awareness: Urdu Poetry and its Critics,* University of California Press, 1994
25. Khurshidul Islam and Ralph Russell, *Three Mughal Poets,* First Indian Impression, OUP Delhi, 1991
26. Ibid
27. Ibid
28. Ibid
29. Ibid
30. Some critics are of the view that this couplet refers to the Quranic story of Yusuf (Prophet Joseph) and Zulaikha. In a conversation with the author, Shamsur Rahman Faruqi agreed with this view.
31. Madhu Trivedi, *The Making of the Awadh Culture,* Primus Books, Delhi, 2010, p. 77

32. Annemarie Schimmel, *Pain and Grace: A Study of Two Mystical Writers of Eighteenth-Century Muslim India*, Brill, Leiden, 1976 India, Brill, Leiden, 1976, p. 42

33. Water-guard

34. Percival Spear, *Twilight of the Mughals*, OUP Karachi,1982 as cited in R.V. Smith, *A Connection So Cool*, The Hindu, New Delhi, March 2, 2014

35. R.V. Smith, *A Connection So Cool*, The Hindu, New Delhi, March 2, 2014

36. Saquib Siddiqui and Anis Ahmed (ed), *Khwaja Mir Dard* [Urdu], Ghalib Institute, Delhi, 1989

37. As quoted in Leonard Lewisohn, *The Sacred Music of Islam: Sam'a in the Persian Sufi Tradition*, British Journal of Ethnomusicology, Vol. 6 (1997)

38. Nasir Nazir Firaq Dehlvi, *Maikhana-e-Dard* [Urdu], Delhi, 1925 (Reproduced by Rekhta Books), https://www.rekhta.org/ ebooks/mai-khana-e-dard-nasir-nazir-firaq-dehlvi-ebooks

39. Nawab Mustafa Khan 'Shefta', *Gulshan e Be-khaar* [Urdu], Delhi, 1832 (Reproduced by Uttar Pradesh Urdu Academy, Lucknow)

40. Some scholars have disputed the authorship of this couplet

41. As quoted by Qazi Obaidur Rahman Hashmi in his monograph for Delhi Urdu Academy, *Khwaja Mir Dard*, Delhi, 2008

42. Ibid

43. Conversation with the author in April 2017

44. As quoted by Rauf Parekh in https://www.dawn.com/ news/1050655

45. CM Naim, Mir in 'Fact' and 'Fiction', paper presented at University of Virginia in September 2008, available on http://www.columbia.edu/itc/mealac/pritchett/00garden/texts/ txt_naim_2009.pdf

46. Original written by Mir in Persian 1783. English Translation with annotation by CM Naim, OUP, 2000

47. A *masnavi* is a long poem, more often than not, following a meter of ten or eleven syllables. It closest equivalent in English literature is the ballad.

48. Supra n. 46

49. Khurshidul Islam and Ralph Russell, *Three Mughal Poets*, First Indian Impression, OUP Delhi, 1991, pp. 235-236

50. Ibid at pp. 96-98
51. Ibid
52. Supra n 45. Also see generally, S.R. Sharma, *Ahwaal-e-Mir: Life, Times and Poetry of Mir*, Partridge India, Delhi, 2014
53. Supra n. 49
54. Supra n. 49
55. Zehra Nigah in a conversation with the author in February 2018
56. As quoted in Shamsur Rahman Faruqi, *Mir Taqi Mir*, Ghalib Institute, Delhi, 1991
57. In some collections, the first misra is thus written: *Ab toh jaate hain butkade se Mir*
58. Ali Sardar Jafri casts a doubt on the authorship of these verses but without explanation
59. Ibid
60. Zehra Nigah's Talk on Mir in the *Hindustani Awaaz* series titled 'Why it Speaks to Me?', Delhi, April 2014 https://www.youtube.com/watch?v=b_q3MM7PoWU (recorded by Aseem Asha Foundation)
61. Frances W. Pritchett, *Journal of South Asian and Middle Eastern Studies*; Vol III, No.1, Fall 1979
62. In some collections, the first misra is thus written: *Rah-e-talab mein girey hote sar ke bal hum bhi*
63. Conversation with the author in April 2017
64. Conversation with the author in April 2017
65. The idiom *apni derh eenth ki masjid banaana* ('to make one's own mosque out of a brick and a half') means to always have a contrary opinion from what people say.
66. Emma Roberts, *Scenes and Characteristics of Hindostan*, with Sketches of Anglo-Indian Society, WH Alle & Co., London, 1835 as cited in C.M. Naim, *Syed Ahmad and His Two Books Called 'Asar-al-Sanadid'*, Modern Asian Studies Vol. 45, 2010
67. C.M. Naim, *Syed Ahmad and His Two Books Called 'Asar-al-Sanadid'*, Modern Asian Studies Vol. 45, 2010
68. Abdur Rehman Bijnori, *Mahaasin-e-Kalaam-e-Ghalib* [Urdu], Delhi, 1921
69. This refers to two couplets by Ghalib—one where he uses the term 'dhaul dhappa' to say that he was engulfed in a

physical tug of war with his beloved and another where he explains why he does not kiss her feet while she is asleep:

Dhaul dhappa us saraapa naaz ka sheva nahin
Hum hi kar baithe thay Ghalib pesh-dasti ek din

Fist-fighting was not the style of that coquettish one
It was I who, one day, wanted to beat her to it

Le toh loon sote mein uske paaon ka bosa magar
Aisi baaton se vo kafir badgumaan ho jaayega

I can kiss her feet while she's asleep, but
Such things would only make her suspicious

70. Again, this refers to another couplet by Ghalib where he wonders how long he would be able to keep writing with his wounded fingers and blood-dripping pen:

Dard-e-dil likhoon kab tak, jaaoon un ko dikhla doon
Ungliyaan figaar apni, khaamah khoon-chakaan apna

For how long should I write (about) the sorrows of my heart?
Should I not go and show her
My wounded fingers, my blood-dripping pen?

71. Pavan K. Varma, *Ghalib: The Man, The Times*, Penguin Books, Delhi, 2008
72. Ibid
73. Narendra Nath Wig, *Ghalib: Ek Nafsiyaati Mata'ala* (Urdu), Ilmi Majlis, Delhi, 1969
74. Daud Rahbar, *Urdu Letters of Mirza Asadu'llah Khan Ghalib*, SUNY Press, New York, 1987
75. As quoted in Gopi Chand Narang, *Ghalib: Innovative Meanings and the Ingenious Mind*, Translated from Urdu by Surinder Deol, OUP, Delhi, 2017, p. 386
76. Azra Raza and Sara Suleri Goodyear, *Ghalib: Epistemologies of Elegance*, Penguin Viking, Delhi, 2009, p. xiii
77. Supra n. 75
78. Supra note 66
79. 'Musaddas' is a genre of poetry in which each verse-set consists of 6 lines. Hali's epic poem is written in this genre
80. Maulana Altaf Husain Hali, *Yaadgaar-e-Ghalib* (Urdu), Delhi, 1897

81. Ibid
82. http://www.dailyo.in/arts/mirza-ghalib-asadullah-khan-urdu-poetry-delhi-revolt-of-1857-ghazal/story/1/ 8087. html
83. In Columbia University's website http://www.columbia.edu/itc/mealac/pritchett/00ghalib/, Frances W. Pritchett has referred to him as 'Mr. Thomason', though elsewhere he is referred to as Mr. Thompson
84. http://www.columbia.edu/itc/mealac/pritchett/00ghalib
85. Literally translated these titles would mean 'Intellectual of the Nation' and 'Star of the Land'
86. The letter is included in the collection of Ghalib's letters in Tanveer Ahmed Alvi, *Khutoot-e-Ghalib ki Raushni mein Ghalib ki Savaaneh Umri* (Urdu), Ghalib Academy, Delhi, 2004,
87. Supra n. 84
88. Supra note 75
89. Ajmal Kamal, noted Urdu scholar and Editor of *Aaj*, maintains that the word 'hindi' here refers to the language in which Ghalib wrote his letters, which is now called Urdu but, back then, was called Rekhta or Hindi.
90. Supra n. 76
91. Tahir Mahmood, *Legal Metaphor in Ghalib's Urdu Poetry*, Islamic and Comparative Law Quaterly (VIII:3), Delhi, 1988
92. www.columbia.edu/itc/mealac/pritchett/00ghalib/
93. Ibid
94. In an Urdu conversation with the author in 2017. Translation mine.
95. Rajiv Shakdher, J in *Shanti Bhushan Vs. CIT* (2011) 336 ITR 26 (Delhi)
96. Mirza Farhatullah Baig Dehlvi, *Dehli ki Aakhri Shama* [Urdu], Delhi, 1910; reproduced by Anjuman Taraqqi-e-Urdu (Hind), 2009, New Delhi, p. 43
97. For a detailed description of Kucha Chelan see the chapter *Mir Taqi Mir: The Incurable Romancer of Delhi* in this book
98. As narrated in Zaheer Ahmed Siddiqui, *Momin: Shakhsiyat aur Fann* [Urdu], Delhi, 1995
99. Supra n. 86
100. Zaheer Ahmed Siddiqui, *Momin: Shakhsiyat aur Fann* [Urdu], Delhi, 1995

101. Supra n. 80
102. Supra n. 97
103. Originally written in Arabic in 1762, the book has later been translated into many languages including Urdu and English
104. Supra n. 98
105. William Dalrymple, *The Last Mughal : The Fall of a Dynasty*, Delhi 1857, Bloomsbury, London, 2006, p. 1
106. C.M. Naim, *Syed Ahmad and His Two Books Called 'Asar-al-Sanadid'*, Modern Asian Studies Vol. 45, 2010
107. Stanley Lane-Pool, *Aurangzib and the Decay of the Mughal Empire*, Dublin, 1908
108. Supra n. 105
109. https://www.youtube.com/watch?v=3hI0jl2HEb4
110. Supra n. 105
111. Literally translated these title would mean 'Intellectual of the Nation' and 'Star of the Land'
112. A.G. Noorani, *Indian Political Trials*, OUP Delhi, 2006, p. 90
113. Hakim Ahsanullah Khan's Accounts of the 1857 Revolt, Pakistan Historical Society, 1958
114. For details see HLO Garrett, *The Trial of Bahadur Shah Zafar*, Indian Edition, Roli Books, Delhi, 2007
115. Percival Spear, *Twilight of the Mughuls: Studies in Late Mughul Delhi*, in Narayani Gupta(ed), *The Delhi Omnibus*, OUP, Delhi, 2002, pp. 218-19
116. Supra note 114
117. Literally the term *Koo-e-yaar* means 'the beloved's lane' or 'the friend's lane' but Zafar has used it in the sense of 'homeland'. He is saying that he is so unlucky that has been denied even the dignity of burial in his homeland.
118. See generally, Aslam Farrukhi, *Lal Sabz Kabootron ki Chhatri*, Scheherzade, Karachi, 2005, p. 249
119. K.C. Kanda, *Bahadurshah Zafar and his Contemporaries*, Sterling, Delhi, 2007, p. 88
120. Referred to as Nawab Lutf-e-Ali Khan in some works
121. Muhammad Husain Azad, *Aab-e-Hayat* [Urdu], Naval Kishore, Lahore, 1907
122. For another description of Kabuli Darwaaza see the chapter *Mirza Mohammad Rafi Sauda: The Great Satirist* in this book

123. Tanvir Ahmad Alvi, *Zauq Dehlavi* [Urdu], Sahitya Akademi, Delhi, 1992

124. Ahmad Husain Lahori, *Hayat-e-Zauq* [Urdu], Lahore, 1895

125. Supra n. 121

126. Supra n. 121

127. Firaq Gorakhpuri, *Andaaze* (Urdu), Idaara Farogh-e-Urdu, Lahore, 1956

128. Conversation with the author in May 2017

129. When Zauq says *par kya karein jo kaam na be-dillagi chaley*, he actually makes a pun. The word *dillagi* also means 'infatuation' or 'flirtation'. Therefore, *be-dillagi* would mean 'without infatuation' or 'without flirtation'. On the one hand, he means that one cannot live without getting attached to this world. On the other, that one cannot live without flirting with women.

130. Kausar Mazhari, *Monograph: Shaikh Muhammad Ibrahim Zauq* [Urdu], NCPPUL, Delhi, 2016

131. When Zauq says *par kya karein jo kaam na be-dillagi chaley*, he actually makes a pun. The word *dillagi* also means 'infatuation' or 'flirtation'. Therefore, *be-dillagi* would mean 'without infatuation' or 'without flirtation'. On the one hand, he means that one cannot live without getting attached to this world. On the other, that one cannot live without flirting with women.

132. In some collections, the first line is written as *Ho umr-e-Khizr bhi, toh ho maloom ba waqt-e-marg*

133. Shamsur Rahman *Faruqi, Kayi Chaand Thay Sar e Aasmaan* (Urdu), Delhi, Penguin Books, 2006; (English version titled 'The Mirror of Beauty')

134. Khalid Ashraf, *Daagh aur Waalida-e-Daagh* in [Urdu] in an anthology on Daagh, Delhi, 2016

135. Supra n. 133

136. Shamsur Rahman Faruqi, *The Mirror of Beauty*, Delhi, Penguin Books, 2006, pp. 5-7

137. For details of Ghalib's pension dispute, see the chapter on Mirza Ghalib in this book.

138. Supra n. 134

139. See more details in the chapter *Bahadur Shah Zafar: An Emperor's Affair with Urdu* in this book

140. Supra n. 136; The original words used in Urdu by Faruqi for 'Hey young fellows' are *Abey o lamdo*

141. *Hawa lagna* is a Hindustani idiom which means 'to get affected by'

142. Supra n. 134

143. Literally, Intellectual of the Land, Eloquent Man of the Nation, Nightingale of India and World Teacher.

144. Brij Narain Chakbast, *Mazameen-e-Chakbast* [Urdu], Allahabad, 1937

145. Conversation with the author in May 2017

146. Preface to a select collection of Daagh's works, *Intikhaab-e-Kalaam-e-Daagh*, Urdu Academy, Delhi, 1988, p. 2

147. Supra n. 144

148. Though translated by some as 'rival', the word *raqeeb* in Urdu poetry has a specific connotation. It is used to refer to a man to whom the poet has lost his beloved and with who she now has a relationship.

149. Mirza Farhatullah Beg, *The Last Musha'irah of Dehli*, (English Translation by Akhtar Qamber), Orient Blackswan, Delhi, 2010

150. Amaresh Misra, *War of Civilizations: India AD 1857*, Volumes 1 and 2, Rupa, Delhi, 2007

151. Pavan K Varma, Ghalib: *The Man, The Times*, Penguin Books, Delhi, 1989, pp.253-54

152. The mushaira could not be held for a few years because of certain political exigencies but was resumed after a short gap and has since been taking place every year.

Lightning Source UK Ltd.
Milton Keynes UK
UKHW020655161221
395648UK00010B/2723